This book constitutes the first sustained, comprehensive, and rigorous critique of contemporary Hobbesian contractarianism as expounded in the work of Jean Hampton, Gregory Kavka, and David Gauthier. Professor Kraus argues that the attempts by these three philosophers to use Hobbes to answer current political and moral questions fail. The reasons why they fail are related to fundamental problems intrinsic to Hobbesian contractarianism: first, the problem of collective action arising out of the tension in Hobbes's theory between individual and collective rationality; second, the classical problem of explaining the normative force of hypothetical action, a problem that can be traced to the conflicting strategies of hypothetical justification found in Rawls's and Hobbes's theories.

Given the deep interest in Hobbesian contractarianism among philosophers, political theorists, game theorists in economics and political science, and legal theorists, this book is likely to attract wide attention and infuse new life into the contractarian debate.

The limits of Hobbesian
contractarianism

The limits of Hobbesian contractarianism

JODY S. KRAUS

UNIVERSITY OF VIRGINIA SCHOOL OF LAW

CAMBRIDGE
UNIVERSITY PRESS

Published by the Press Syndicate of the University of Cambridge
The Pitt Building, Trumpington Street, Cambridge CB2 1RP
40 West 20th Street, New York, NY 10011–4211, USA
10 Stamford Road, Oakleigh, Victoria 3166, Australia

First published 1993

Printed in the United States of America

Library of Congress Cataloging-in-Publication Data
Kraus, Jody S.
The limits of Hobbesian contractarianism / Jody S. Kraus.
p.   cm.
Revision of the author's thesis (Ph. D.) – University of Arizona,
1987.
Includes bibliographical references and index.
ISBN   0-521-42062-8
1.   Hobbes, Thomas, 1588–1679 – Contributions in political
philosophy.   2.   Social contract.   3.   Political science – History.
4.   Political science – Philosophy.   I.   Title.
JC153.H66K73   1993   93-9015
320'.01 – dc20   CIP

A catalog record for this book is available from the British Library

ISBN 0-521-42062-8   hardback

For Paré

Contents

Contents

Acknowledgments

I produced the first incarnation of this manuscript as my dissertation in the Department of Philosophy at the University of Arizona in 1987, and following three years as a student at Yale Law School, turned my attention to it again in 1991. In 1987, an earlier form of Chapter 5, coauthored with Jules Coleman, appeared in *Ethics* under the title "Morality and the Theory of Rational Choice." The arguments and structure throughout the manuscript have so dramatically changed and, I hope, improved over the years that it is now only a distant relative of its former self. I am grateful to David Brink, Allan Buchanan, Joel Feinberg, David Gauthier, Greg Kavka, Ron Milo, Keith Quillen, Glen Robinson, George Rutherglen, Steven Schiffer, David Schmidtz, Bob Scott, Chris Shields, Bill Stuntz, Holly Smith, and Steve Walt for their helpful comments. I am especially grateful to Jules Coleman not only for his incisive comments, but for his extraordinary personal and professional support from the first day I arrived in Tucson, Arizona, in 1982. Jules has been a mentor, a coauthor, and above all, a great friend. I would like also to acknowledge the profound debt this present work owes to David Gauthier, Jean Hampton, and Greg Kavka. Without the groundbreaking work of these founders of contemporary Hobbesian contractarianism, this book quite literally would not have been possible. I have received much appreciated research support from the Woodrow Wilson Foundation during the 1985–86 academic year through the Charlotte W. Newcombe Dissertation Fellowship, as well as

Acknowledgments

from The University of Virginia Law School Foundation research stipend and summer research grants. I would also like to thank Carolyn Viola-John for her excellent editorial assistance, and Kirby Griffis for his superb assistance in proofreading and creating the index for this book.

I have drawn inspiration from many sources over the years. Michael Brecker's music has meant more to me than words can say – it has made bad times bearable and good times great. Among the many others on whom I regularly depend, there are my friends Doug Arnson, Larry Badler, Steven Dow, John Russell, and Alex Whiting, as well as my brother and sister, Ken Kraus and Pam Richardson. Credit for any success I might have as a scholar should be given to my parents, Drs. Sidney and Cecile Kraus, who taught me academic excellence by their example. Finally, words cannot express my gratitude for the incredible love and support of my wife, Paré.

Selected bibliography

Brink, David. 1989. *Moral Realism and the Foundations of Ethics*. Cambridge University Press.

Gauthier, David. 1986. *Morals by Agreement*. Oxford: Clarendon Press.

Hampton, Jean. 1986. *Hobbes and the Social Contract Tradition*. Cambridge University Press. (All references to Hampton refer to this work, unless otherwise specified.)

  1987. "Free-Rider Problems in the Production of Collective Goods." *Economics and Philosophy*. 3:245–73. (Cited as "Free Rider.")

Hardin, Russell. 1982. *Collective Action*. Baltimore: Johns Hopkins University Press.

Hobbes, Thomas. 1968 (originally published 1651). *Leviathan*. Edited by C. B. Macpherson (using the 1651 "Head" edition). Harmondsworth: Penguin.

Kavka, Gregory. 1986. *Hobbesian Moral and Political Theory*. Princeton University Press.

Lewis, David. 1969. *Convention: A Philosophical Study*. Cambridge, Mass.: Harvard University Press.

Luce, R., and H. Raiffa. 1957. *Games and Decisions*. New York: Wiley.

Selected bibliography

Olson, Mancur, Jr. 1965. *The Logic of Collective Action.* Cambridge, Mass.: Harvard University Press (reprinted 1971).

Rawls, John. 1971. *A Theory of Justice.* Cambridge, Mass.: Harvard University Press.

(All cited throughout by last name only.)

Chapter 1

Introduction

In *Leviathan*, Thomas Hobbes constructs a theoretical apparatus that promises to unify the fields of human psychology,
ethics, and political philosophy. Hobbes's grand project is
to found an "objective science of moral philosophy," firmly
grounded on truths of human psychology, from which a
moral obligation to obey an absolute political sovereign can
be generated. Though such an ambitious and far-reaching
theory usually attracts considerable and long-lasting attention, Hobbes's social contract theory seems to have been
almost entirely dismissed by his contemporaries and largely
ignored by political philosophers in the twentieth century
until Rawls published *A Theory of Justice* in 1971. Since then,
interest in Hobbesian contractarianism has grown steadily.
Alongside the critical discussion of Rawls's theory, a substantial body of contemporary Hobbesian scholarship has
developed in both political and moral theory. In the last
decade, this research has culminated in the publication of
three major works inspired by Hobbes's social contract theory. This book attempts to provide an overarching and detailed critical analysis of these works in an effort to explore
both the insights and limits of political and moral Hobbesian
contractarianism.

Before presenting this analysis, however, I provide the
backdrop from which these theories have emerged. My objective in this chapter is to introduce contractarian theory in
general, to provide one view of why Hobbesian contractarianism is enjoying a contemporary renaissance in moral and

1

political theory, and to anticipate some of the themes which emerge from the analysis in the subsequent chapters.

A GENERAL CHARACTERIZATION OF CONTRACTARIANISM

Contractarian theories can be versions of either political or moral contractarianism. "Political contractarianism" constitutes a theory of political legitimacy and obligation. Political contractarianism sets forth conditions under which political institutions are morally legitimate and under which individuals may have political obligations.[1] "Moral contractarianism" constitutes a meta-ethical theory which sets forth a criterion of assessment for moral principles. As a meta-ethical theory, moral contractarianism proposes a theory of the nature of moral justification and the meaning of moral terms.

There are two basic categories into which political and moral contractarian theories seem to fall. First, contractarian theories can be *analytical*. Analytical contractarian theories provide a reconstruction of the genesis and continuity of political authority or the genesis of moral principles. Such theories do not make any claims concerning the historically accurate nature of the evolution of political institutions or any actual genesis of moral principles. Rather, they impose an artificial and alternative scenario on political evolution, or adopt a theoretical framework to reconceive of moral principles as the outcome of some hypothetical scenario. Contractarian reconstructions treat a set of political institutions or moral principles *as if* they were the outcome of some

---

1 There is an interesting literature which separates the issue of political legitimacy from that of political obligation (e.g., A. John Simmons, *Moral Principles and Political Obligation* [Princeton: Princeton University Press, 1979] and Kavka [p. 399]). For simplicity, I will treat the issues of political legitimacy and obligation *as if* they were the same, and thus I will proceed *as if* political legitimacy entailed political obligation, and *vice versa*. Though this view is controversial, no substantive claims will depend essentially on its truth.

2

contract, agreement, convention, or choice. The aim is to show that political society can be understood in terms of some theoretical, sometimes hypothetical, model, or that moral principles can be understood as resulting from a choice of some kind. Second, contractarian theories may be *normative*.[2] Normative theories in general conclude that something ought to be the case, is justified, or is legitimate or not. In contrast to analytical contractarian theories, which merely reconstruct or reconceive the origins of political association or moral principles, normative contractarian theories argue in favor of or against political association or moral principles. An analytical reconstruction of political association which holds that political authority can be understood, for example, as the outcome of a bargain is either plausible or not, depending on the nature of the reconstruction offered. But even if plausible, such an analysis by itself is neutral with respect to the legitimacy, desirability, or defensibility of political authority. It is possible to admit that political authority can be reconstructed or modeled as the outcome of some hypothetical scenario or other, but to deny the relevance of this reconstruction for purposes of establishing the legitimacy of political authority. Likewise, it is possible to agree with an analytical theory asserting that certain principles can be understood as the outcome of some hypothetical bargain, but to deny either that such principles qualify as moral principles or that even if moral, such principles are therefore in any sense correct, or ones with which we have reason to conform. Normative contractarian theories go beyond the merely analytical to draw certain normative conclusions about the legitimacy of political authority or the correctness of moral principles.

I have distinguished among political, moral, analytic, and normative contractarian theories. Any given contractarian theory may fall into all or any combination of these categories. But I have not yet indicated what makes a theory,

2 See Alan Nelson, "Explanation and Justification in Political Philosophy," *Ethics* 97 (1986):154.

whether political, moral, analytic, or normative, a contractarian theory.

Contractarianism can be characterized by singling out certain structural elements common to all versions of contractarianism, elements which together may be regarded as constitutive or definitive of the contractarian approach. These essential elements of contractarian theory take the form of a three-stage argument schema.

The first stage of the contractarian argument

The first stage of the contractarian argument is the specification of a hypothetical scenario. In this stage, the contractarian merely stipulates a set of hypothetical individuals and characterizes a hypothetical environment in which we are to imagine the hypothetical individuals interacting. There is no definitive set of characterizations of the hypothetical scenario which must be provided. Contractarian specifications of a hypothetical scenario are many and varied, and thus can range from the general and broad to the detailed and narrow. But there are certain parameters within each characterization task to which contractarians typically attend. These parameters will serve to illustrate the nature of the specification of the contractarian hypothetical scenario.

The characterization of a set of hypothetical individuals. A contractarian begins specification of the hypothetical scenario by defining the characteristics of the hypothetical individuals which would significantly affect, if not determine, the nature of their decisions, choices, and interactions in the hypothetical environment. Thus, contractarians characterize their hypothetical individuals in terms of their rationality, risk aversion, future utility discount rate, interests, information, and physical and intellectual capacities.

The nature and extent of an individual's rationality will have a profound effect on the choices he will make. Contractarians determine the nature of their hypothetical individuals' rationality by endorsing some definition of rationality. One of the most theoretically fruitful definitions of rationality is the narrow economic definition of rationality as utility maximization. According to this definition, a rational actor seeks to maximize his utility, or in the parlance of economic and game theory, is a maximizer of his utility function. It is standard practice in microeconomic theory to understand this utility function as generated from the actor's set of preferences, which are assumed to be complete, transitive, and asymmetrical.[3] The advantage of attributing rationality so construed to the hypothetical actors in the contractarian choice problem is that their choices may be determinable as a matter of mathematical calculation. But contractarians need not claim their hypothetical actors are rational in this economic sense of rationality, and may either attribute a weaker version of the economic definition of rationality to the actors or employ a different notion of rationality entirely.

Whatever the conception of rationality contractarians endorse, they seem to agree as to the extent of rationality which must be attributed to their hypothetical individuals. These individuals must be, in general, at least minimally rational, however one construes rationality. For all contractarians hope to make generalizations concerning the nature of the decisions, choices, and interaction of the individuals

---

3 If we let x, y, and z be alternatives, and define the relation xP_iy to mean "Person i prefers x to y," then completeness, transitivity, and asymmetry can be defined as follows:

Completeness: For any pair of alternatives x and y, either xP_iy or yP_ix

Transitivity: For any three alternatives x, y, and z, if xP_iy and yP_iz, then xP_iz.

Asymmetry: For any pair of alternatives x and y, if xP_iy then not yP_ix.

in the hypothetical scenario.[4] The minimal rationality assumption enhances the tractability of analysis of individual choice and collective action problems in the hypothetical scenario. For example, suppose we stipulate that on the economic model of rationality defined above, a minimally rational individual is one who at least seeks to maximize expected utility (even if she does so imperfectly). If we can assume that every individual in the hypothetical scenario is minimally rational in this sense, we can at least deduce the optimal strategies and outcomes for the actors in the scenario, if not the strategies likely to be adopted and the outcomes likely to result. The stronger the rationality assumption, of course, the higher the certainty of the analysis of interaction in the hypothetical scenario. But if the threshold of minimal rationality is not met, it would be extraordinarily difficult even to undertake analysis of the problems in the hypothetical scenario, much less to determine their solutions. If individuals cannot be assumed even to be minimally rational (i.e., and thus cannot be assumed at least to be seeking to maximize their expected utility), then there appears to be no way to generalize about their behavior. Even a complete and accurate description of their beliefs and desires would provide an inadequate basis for predicting their behavior. If, for example, a contractarian's strategy is to construct a hypothetical scenario in which individuals are to make some choice, there would be no straightforward way reliably to predict which choice such individuals would make (or for that matter, whether the individuals would make a choice at all).

In addition, the degree of rationality attributed to the

---

4 Speaking of the justification of a narrow rationality assumption in economic and game theory, Russell Hardin notes that "the assumption of narrow rationality is almost methodological: it is easy to accommodate in analysis, and it is relatively easy to assess in generalizable behaviors. . . ." Hardin also observes that "often the assumption of narrow rational motivation yields predictions that are the most useful benchmark by which to assess the extent and the impact of other motivations" (Hardin, p. 11).

individuals in the hypothetical scenario may also play a substantive role in the ultimate normative argument contractarians make. The contractarian argument might, for example, rely on the claim that the outcome of interaction in the hypothetical scenario is ideally rational because it would result from ideally rational interaction in the hypothetical scenario. Obviously, such a claim can be vindicated only if the contractarian characterizes the hypothetical actors in the hypothetical scenario as ideally rational. The role of the rationality assumption in the overall normative contractarian argument will be discussed in more detail when I consider the construction of the contractarian hypothetical scenario, and again in the course of previewing the specific contractarian theories which will concern us.[5]

The level of rationality attributed to individuals by itself, however, is far from determinative of their decisions, choices, or behavior. Another important factor is the extent to which the hypothetical individuals are characterized as risk averse, risk neutral, or risk inclined, and the extent to which such dispositions toward risk differ among these individuals. For equally rational individuals will make dramatically different choices in the same situation depending on their risk aversion. For the contractarian's analysis of the hypothetical scenario, the specification of risk aversion will affect, for example, what formal rule of choice the hypothetical individuals would employ. Two equally rational individuals, as defined by the economic conception of rationality sketched previously, and in the same situation, may nonetheless employ different choice rules and thus make different decisions. For example, a risk-averse individual might employ the maximin rule in order to maximize his minimum possible gain (or minimize his maximum possible loss), while forfeiting the possibility of higher gains, while a risk-inclined individual might employ the maximax rule in order to maximize his possible gain, at the expense of risking a lesser gain (or greater loss) than he could otherwise guarantee himself.

5 See the section "Construction and Fit" in Chapter 1.

Introduction

An equally important factor in determining individual decisions and behavior is the rate at which individuals discount future utility. The "discount rate" for individuals is the economic term for what is colloquially referred to as "farsightedness" or "shortsightedness." Equally rational individuals may differ with respect to their current or present valuation of future gains. One rational individual may value, for example, one dollar today four times as much as one tomorrow, while another equally rational individual may value one dollar today only twice as much as one tomorrow. As a result, these individuals will calculate their utility gains very differently and make very different choices. Whether and to what extent individuals are shortsighted or farsighted will play a crucial role in the theories we will later consider.

The nature and scope of the interests of the hypothetical individuals also significantly affect their decision process and behavior. Equally rational individuals may have radically different interests which range over radically different areas. Contractarians sometimes characterize the nature of their hypothetical individuals' interests in a highly theoretical manner. They sometimes, for example, endorse the economic conception of rationality we have seen, but further define "true" or "ideal" rationality as the maximization of a utility function generated from a set of purified or idealized interests.[6] Contractarians may have different theories regarding the purification or idealization of these interests. They must, then, specify whether their hypothetical individuals have these idealized or nonidealized sets of interests. When contractarians specify the scope of the interests of their individuals, they must explain, for example, the extent to which the individuals have interests only in themselves, or what we might call "self-regarding" interests, or interests

6 Cf. David Brink's description of a purified desire-satisfaction theory: "A counterfactual desire-satisfaction theory claims that what is valuable is what would satisfy one's desires in some preferred epistemic position, for instance, if one's beliefs and desires were consistent and one's desires were based on full (nonevaluative) information" (Brink, p. 221).

8

in the well-being of others, or what we might call "other-regarding" interests.[7] In economic terms, the issue is whether individuals have interdependent utility functions. Here, the contractarian specifies whether the hypothetical individuals are, for example, egoistic, altruistic, or some combination of both.

Contractarians typically also characterize the individuals in the hypothetical scenario in terms of the nature and scope of their information and uncertainty. The information typically specified in the hypothetical scenario concerns self-knowledge, social knowledge, and general knowledge. Self-knowledge includes individuals' knowledge of their personal characteristics, such as height, weight, sex, physical and mental abilities and disabilities, and so on. Social knowledge includes knowledge of their cultural values and norms, social and political institutions, economic strata and institutions. General knowledge includes knowledge of economics, sociology, criminology, political science, medicine, and all other standard areas of academic and common knowledge.

Finally, contractarians will characterize the physical and mental capacities of the hypothetical actors. Traditional contractarians typically follow Hobbes in characterizing the hypothetical individuals as roughly equivalent in physical and intellectual capacities, or at least sufficiently so to make it very unlikely that any one individual would, on her own, be capable of systematically dominating the others. And with the exception of those who attribute ideal or perfect rationality to the hypothetical actors, most contractarians attribute roughly the same intellectual capacities to their hypothetical actors as ordinary people have.

The characterization of the hypothetical environment. Once a set of hypothetical individuals has been defined, the contractarian then constructs a hypothetical environment in

7 The distinction between "self-regarding" and "other-regarding" interests is drawn nicely in Joel Feinberg's *Harm to Others: The Moral Limits of the Criminal Law* (New York: Oxford University Press, 1984), pp. 70–9.

which these individuals are to interact. The characterization of the hypothetical environment includes such features as the availability of resources, the availability of certain technologies, and the size of the population of individuals.[8] Contractarians often characterize their environment as one in which the existence of various technologies does not affect the approximate physical equality of individuals in it, and the population is large enough to create moderate scarcity of resources and significant coordinative and informational problems which confront large groups of people. Further, the physical characterization also determines whether the environment is supposed to be a prepolitical setting designed to model a hypothetical anarchy preexisting any political association, a postpolitical setting designed to model a hypothetical anarchy ensuing upon the end of a preexisting political association, or more of a "thought experiment," which is neither.

Summary

The first stage of the contractarian argument, characteristic of contractarian theories in general, requires the specification of a hypothetical scenario. This requires the characterizations of a set of hypothetical individuals and a hypothetical environment in which they are to interact. The contractarian typically attributes to the hypothetical individuals a certain level of rationality, risk aversion, farsightedness, self- and other-regarding interests, information, and physical and mental capacities. The hypothetical environment is characterized according to the resources and technologies available, and the size of the population of individuals in it. Once contractarians provide these characterizations, they begin the second stage of the contractarian argument.

8 See Hampton, pp. 254–5 for the significance of the existence of varying degrees of technologies in the contractarian choice problem.

Three-stage contractarian argument schema

The second stage of the contractarian argument

The second stage of the contractarian argument contains the theoretical analysis of interaction in the hypothetical scenario. The first step in providing such an analysis usually consists in demonstrating the existence of some problem the individuals face in the hypothetical scenario. The second step is demonstrating the existence of some solution to this problem. Contemporary contractarians use game theory to make their claims concerning the nature of interaction and decisions among the individuals in the hypothetical scenario. Although the game-theoretic characterization of the hypothetical scenario has only recently become part of the formal apparatus of contractarianism, the traditional contractarian theories created long before the onset of game theory employed arguments which can now be reconstructed and formally tested by game theory.

The analysis of the problem in the hypothetical scenario. Among the game-theoretic models of interaction in the hypothetical scenario available to contractarians are the single-play prisoner's dilemma (the PD), the quasi-PD, the iterated PD, and pure and mixed coordination games. Though these will be explained in detail in subsequent chapters, the game-theoretic modeling of the hypothetical scenario can be illustrated by considering the single-play PD as one possible model of the problem in the hypothetical scenario.[9] In the single-play PD, two or more rational actors face a choice in which the maximization of individual utility yields a collectively suboptimal result (i.e., everyone could be made better off without making anyone worse off). As a result of every chooser's utility-maximizing choice, everyone is made worse off than if he or she did not, paradoxically, act to maximize utility. In the original example of the prisoner's dilemma, two prisoners are captured and interrogated in separate

---

9 According to Hardin, Merrill Flood and Melvin Dresher discovered the game later given the name "prisoner's dilemma" by A. W. Tucker (see Hardin, p. 24). The PD is explained in detail in Luce and Raiffa.

rooms. Each is told that if he confesses and the other does not, he will get a three-month sentence while the other gets a ten-year sentence. If he does not confess, and the other does, he will get a ten-year sentence while the other gets a three-month sentence. If neither confesses, both will get a one-year sentence, while if both confess, both will get an eight-year sentence. In this example, each individual can maximize his utility only by confessing, irrespective of whether the other individual confesses. This game is represented by the following matrix:

	B	
	Not confess	Confess
A		
Not confess	1, 1	10, .25
Confess	.25, 10	8, 8

Figure 1.1. The prisoner's dilemma

In game-theoretic terms, this means that confessing, or not cooperating (i.e., by not pursuing the cooperative strategy, the strategy which requires not confessing), is a "dominant strategy" for each party. In the single-play PD, if both individuals were able to cooperate, they would be better off (each would have only one year to serve) than if each does not cooperate and confesses instead (each ends up with eight years in prison). The single-play PD illustrates the divergence between individual rationality (economically construed) and collective rationality.

The PD is just one possible cause of what more generally may be called "collective action problems." Collective action problems are barriers to the provision of collective goods. We can define a "collective good" as a good which benefits every member of a given group, but from whose consumption it is impractical or impossible to exclude any individuals in that group (no individuals in that group can be prevented from benefiting from the good). Collective goods thus have two essential characteristics: nonexcludability and jointness of supply. A good is "nonexcludable" if it is impossible, infeasible, or uneconomical to exclude others from consuming it. A good is "purely joint in supply" (what some have called "purely nonrivalrous") if "additional consumption of it by one individual does not diminish the amount available to others."[10] Because a collective good is nonexcludable, it is either not possible or not practical to prevent those who do not contribute to its production or maintenance from consuming it. Thus, individuals have an incentive to take a free ride on the contributions of others – to gain at no cost to themselves. This has been called "the free rider problem." In addition, even those individuals not inclined to free ride will fear that sufficiently many others will free ride, that the good will not be produced, and their contribution will be wasted. This has been called "the assurance problem." The free rider and assurance problems together explain why collective goods often have the structure of a single-play PD, and therefore often result in a suboptimal outcome – one in which all are worse off than they would have been had they cooperated (not taken a free ride) and succeeded in creating the collective good.[11] A standard example of a collective good is national defense.

Formally, a collective action problem has been defined in terms of a simple equation of costs and benefits. Russell Hardin, following Mancur Olson, Jr., defines a collective action problem as an "equation of [total] costs [of providing the entire collective] good (C), gross benefits (V_i) to the individual i, and net benefits (A_i) to the individual from i's

---

10 See M. Olson, Jr., *The Logic of Collective Action*, p. 14, n. 21 (1965) and J. Head, "Public Goods and Public Policy," *Public Finance* 17, no. 3 (1962):197–219. In this literature, a "pure public good" is defined as one which is nonexcludable and purely joint in supply. A collective good, however, may admit of various degrees of jointness in supply.

11 The connection between the free rider and assurance problems and the structure of the prisoner's dilemma was first made by David Schmidtz. See D. Schmidtz, *The Limits of Government* (Boulder: Westview Press, 1991), ch. 4.

own contribution to a group's collective good: $A_i = V_i - C$. If $A_i > 0$ for some i, the group is *privileged* and presumably will succeed [(i.e., the collective good will be produced unless strategic bargaining occurs)]. If $A_i < 0$ for *all i*, the group is *latent*, and it will fail unless other noncollective-good (selective) incentives are available to induce contributions" (Hardin, p. 20).[12] As I have said, the PD is one possible cause of collective action problems. In fact, the n-person PD has been used as a formal model of the logical structure of certain collective action problems.[13] But we will see later that the precise nature of various collective action problems is a substantive point of contention, and the assimilation of collective action problems in general to the structure of the n-person PD is controversial. In particular, whether or not a group will be latent is now understood to depend upon the extent to which each group member derives utility from benefiting others. Some otherwise latent groups might be able to provide a collective good because they are, for example, sufficiently altruistic.[14] In addition, it is clear that some collective action problems do not result directly from the incompatibility of individually rational actions and collectively rational (i.e., mutually beneficial) results. Some collective action problems are caused by lack of information (e.g., regarding the rationality, expectations, or beliefs of others) or lack of group coordination (i.e., individuals in a group being unable to coordinate their actions to secure a mutually desired outcome).

Thus, contractarians cannot merely stipulate that their hypothetical scenario produces a collective action problem. Rather, they must prove that their hypothetical actors and environment, as they have characterized them, would necessarily (or probably) create a collective action problem. Oftentimes, this is no mean feat. It requires a formal structuring

12 See Olson, Jr., 1965, pp. 23, 49–50.
13 See Hardin, pp. 25–8.
14 See e.g., Kavka, pp. 154–6 and D. Schmidtz, *The Limits of Government*, ch. 4.

of the interactions of individuals in the hypothetical scenario which takes into account the many different features of the individual and environmental features which define it. Quite often, numerous distinctions and qualifications must be advanced before the game-theoretic picture of the hypothetical scenario becomes clear and defensible. Usually, even if a contractarian can prove that some interaction in his hypothetical environment constitutes, for example, a PD, he will also have to recognize that some interaction in that environment will not have the structure of a PD. Few categorical game-theoretic truths naturally fall out of even the most carefully characterized choice problems.

The game-theoretic modeling of the hypothetical scenario is very sensitive to the variations in the characterizations of the hypothetical individuals and environment. For example, if interaction in the choice environment has, in general, the structure of a PD, then one major problem minimally rational individuals in it will confront is their inability to cooperate. Moreover, their rationality, risk aversion, information, and interests may well result in a war-scale conflict. In other hypothetical environments, PD's might not arise because, for example, the individuals in it are defined as sufficiently altruistic to eliminate any PD's which would otherwise arise. In this situation, individuals might find it rational to cooperate if they knew their cooperation would lead to benefiting others. But even if individuals find cooperation rational, they might face, for example, an information or coordination problem which prevents cooperation. Thus, everyone might be willing to cooperate but be unable to effect the coordination required to achieve the desired cooperation.

Alternatively, the problem in the hypothetical scenario might not arise out of its game-theoretic structure, but might instead be built into the environment directly by the theorist. For example, a contractarian might simply stipulate that the actors in his hypothetical environment must formulate and choose principles of justice.[15] By definition, the problem the hypothetical individuals face is to make their choices under the constraints imposed upon them in the hypothetical scenario. Here, their problem is not one of cooperation or agreement, but is strictly decision-theoretic (though the contractarian's problem may well be to show that all individuals in such an environment would come to an agreement through their separate decision-making procedures).

The analysis of the solution to the problem in the hypothetical scenario. There are two kinds of solutions available to solve the problem in the hypothetical environment. "External solutions" invoke a *deus ex machina* to solve the problem in the contractarian hypothetical scenario. These sorts of solutions introduce a new, foreign element into the formal model of the hypothetical scenario from which the problem arises, an element which itself is unavailable from within the model. Political contractarians, for example, might hold that the importation or imposition of some already established political authority would solve the problems individuals face in the hypothetical setting (e.g., lack of cooperation due to the PD structure of interaction). But they might concede that such a solution would be unavailable to the individuals in the hypothetical scenario. The solution would be available only by assuming its existence independently, rather than demonstrating its emergence internally, from within the model. External solutions nonetheless can be quite useful. Political contractarians might hope, on the basis of external solutions, to demonstrate that political institutions can be viewed as collectively rational, in virtue of their potential for bringing about a mutually advantageous solution to a particular problem. Here, the political contractarian's second-stage task might be described as that of providing a "weak rational reconstruction" of political authority. It is a rational reconstruction because it shows how political association can be

---

15 However, a contractarian would not, of course, simply stipulate that the parties must choose a particular substantive principle. This would blatantly beg the question.

viewed as a (collectively rational) solution to a problem individuals would face. It is weak because it does not claim
that individuals in the hypothetical setting themselves would
be able to bring about such a solution (e.g., political association) to their problems. A weak rational reconstruction might
be all that is available to the contractarian who concedes, for
example, that the individually rational actions of individuals
in the hypothetical scenario would lead inevitably to collectively irrational results (as they do in the PD).

An "internal solution" is one that would be available to
the individuals in the hypothetical scenario. By arguing that
an internal solution exists, the contractarian is claiming that
the individuals in the hypothetical scenario independently
would be able to solve the problems they face. In effect, the
claim is that the model which generates the problem in the
first place itself embeds a solution to that problem. By offering an internal solution to the hypothetical scenario problem, the political contractarian is purporting to provide a
"strong rational reconstruction" of the emergence of political authority. This reconstruction hopes to show that individuals in their hypothetical environment could or would
find the creation of a political authority individually rational
as well as collectively rational, and thus that a set of political
institutions could or would emerge as the result of minimally rational interaction in the hypothetical setting. A strong
rational reconstruction therefore requires the characterization of an internal method of resolution of the problem in
the choice environment. The contractarian must propose
some method which the hypothetical individuals could or
would use to solve their problem. Among the various methods proposed for solving, for example, coordination problems (or elements in proposed solutions to PD's) are voting,
explicit agreement (i.e., explicit contract), conventions, and
discussions. All of these methods constitute various ways in
which groups of individuals might jointly bring about some
change in the nature of their interaction. For example, if the
choice problem is defined as one in which individuals face
PD interactions, the contractarian who hopes to prove that

political authority would emerge as the result of individually rational behavior must show that individuals could create a political authority despite the fact that their interactions have the structure of a PD. This particular problem has often vexed political contractarians and is the focus of much of Hobbesian contractarianism.[16]

The moral contractarian might, in the second stage of his argument, hope to demonstrate that a certain substantive set of moral principles would be chosen in the hypothetical environment. Such a moral contractarian must invoke some decision-theoretic principles according to which the individuals he has characterized in the hypothetical environment specified would necessarily, or at least possibly, choose or agree upon that set of moral principles. If the individuals in the moral contractarian's hypothetical scenario are minimally rational, then this task can be described as that of providing a rational reconstruction of moral principles, rather than of political institutions. It provides one model in which certain principles would result from rational choice or interaction. Among the various methods proposed for solving strictly decision-theoretic problems (as opposed to interdependent, cooperative problems), are the maximin, minimax, expected utility maximization, and disaster avoidance principles of formal decision theory. Any of these methods might be advocated as the best way for an individual to make a choice on his own, a choice which is intended to solve some problem that individual faces (e.g., choosing the rules of the society in which he will live).

Summary

Although stage one of the contractarian argument is strictly definitional, simply stipulating a particular characterization

---

16 Note that weak and strong rational reconstructions are not in themselves justifications of political authority. Instead, they are analytical *strategies* contractarians might use in the second stage of their argument in order to provide a crucial premise in a third-stage justificatory argument.

of a hypothetical scenario, stage two is strictly analytical. In stage two, the contractarian draws conclusions regarding the results of interaction in the hypothetical environment. These conclusions are, therefore, only conditional in form: if there were individuals characterized as I have characterized them in stage one, living under conditions I have specified in stage one, then these individuals would face a certain set of problems which would be amenable to certain sorts of solutions. The problems alleged to exist in the hypothetical scenario are either proved to follow necessarily from the description of the scenario (as in the claim that the scenario would generate widespread, PD-structured collective action problems), or are stipulated by contractarian definition (as in the problem of choosing principles of justice in the hypothetical scenario). In either case, the contractarian hopes to demonstrate the existence of either an external or internal solution to this problem. The former supports a weak rational reconstruction of political authority or moral principles, while the latter supports a strong rational reconstruction of the same.

The third stage of the contractarian argument

The third and final stage of the contractarian argument draws the ultimate contractarian conclusions regarding the normative status of political authority or the nature of morality. The contractarian constructs some argument according to which the results of the first and second stages of his argument serve as some of the premises in establishing the truth of the overall contractarian claim. Political contractarians, for example, might argue on the basis of a second-stage demonstration of the individual and collective rationality of creating and maintaining a political sovereign in the hypothetical scenario that contemporary political authority is thus rational. Moreover, it might be argued that a demonstration of the rationality of political institutions in the hypothetical scenario somehow establishes the moral legitimacy of contemporary institutions which are themselves either individually or collectively rational. The moral contractarian might argue from the fact that individuals in the hypothetical scenario would choose certain principles to the claim that those principles constitute the correct set of moral principles which bind actual individuals. Or he might argue that it is individually rational to comply with morality on the basis of a second-stage demonstration of the individual rationality of complying with morality in the hypothetical environment.

These final arguments can be very different from one another. Some final arguments rely upon independently supported meta-ethical views to establish normative political results. Others rely upon pretheoretic moral intuitions to establish meta-ethical conclusions, which then serve as the basis of political conclusions. Still others endorse novel principles according to which actual, tacit, or hypothetical agreement binds actual (i.e., nonhypothetical) individuals. There are two criteria for assessing these final contractarian arguments. These are the straightforward logical criteria of validity and soundness.[17] The soundness of the final contractarian argument will depend on how well its premises have been defended in the prior stages of the contractarian argument. The assessment of the soundness of the final contractarian argument depends, then, on what I shall call "fit." A final argument fits in its contractarian theory when it relies upon premises established in the first two stages of the theory. A final argument which relies upon substantive premises not established in the first stages of the contractarian theory does not fit in its theory. A contractarian theory whose first and second stages fail even to purport to establish the truth of the premises of its final argument has argument stages which do not fit together. The first and second stages of such an argument are rendered idle and useless,

---

17 A "valid" deductive argument is one such that if its premises are true, then its conclusion must be true. A "sound" argument is a valid deductive argument with all true premises. See W. Salmon, *Logic* (Englewood Cliffs, N.J.: Prentice-Hall, Inc., 1984), p. 19 and H. Kahane, *Logic and Philosophy* (Belmont, Ca.: Wadsworth Publishing Co., Inc., 1978), pp. 6–8.

and the soundness of the final argument remains unproved. The criterion of fit reveals that contractarians cannot, for example, randomly substitute each other's stage-three arguments. For one argument may rely for its crucial premises on the demonstration of the possibility of cooperation in the face of the single-play PD, while the other may rely crucially on the impossibility of cooperation in the single-play PD. Each stage of the contractarian argument builds on the prior, and so each stage must be designed to fit the one which follows it.

Summary

I have characterized the central feature of contractarian theories in terms of a three-stage argument schema which all contractarians endorse. Though this schema allows for considerable variation among particular contractarian arguments, it reveals the common denominators to all contractarian theories: each must specify a hypothetical scenario, provide an analysis of the problems and solutions in that scenario, and finally provide an argument according to which that hypothetical scenario and its analysis yield some ultimate conclusion regarding the legitimacy of political authority or the nature of morality.

The characterization of contractarianism provided above illustrates the way in which traditional contractarianism has been adopted as a general framework for undertaking political and moral theory. Traditional contractarianism, as its name suggests, takes the idea of hypothetical agreement, even unanimous hypothetical agreement, to be central, if not definitive, of contractarianism. But in the contractarian argument schema I have sketched, hypothetical agreement is present only in those contractarian theories which choose to include it in their first-stage characterization of the hypothetical scenario or their second-stage conclusions regarding the results of interaction or choice in that setting. Traditional political contractarian theories generally characterize individuals in the choice environment as unanimously agreeing, or contracting, among each other to institute a political sovereign. The third stage of their argument often relies upon the normative significance of this hypothetical agreement in legitimating political regimes whose subjects have never given to them their actual or even tacit consent. Contemporary contractarian theories need not even address the legitimacy of political authority, and those that do need not rely upon hypothetical agreement in the hypothetical environment for their ultimate normative conclusions.[18] Instead, as we have seen, some might merely hope to show political authority to be collectively rational (e.g., by providing a weak rational reconstruction of political authority). Others might hope to show that a political authority would indeed emerge from the hypothetical contractarian setting (e.g., by providing a strong rational reconstruction of political authority), but as a result of coordinative conventions rather than agreements. The overall framework of the traditional contractarians has been refined, deepened, and broadened in its application. As a result, the role of contract in contractarianism is no longer viewed as essential to contractarianism in general, and is viewed as central only to certain contractarian theories.

REALISTIC AND IDEALISTIC CONSTRUCTIONISM

From the foregoing characterization of contractarianism, it is clear that the most fundamental theoretical task every contractarian faces is that of specifying the hypothetical scenario. I shall call this first-stage process the "construction" of the hypothetical scenario. It is useful to characterize differences among contractarians' first-stage arguments as one of "construction strategies or principles." Construction strategies range from what I shall call "realistic construction-

---

18 Thus, it is not necessarily the case that a proof of a political regime's collective rationality is itself a proof of its moral legitimacy. Some moral theories might hold that collective rationality entails legitimacy, but others might not. An argument is needed to move from a claim about rationality to a conclusion about moral legitimacy.

ism" to "idealistic constructionism." "Realistic construction-ism" is the view that the contractarian's hypothetical setting should be, in as many respects as is possible, realistic. The characterization of the choosers should be based upon a true characterization of human beings. They should be, for example, no more or less rational, risk averse, informed, selfish or altruistic, or numerous than are actual human beings, past or present. The characterization of the hypothetical environment should serve as an accurate model of prepolitical or postpolitical association.

Realistic constructionism is the underlying strategy of the traditional political contractarians of the seventeenth and eighteenth centuries. The choice environment of their contractarian theories is the "state of nature," which is supposed to constitute a hypothetical reconstruction of human interaction before political association. It is supposed to enable us to "deduce" what life would have been like for individuals without political government. The traditional contractarians hope to show that ordinary individuals living in a world without political institutions would voluntarily consent to adopt or create political institutions. Thus, the state of nature each imagines is constructed to accord with certain alleged realities of human nature and environment. Each theorist agrees that the individuals in the state of nature are ordinary human beings with the same knowledge and capacities that human beings normally have. The traditional state of nature is quite "natural." The conclusions each theorist reaches concerning the results of interaction in the state of nature are supposed to constitute true predictions of what would have occurred were human beings once to have interacted over an extended period of time in a prepolitical setting.

The opposite strategy in constructing the contractarian choice problem is to characterize the hypothetical individuals and their environment so that the choice problem can be understood as embedding certain of our most fundamental normative values. This is the strategy of "idealistic constructionism." Here, the characterization of the hypothetical individuals and their environment is guided by ideals of persons and ideals of human interaction. Individuals are defined to embed certain normative ideals, and their environment is designed to insure that their choices and interactions are normatively ideal. The chief contemporary proponent of idealistic constructionism is John Rawls. In *A Theory of Justice*, Rawls quite clearly rejects the traditional construction of the contractarian hypothetical scenario and even explicitly rejects the name "state of nature" for his scenario. Instead, Rawls calls his hypothetical scenario "the original position." The original position is not supposed to provide an accurate model of what human interaction would consist of before or after political association. The hypothetical individuals in it are not as rational, risk averse, and informed as actual individuals in a historically accurate or contemporary society. Rather, they are ideally rational, arguably risk-averse, individuals stripped of all knowledge of their personal characteristics and social environment. They are placed, as Rawls puts it, behind a "veil of ignorance." Individuals in this setting are to choose principles of justice to govern their lives after they leave this setting. The veil of ignorance is justified on the ground that it makes unavailable to individuals choosing principles of justice features of their selves and society that are irrelevant from a moral point of view. For Rawls, considerations of morality require that individuals in the original position be placed behind a veil of ignorance. The original position is intended to provide a morally ideal environment in which to choose principles of justice. It insures that the choices individuals make in it will be fair, and thus gives expression to Rawls's conviction that our conception of justice is founded on our conception of fairness.

In the first stage of the contractarian argument, then, we see that either realistic or idealistic constructionism guides the construction of the contractarian hypothetical setting. And although traditional contractarian theories and Rawls's theory seem to define different ends of the spectrum, ranging from realistic to idealistic construction of the hypothetical scenario, theories need not be exclusively realistic nor idealistic. Contractarians can design their hypothetical scenario to represent certain realities while including in or excluding from it certain features which serve to embed some normative ideals. Contractarian scenarios can, in other words, fall anywhere on a continuum from the realistic to the idealistic.

Construction and rationality

The strategies of idealistic and realistic constructionism provide two further rationales for characterizing the individuals in the hypothetical setting as at least minimally rational.[19] Realistic constructionism requires that the individuals in the contractarian hypothetical setting be at least as rational as actual human beings are, and if we assume that most human beings are minimally rational, then we must assume the same of the individuals imagined in the hypothetical scenario. Idealistic constructionism requires that the individuals in the scenario embed certain normative ideals, and thus may require that these individuals be ideally rational. Thus, we see that various versions of the rationality assumption of contractarianism can be justified not only by the general theoretical goal of deriving generalizations, but on the ground that it is required either by realistic or idealistic constructionism.

Construction and fit

The paradigms of realistic and idealistic construction can also serve in an illustration of the notion of fit earlier introduced as a criterion for assessing the third stage of the contractarian argument. Realistic construction in the first

19 The earlier discussion of the rationality assumption takes place in the subsection of this chapter entitled "The characterization of a set of hypothetical individuals" in the section entitled "The First Stage of the Contractarian Argument."

stage of the contractarian argument requires that the third-stage argument rely on the realistic characterization of the choice problem. For example, the third-stage argument might hold that the choice problem is designed to reconstruct the choices actual individuals might make if they were suddenly to be placed in a postpolitical anarchy. It might provide an argument according to which hypothetical choices can, under certain circumstances, bind actual individuals and that we can therefore understand ourselves as bound by the hypothetical choices made in the hypothetical scenario. Alternatively, the hypothetical inquiry might simply serve to demonstrate that in the absence of the state, current society would degenerate into an environment in which everyone would be worse off than they currently are living under political authority. The point may simply be to demonstrate that the state is mutually advantageous relative to the current anarchic alternative. Both of these strategies exploit the fact that the hypothetical individuals and environment are designed to be realistic. Their realism enables the contractarian to claim that the choices and behavior of the hypothetical individuals in the hypothetical environment reflect the choices and behavior of actual individuals in a realistic, or actual setting.

Idealistic construction in the first stage of the contractarian argument provides the basis for a completely different third-stage argument. A contractarian argument in which the first stage is guided by idealistic constructionism might rely upon the normatively ideal nature of the hypothetical individuals and their environment. These theories hold the view that if a basic ideal like rationality is absent in the choice setting, then a special normative significance might not be expected to attach to the choices made in it. The fact that the individuals and their environment are ideal enables the contractarian to argue that the choices are especially normatively significant. These choices might be understood as fleshing out the logical implications of our basic normative intuitions.

Thus, the third-stage arguments must fit the first-stage construction of the hypothetical scenario and the second-stage analysis of it. A third-stage argument which claims, for example, that the choices of ideal individuals in an ideal setting are themselves normatively ideal, and thus binding on us, cannot use as its premise the second-stage demonstration that realistic, nonideal individuals in a realistic, nonideal setting of the first stage would make certain choices. Nor can a third-stage argument which claims that individuals are bound by their hypothetical choices rely on a second-stage demonstration of the hypothetical choices of idealistic, unrealistic individuals in an idealistic, unrealistic setting provided in the first stage. For such choices could not qualify as reconstructions of actual individuals' choices. The third stage of the contractarian argument must fit with the construction of the hypothetical scenario in the first stage and the subsequent analysis of it in the second stage.

Summary

I have characterized different contractarian strategies for designing the first stage of the contractarian argument as ranging from realistic to idealistic constructionism. These strategies serve not only to place all contractarian theories along a theoretical continuum characterizing the nature of their method, but also serve as the underlying principles supporting the typical contractarian rationality assumption. In addition, I have used these paradigms to illustrate the criterion of fit used in assessing the third stage of the contractarian argument.

THE RENAISSANCE OF HOBBESIAN CONTRACTARIANISM

Every so often in an academic discipline, one innovative individual will fundamentally change the direction of the field. In political philosophy, the most recent instance is, without doubt, John Rawls. Rawls's *A Theory of Justice* is a well-developed contractarian theory of moral principles and political legitimacy inspired by Kant's idealistic contractarian theory. It would not be an exaggeration to say that the last twenty years in political philosophy have been dominated by Rawls's theory. There can be no underestimating the importance of his work, not only in political and moral philosophy, but in other fields as well. Kant's political theory, along with virtually every other contractarian theory, previously had gone largely ignored. Rawls's theory served, at the very least, to bring about a contemporary renaissance of contractarian theories. But since the publication of *A Theory of Justice*, no contractarian theory has enjoyed as much renewed attention and redevelopment as has Hobbes's. Hobbes's theory seems to have emerged as the dominant contractarian alternative to Rawls's theory. In what follows, I shall provide one explanation for the contemporary juxtaposition of Hobbes and Rawls, and account for the present interest in Hobbes's theory.

Perhaps the most fundamental philosophical problem contractarianism seeks to address is the problem of justifying normative conclusions. On the one hand, if one hopes to prove the truth of a normative proposition, one can adduce as premises other normative propositions from which the normative proposition in question can be inferred. But unless everyone (or at least the opponent for whom the normative proposition is to be proved true) is prepared to grant without further question the truth of this prior normative proposition, the proof is incomplete, for it is only as strong as the normative premise on which it rests. Should the truth of that proposition be called into question, another proof would be required. Unless this process is to continue *ad infinitum* or become viciously circular, some premise must be demonstrable on the basis of an argument which itself does not presuppose any normative truths. By reducing normative propositions to nonnormative ones, we might hope to avoid either resting the proof of normative propositions on an endless or circular normative chain, or simply stipulating some foundational normative proposition in virtue of which all others may be proved. The former is theoretically inadequate and the latter ultimately begs the question against those who do not accept the foundational normative proposition endorsed. But reductions of normative propositions to nonnormative ones – or attempts to derive normative conclusions exclusively from nonnormative premises – have proved notoriously difficult to defend. "Hume's Hurdle" and G. E. Moore's "naturalistic fallacy" name the problem which has continually plagued normative philosophy. Following Hume and Moore, philosophers have generally recognized an apparent "naturalistic gap" between "is" and "ought" propositions.[20]

20 See G. E. Moore, *Principia Ethica* (Cambridge University Press, 1960), pp. 5–21. See also D. Hume, *A Treatise of Human Nature*, edited by L. A. Selby-Bigge (New York: Oxford University Press, 1960). Hume asserts the logical argument that no "ought" statement is deducible from an "is" statement:

> In every system of morality, which I have hitherto met with, I have always remark'd, that the author proceeds for some time in the ordinary way of reasoning, and establishes the being of a God, or makes observation concerning human affairs; when of a sudden I am surpriz'd to find, that instead of the usual copulations of propositions, *is*, and *is not*, I meet with no proposition that is not connected with an *ought*, or an *ought not*. This change is imperceptible; but is, however of the last consequence. For as this *ought* or *ought not*, expresses some new relation or affirmation, 'tis necessary that it shou'd be observ'd and explain'd; and at the same time that a reason should be given, for what seems altogether inconceivable, how this new relation can be a deduction from others, which are entirely different from it. (Hume, 469)

Moore's "naturalistic fallacy" underscores Hume's point: as a matter of logical deduction, "ought" propositions seem not to be entailed by any set of "is" propositions. According to Hare's somewhat more nuanced interpretation of the naturalistic fallacy, its point is that any non-normative definition of a normative term will be inconsistent with recognizing the commendatory force of the normative term being defined. For example, if one offers the definition of a "good act" (a normative proposition) as (equivalent or identical in meaning to) an "act which increases happiness" (a descriptive proposition), then it becomes impossible to commend an act which increases happiness by saying that the act is a good one. For the statement, "That act is a good act," just means "The act which increases happiness is an act which increases happiness." But surely, Hare argues, the meaning of the sentence praising the act as good is not analytic, but instead is

Introduction

Political and moral theory are concerned to establish the truth of certain normative propositions. Given the dilemma posed by the naturalistic gap, political and moral theorists must risk either begging the question against certain normative views (or they might avoid this risk by restricting the application of their theories to those who share certain fundamental normative precommitments), or failing to bridge the gap between descriptive premises and normative conclusions. In fact, two strands of contractarian theories have evolved, each of which seems to avoid one risk only at the expense of taking the other. We can define such theories by locating Hobbes and Rawls on opposite ends of a contin-

supposed to accomplish more than mere redundancy or definition. It is intended, and in fact succeeds, in commending the act by calling it good. But this would be impossible if a "good act" simply meant "an act which increases happiness." See R. M. Hare, *The Language of Morals* (New York: Oxford University Press, 1952), ch. 5.

Philosophers generally credit Moore with having initiated this century's meta-ethical inquiry. Darwall, Gibbard, and Railton write, "the controversy began with Moore's charge that previous moral philosophy had been disfigured by a fallacy – the fallacy of defining Good in either naturalistic or metaphysical terms." But at the same time, they note that "it has been known for the last fifty years that Moore discovered no *fallacy* at all." Despite the dubious and now discredited semantic and epistemic views on which Moore's claim arguably rests, Darwall, Gibbard, and Railton acknowledge that "it seems impossible to deny that Moore was on to something." S. Darwall, A. Gibbard, and P. Railton, "Toward *Fin de siècle* Ethics: Some Trends," *The Philosophical Review* 101, no. 1 (January 1992):115–16. Whether Moore's naturalistic fallacy is a fallacy at all, can be revised to constitute a fallacy, or merely points to an unresolved difficulty in meta-ethics is a matter of substantial disagreement among moral philosophers. For present purposes, I endorse only the view that inferences from descriptive premises to normative conclusions seem to present logical difficulties different in kind from those presented by inferences either from descriptive premises to descriptive conclusions or from normative premises to normative conclusions.

For some of the standard discussions of Moore's argument, see A. Prior, *Logic and the Basis of Ethics* (Oxford: Clarendon Press, 1949), ch. 1, and J. J. C. Smart, "An Outline of a System of Utilitarian Ethics," in J. J. C. Smart and Bernard Williams, *Utilitarianism: For and Against* (Cambridge University Press, 1973).

uum. This continuum ranges from theories which are highly idealized and thus highly normatively precommitted (theories whose first stage is likely to be guided by idealistic constructionism), to those which are minimally idealized, and thus minimally normatively precommitted (theories whose first stage is likely to be guided by realistic constructionism). Although the former avoid the naturalistic fallacy, they face the charge of begging the question. Although the latter beg no questions, they face the problem of deriving a normative proposition either from a nonnormative one or from a normatively minimal proposition without committing a *non sequitur*. In the section that follows, I will suggest that Hobbes's theory has been viewed as the embodiment of all the strengths of contractarianism without the substantive, normative precommitments found in Rawls's theory. Rawls has convinced many philosophers that the contractarian analysis of normative issues is powerful and productive, and may offer a fruitful approach to the problem of bridging the naturalistic gap, or at least considerably mitigating its effects. But criticism of Rawls has equally convinced some philosophers that Rawls's version of contractarianism begs central normative questions by presupposing an entire Kantian normative framework. Hobbesian contractarianism promises to avoid this problem. But as I have suggested, it cannot avoid this problem without encountering another of equal importance.

Rawls and normative precommitment

There is considerable disagreement regarding the extent to which Rawls's theory in *A Theory of Justice* is precommitted to controversial normative ideals. Some hold that Rawls presupposes too much, while others argue that he does not presuppose enough. Virtually every aspect of Rawls's initial theory has been criticized, but criticism of his theory of primary goods and his characterization of the original position stand out as examples of the controversial nature of his normative presuppositions. But we need not examine the details of these criticisms to reveal his normative precommitments. In his series of articles entitled "Kantian Constructivism in Moral Theory," Rawls makes explicit the normative framework he takes to be operative in his contractarian theory. Though an adequate explication of his view in these articles would take us far afield, a brief sketch of the normative framework he presupposes will serve to illustrate the nature and extent to which Rawls regards his theory as normatively precommitted. The following provides this brief sketch.

Rawls claims that his theory proposes a specific model of both a well-ordered society and the moral person. These conceptions are determined prior to his theory, and thus are presupposed, rather than demonstrated, by it. Rawls claims that a well-ordered society contains political institutions which mirror the public conception of justice. The members of such a society view themselves as free and equal moral persons. They are entitled to make claims on the designs of their institutions in the name of their own fundamental aims and highest order interests. They are free to revise their systems of ends. They have equal rights to determine and assess the principles of justice with which their institutions are to accord. And each person, as a moral person, has an effective sense of justice and a conception of the good (i.e., a system of ends). The original position is designed to connect the models of a well-ordered society and the moral person with principles of justice.

In the original position, individuals are assumed to make decisions based on their "highest order interests," since these are the interests, according to the concept of a well-ordered society, in the name of which persons are entitled to make claims against their institutions. Individuals are viewed as having highest order interests (supremely regulative and effective interests) in realizing and exercising their moral powers. Their moral powers are their capacities to understand, apply, and act from an effective sense of justice, and to form, revise, and rationally pursue their conception of the good. But individuals in the original position can pursue their highest order interests only if there is some good such that no matter what one's conception of the good is, its maximization is uniquely rational. This maximand in the original position is provided by what Rawls calls "primary goods." Primary goods are of general use for the pursuing of ends contemplated by, or possible for, *moral persons,* not actual persons, in the original position. Rawls claims that autonomous, rational agents in the original position will seek to maximize their own share of primary goods. The construction of the original position, and in particular, the conception of individuals in it as rationally autonomous, is guided by what Rawls claims are the two necessary elements of any notion of social cooperation: the Reasonable and the Rational. The Reasonable requires that terms of cooperation be fair, and that burdens and benefits of cooperation be distributed according to the principles of reciprocity and mutuality. The Rational requires that cooperation be beneficial to every individual.

In sum, Rawls's theory presupposes, rather than argues for, a conception of the well-ordered society and the moral person. Moreover, it presupposes that individuals have as their highest order interests the fulfillment of a particular conception of justice. In generating the specific content of principles of justice, Rawls presupposes that the choice of principles of justice must be both reasonable and rational, as he understands those concepts. Thus, the original position must insure that cooperation is fair, reciprocal, and mutual. If we take Rawls at his word, his view can hardly be understood to be normatively minimal. Instead, it constitutes a rather elaborate fleshing-out of some very complex, highly controversial, Kantian notions of morality and persons.[21] In

21 Rawls claims, for example, that
> [w]hen fully articulated, any conception of justice expresses a conception of the person, of the relations between persons, and of the general structure and ends of social cooperation. To accept the principles that represent a conception of justice is at the same

later work, Rawls has explicitly conceded that his theory presupposes certain intuitions and conceptions shared by members of modern democracies and not necessarily shared by others.[22] Understandably, philosophers who are none-

> time to accept an ideal of the person; and in acting from these principles we realize such an ideal. Let us begin, then, by trying to describe the kind of person we might want to be and the form of society we might wish to live in and to shape our interests and characters. In this way we might arrive at the notion of a well-ordered society. ("A Well-Ordered Society." in P. Laslett and J. Fishkin, eds., *Philosophy, Politics, and Society,* 5th Series [New Haven, Conn.: Yale University Press, 1979.])
>
> Commentators on Rawls's work have long emphasized the foundational role of the conceptions of the person and of the well-ordered society as essentially pretheoretic commitments in Rawls's later work. See e.g., Brink, *Moral Realism,* pp. 314–16 and accompanying notes ("Rawls concludes that determinacy in theory choice in ethics is possible only if we appeal to the morally more robust ideal of the person. [314] . . . A Kantian Ideal may require Rawls's two principles of justice, but there are alternative ideals of the person (e.g., utilitarian and libertarian ideals) that require other moral principles." [317].

22 This is quite explicitly Rawls's strategy in articles he has published after *A Theory of Justice.* In "Justice as Fairness: Political Not Metaphysical," (in *Philosophy and Public Affairs* 14 [1985]), Rawls argues that his theory applies only to modern constitutional democracies and may not apply elsewhere:

> [J]ustice as fairness is framed to apply to what I have called the 'basic structure' of a modern constitutional democracy. . . . Whether justice as fairness can be extended to a general political conception for different kinds of societies existing under different historical and social conditions, or whether it can be extended to a general moral conception, or a significant part thereof, are altogether separate questions. I avoid prejudging these larger questions one way or the other. (pp. 224–5)
>
> [S]ince justice as fairness is intended as a political conception of justice for a democratic society, it tries to draw solely upon basic intuitive ideas that are embedded in the political institutions of a constitutional democratic regime and public traditions of interpretation. Justice as fairness is a political conception in part because it starts from within a certain political tradition. (p. 225)

It is worth noting, however, that Rawls insists that his theory does not presuppose any controversial metaphysical, psychological, or epistemological views. It does not, he claims, presuppose the truth of any

theless convinced that contractarianism is a fruitful normative enterprise might well be reluctant to accept this entire
Kantian package which I have just barely sketched. Both
criticism of Rawls's normative commitments in *A Theory of
Justice*, and especially reaction to the commitments made
in his subsequent works, have given philosophers incentive to seek other contractarian frameworks devoid of the
presupposition of complex and controversial normative
ideals.

Hobbes and normative minimalism

No extant contractarian theory is more normatively minimalistic than Hobbes's theory in *Leviathan*. Hobbes's theory shares
with other contractarian theories the minimal rationality assumption I have previously discussed. But even this as-

> controversial theory of the person, for example:
>> a conception of the person in a political view, for example, the
>> conception of citizens as free and equal persons, need not involve,
>> so I believe, questions of philosophical psychology or a metaphys-
>> ical doctrine of the nature of the self. No political view that de-
>> pends on these deep and unresolved matters can serve as a public
>> conception of justice in a constitutional democratic state. (p. 231)
> But at the same time, Rawls admits that
>> a conception of the person, as I understand it here, is a norma-
>> tive conception, whether legal, political, or moral, or indeed also
>> philosophical or religious, depending on the overall view to which
>> it belongs. In this case the conception of the person is a moral
>> conception, one that begins from our everyday conception of per-
>> sons as the basic units of thought . . . and adapted to a political
>> conception of justice and not to a comprehensive moral doctrine.
>> (p. 232, n. 15)
> The extent to which the political conception of the person upon which
> Rawls's theory depends is normatively controversial is itself a matter
> of controversy. The above passages from Rawls make clear that some
> theory of the person is presupposed. But the question remains whether
> this theory is somehow uncontroversial, because it alleges not to be a
> conception of the person for purposes of a full-fledged general moral
> theory, or is nonetheless controversial because it assumes a certain
> ideal not universally shared (even in Rawls's view, the conception is
> shared at most among citizens of modern constitutional democracies).

sumption is not idealistic. For Hobbes claims that individuals are, for the most part, only minimally rational, and on some accounts, even relies on the claim that many individuals are sometimes irrational. Hobbes's realism extends to every part of his theory. The state of nature, as I have mentioned, is designed to portray accurately the nature of prepolitical human interaction and the bargaining that takes place in it is unfettered by any moral constraints. The ultimate social contract in Hobbes's theory is a product of hypothetical interaction that contains no normative assumptions beyond that of minimal rationality. In fact, it represents an attempt to generate normative conclusions from virtually no normative assumptions at all.[23] And although the absence of normative presupposition from Hobbes's theory insures that no normative questions will be begged, it is this fact, I will argue, that contributes to the demise of pure Hobbesian contractarianism.

OVERVIEW: THEMES AND THEORIES

This book is focused exclusively on Hobbesian contractarianism and does not purport to contribute to classical Hobbesian scholarship. Classical Hobbesian scholarship concerns itself as much with what Hobbes said as with what can be said on Hobbes's behalf. I shall be exclusively concerned with the latter. In recent years, three book-length contractarian positions have been advanced, each of which adopts a Hobbesian approach to political or moral philosophy. These are Jean Hampton's *Hobbes and the Social Contract Tradition*, Gregory Kavka's *Hobbesian Moral and Political The-*

---

23 Hobbes does claim that individuals in the state of nature are bound by "the laws of nature." But he understands these laws to be requirements of individual rationality rather than requirements of an objective morality distinct from rationality. Moreover, he claims that in the state of nature, these laws are binding *in foro interno* only, and bind *in foro externo* only when adherence to them is individually rational. (See *Leviathan*, ch. 15.)

ory, and David Gauthier's *Morals by Agreement*. The first two of these are political contractarian theories, while the third is a moral contractarian theory. Each of these works shares a commitment to utilizing the fundamental contractarian approach found in Hobbes's work. Each reflects, in my view, a rejection of much, if not all, of Rawls's normative precommitments, and takes on the task of rebuilding Hobbes's theory with the help of contemporary game and economic theory. In this final section, I first explain why these theories together constitute a unified exploration into the foundations of Hobbesian contractarianism. I then provide an overview of the critique which follows and anticipates the major themes of the book.

In order to provide a critical evaluation of Hobbesian contractarianism, I have chosen the works of Hampton, Kavka, and Gauthier. Considered in the order they are presented, these theories represent a progression from Hobbes's traditional position, to a modified Hobbesian position, to a radical reinterpretation of Hobbes's theory. The first two theories use Hobbes's theory as a point of departure for establishing the legitimacy of political authority. The third theory uses Hobbes's framework to launch a moral contractarian theory. Together, these theories illustrate the richness of the Hobbesian approach to normative theory, and seem to define the spectrum of variations and uses to which Hobbesian contractarianism can be put. In addition, these are, analytically speaking, "state-of-the-art" Hobbesian contractarian theories. As I have mentioned, each author utilizes the most rigorous analytical tools available in developing their contractarian position, and attempts to construct a comprehensive Hobbesian contractarian theory. Moreover, these three theories are presently the only well-developed, full-length contemporary versions of Hobbesian contractarianism. Finally, the analysis of these theories brings to light certain common problems that, I will argue, face any Hobbesian contractarian. These themes help define the limits of Hobbesian contractarianism.

Introduction

The themes

Two major themes will emerge from the critique of these Hobbesian theories. The first is that the problem of collective action poses a formidable, if not insurmountable, barrier to the success of Hobbesian contractarianism. Hobbesian contractarian theories attempt to demonstrate that individuals facing collective action problems in the hypothetical scenario can provide themselves with solutions to their own collective action problems, either by creating a political sovereign or by voluntarily constraining their utility-maximizing behavior. Such solutions are, as explained previously, "internal solutions," ones which must arise from within the population facing the collective action problems. An external solution can solve collective action problems by imposing certain constraints on the behavior of individuals facing the collective action problem. But external solutions to collective action problems cannot, by definition, arise from the voluntary interaction of the group facing the problem. Notwithstanding the creative efforts of Hobbesian theorists, the lesson of my critique is that collective action problems are extraordinarily resistant to internal solutions. The task of surmounting collective action problems barring cooperation in the state of nature appears to be beyond even the most ingenious and inventive of arguments. Arguments purporting to demonstrate the viability of an internal solution either misconceive the collective action problem in the choice problem, and so misconceive its solution, or solve the initial collective action problem in the choice environment only to create another.

The second and more fundamental theme calls attention to the chief liability of normatively minimalistic contractarian theories like Hobbesian contractarianism. Attempts to connect the first stage of the Hobbesian contractarian argument with the contractarian's ultimate moral or political conclusion are undermined by the normative poverty of the hypothetical scenario. Unlike Rawls's theory, normatively minimalistic theories presuppose few normative truths in the construction of their hypothetical scenario. In light of the paucity of normative inputs in the first stage of Hobbesian contractarianism, it is difficult to generate strong normative conclusions in the third stage. The distance between the normatively minimal premises and normatively rich conclusions of Hobbesian contractarianism is difficult to span. Given the Scylla of the naturalistic gap and the Charybdis of begging the question which face any attempt to establish the truth of normative propositions, this result should be unsurprising.

The theories

Before previewing the details of the three contractarian theories, I should note one feature all three have in common. They share the view that political authority is to be justified, if at all, on the ground that it constitutes a solution to certain problems in the hypothetical scenario which each refers to as the "state of nature." They disagree, however, over the nature and causes of problems in the state of nature. Hampton argues, on Hobbes's behalf, that most interaction in the state of nature is correctly modeled as an iterated PD. She claims that shortsightedness causes individuals to fail to appreciate the rationality of cooperation in such situations, and is thus responsible for the resulting conflict and noncooperation of the state of nature. The state, she argues, is necessary to force individuals to cooperate, as individual rationality requires. The state, in Hampton's view of Hobbes's theory, forces individuals not only to act in a collectively rational manner, but in a manner which is individually rational as well. Kavka agrees that the state of nature is a state of conflict and noncooperation but disagrees about its cause. This is because Kavka's state of nature is populated by ideally rational, farsighted individuals. He thus cannot claim that conflict and noncooperation are the result of the shortsightedness of individuals in the state of nature. Instead he argues that cooperation in the state of nature has the game-theoretic structure of a quasi-PD, in which defection (noncooperation) is quasi-dominant. According to Kavka's entire analysis of the state of nature and his definition of a "quasi-PD" (described in detail in Chapter 4), this means that it will be unlikely for cooperation to be individually rational in the state of nature. Kavka thus views political authority as the means for enforcing cooperative agreements in which defection would otherwise be quasi-dominant, agreements in which cooperation, therefore, would otherwise be likely to be individually irrational. Gauthier, unlike Hampton and Kavka, is most concerned with the single-play PD in the state of nature. As we will see, Gauthier is concerned to show not that political authority is legitimate, but that the game-theoretic problems of the state of nature disappear once we understand the true nature of the requirements of individual rationality. He hopes to demonstrate this by showing cooperation to be individually rational even in the single-play PD. Thus, the game-theoretic understanding of the state of nature least conducive to achieving voluntary cooperation and collectively rational outcomes (i.e., a single-play PD) would still not succeed in demonstrating the need for political authority. Cooperation would be possible in the state of nature without political enforcement of agreements. So we see that each of these contractarians has a different understanding of the nature and causes of interaction in the state of nature. Hampton and Kavka agree that there is conflict and noncooperation, but disagree as to their game-theoretic explanation, while Gauthier argues that even if interaction in the state of nature has the game-theoretic structure of a single-play PD, it can be nonetheless individually rational to cooperate in the state of nature. Each accepts the paradigm of the state of nature but provides a different account of its correct analysis.

Hobbes and the Social Contract Tradition. The first book I will consider is Jean Hampton's *Hobbes and the Social Contract Tradition.* Her book represents, to date, the most thorough and compelling attempt to provide an accurate reconstruction of Hobbes's theory. Instead of advocating a substantive position herself, Hampton undertakes a defense of Hobbes's original argument as an exercise in its own right. Although she nowhere endorses Hobbes's theory, even in the refined form of the position she advances on his behalf, she does claim to have vindicated Hobbes as far as is theoretically possible.[24] Hampton claims that the Hobbesian state of nature is supposed to serve as a model of what would happen to contemporary, actual individuals were society's political institutions suddenly removed. It is supposed to provide a model-theoretic illustration of the anarchy to which all human beings, necessarily, would return should they succeed in removing their political authorities from power. This state of anarchy, she argues, would consist in a war of all against all in which only conflict, and not cooperation, would be possible. On the basis of this claim, she argues that individuals in the state of nature would find it rational to adopt or create political institutions and that political institutions would thus emerge as the result of rational interaction in the state of nature. Her argument for the rational emergence of political association in the state of nature takes place in the second stage of her contractarian argument. Once she establishes that claim, she offers, in the third stage of her contractarian argument, an argument according to which contemporary political institutions are legitimate. This argument is two-part. In the first part, Hampton employs what I call "the inferential argument" to conclude that contemporary, collectively rational, political institutions are individually rational to maintain. The argument holds that institutions which individuals would find rational to create and maintain in the state of nature are justified, because of their rationality, for actual individuals in contemporary society. She claims that:

24 Throughout the book, however, I will treat Hampton's arguments on Hobbes's behalf as if they were advanced as Hampton's own position. It should be understood, however, that references to Hampton's position would be more accurately, though more cumbersomely, described as "Hampton's Hobbes" position, and not as Hampton's own views of the correct answer to the questions Hobbes's theory addresses.

> human beings are justified in creating and maintaining the
> state [because] rational people [in the state of nature] have
> a certain compelling reason (either self-interested or other-
> interested or a combination of both) for leaving the state of
> nature by creating government, where that reason is (or should
> be) *our* reason either for creating government if one does not
> exist or for maintaining it in power if it does. (Hampton, 272)

Furthermore, that compelling reason which individuals in
the state of nature have for creating and maintaining a state
"constrains the *kind* of state we should create and maintain
(i.e., it tells us what kind of state is a justified political
regime)" (Hampton, p. 273).

Hampton follows Hobbes and argues that the reason individuals in the state of nature have for creating and maintaining a state, and thus our reason for the same, is that
doing so is individually rational. So the third stage of Hampton's argument relies upon the second stage project of demonstrating the creation and maintenance of the state in the
state of nature to be individually rational. Then based on the
inferential argument, she concludes that the state is rational
for contemporary individuals. But even if this claim succeeds, Hampton must provide some reason for thinking that
a demonstration of the (individual) rationality of a state
constitutes a demonstration of its moral justification or legitimacy. That reason is supplied by Hobbes's meta-ethical
view according to which morality is redefined in terms of
individual rationality. This view is supported in the second
part of the third stage of her contractarian argument. For it
connects the results of the second stage with the ultimate
justification of the state. It shows the normative value of
demonstrating the individual rationality of political association in the state of nature.

My criticism of Hampton's view is two-part. In Chapter 2,
I challenge the third stage of her argument. I first point out
that the inferential argument she defends is problematic,
and that what individuals find individually rational in the
state of nature need not be found individually rational by

actual individuals in contemporary or postpolitical society. I
then reject the claim that Hobbes's redefinition of morality
in terms of individual rationality is motivated by sound arguments. In Chapter 3, I reject her claim that the creation
and maintenance of a political sovereign in the state of nature is individually rational, and thus reject the second stage
of her argument. The crux of the argument here reveals the
theme that standard problems of collective action are the
ruin of attempts to show the individual rationality of providing collective goods like the state.

Finally, in the last section of Chapter 3, I waive my objections against her second-stage argument, and return to criticism of her third-stage meta-ethical argument. I grant that it
is individually rational to create and maintain a state in the
state of nature and thus in contemporary society. Even so, I
argue that a demonstration of a regime's individual rationality cannot provide its justification. This is because the
Hobbesian redefinition of morality in terms of individual
rationality is not only unmotivated, but is also subject to a
reductio ad absurdum. I claim that her arguments for the individual rationality of creating and maintaining a political sovereign, if successful, unfortunately would serve to demonstrate that a collectively irrational regime may be individually
rational to maintain as well. And if this is so, surely the
mere individual rationality of maintaining a regime cannot
serve as its justification. This argument demonstrates that
standard collective action problems are, at yet another level,
ultimately responsible for the undoing of Hampton's theory.
This signals the failure of the meta-ethical theory which
identifies morality with individual rationality, and reiterates
one of the general themes of this book: the problem of
collective action undermines the second and third stages of
the standard Hobbesian argument.

Hobbesian Moral and Political Theory. The next book I consider is Kavka's *Hobbesian Moral and Political Theory.* Like
Hampton's theory, Kavka's is a version of political contractarianism. But Kavka's strategy is to combine the insights of
Hobbes and Rawls in a theory which blends realistic and

43

idealistic constructionism. His theory reconceives the Hobbesian project, creating a hypothetical bargaining scenario reminiscent of Rawls's original position, but defined in part by the state of nature. Recognizing the danger of circularity surrounding purely idealistic theories, and the difficulty of generating normative conclusions attending purely realistic theories, Kavka's hybrid theory represents an ambitious attempt to avoid the pitfalls and reap the benefits of both approaches. As a result, Kavka is able to advance a number of stage-three arguments – arguments which purport to explain the normative significance of the hypothetical analysis of his contractarian theory – some of which are unavailable to pure realistic theories like Hobbes's. The principal aim in considering Kavka's theory, for the purposes of the present inquiry, is to evaluate these arguments. Analysis of Kavka's theory reveals, however, that his attempt to blend the two opposed theoretical approaches of idealism and realism leads to a number of conceptual confusions surrounding the structure of his theory. Consideration of his theory therefore first requires an unraveling of the threads of realism and idealism in the construction of his hypothetical scenario. Once the realistic and idealistic elements in his theory are clearly separated, his stage-three arguments can be evaluated. The first, I argue, fails for lack of fit: It is premised on the outcome of a realistic hypothetical setting, but Kavka's hypothetical scenario contains idealistic elements. The second two rely principally on the idealistic elements included in Kavka's hypothetical setting and fail for independent reasons. Unlike Rawls, Kavka does not fully embrace idealistic constructionism and thus cannot turn to Kantian notions for normative justification. Instead, Kavka's partial embrace of realistic constructionism requires alternative arguments to explain the normative significance of the outcomes of his quasi-idealistic hypothetical scenario, arguments which I claim cannot withstand critical scrutiny.

Morals by Agreement. David Gauthier's *Morals by Agreement* is, as I have said, a moral contractarian version of

Hobbes's theory. Its principal aim is to demonstrate that morality can be derived from individual rationality, once the latter is properly analyzed. His analysis of rationality, and its relationship to morality, takes place within a Hobbesian state of nature. There are two parts to Gauthier's theory. The first is a substantive theory of morality. Here, Gauthier hopes to show that the content of moral principles can be understood as the outcome of a rational bargain in the state of nature. The second is a motivational theory of morality. Here, he hopes to show that it will be individually rational to comply with moral principles so understood. This requires Gauthier to explain how cooperation in the single-play PD can be individually rational. In the discussion of Gauthier, I suppose, *arguendo,* that he has successfully demonstrated the possibility of the individual rationality of cooperation in the single-play PD, and thus that cooperation is possible in the state of nature. I deny, however, Gauthier's substantive claim that cooperation in the state of nature will be fair and thus moral. My strategy for demonstrating the failure of Gauthier's substantive moral theory is to show that if it is individually rational to cooperate in the state of nature, it will be individually rational to cooperate even on unfair terms. The crux of the argument here relies, once again, on the problems of collective action that plague, in this case, Gauthier's attempts to show that compliance on fair terms, or what Gauthier calls "narrow compliance," is uniquely rational in the state of nature. The theme of collective action problems emerges throughout the consideration of Gauthier's theory. In addition, Gauthier's theory is seen as yet another attempt to traverse the naturalistic gap, for Gauthier hopes to generate both a substantive and motivational theory of morality from a purely nonmoral characterization of the state of nature. From such a characterization, it is supposed to be demonstrable that it is individually rational to cooperate on, and only on, fair terms with other individuals. I will argue that it is therefore unsurprising that Gauthier's argument does not succeed.

Though my principal aim in considering Gauthier's theory

is to assess an outstanding example of Hobbesian moral contractarianism, his theory also has implications for political contractarianism. In the introductory section of the discussion of Gauthier, I will highlight the connections between Gauthier's theory and political Hobbesian contractarianism.

Summary

In the following chapters, we begin our investigation into Hobbesian contractarianism. We explore Hampton's, Kavka's, and Gauthier's attempts to revitalize Hobbes's contractarian argument. Their works are the best and most comprehensive representatives of the Hobbesian contractarian framework. All are committed to rigorous game-theoretic analysis and all are, to various extents, normatively minimalistic. My critique of these theories is not intended to exhaust the "logical space" even for Hobbesian contractarianism, much less for all of contractarianism. Rather, my hope is that by examining these well-developed works in detail, the discussion will illuminate and guide future Hobbesian contractarian work while informing the contractarian approach in general.

Chapter 2

Hampton's justificatory strategy

In *Hobbes and the Social Contract Tradition*, Jean Hampton first presents Hobbes's well-known argument for the legitimacy of a political sovereign with absolute power and authority. This argument concludes that individuals must completely alienate all of their rights to a sovereign who shall be free to rule as she sees fit. It invites us to understand the fundamental relationship between subject and sovereign as that of slave and master. Hampton argues that the fundamental flaw in this position, or "alienation theory" as she refers to it, is that Hobbes's views on psychology and ethics, both discussed in this chapter, entail an inalienable right to self-defense, one which would therefore survive the transition from the state of nature to political association. In order to reconcile Hobbes's psychological and ethical theories, which together entail an inalienable right to self-defense, and Hobbes's political theory, which entails the alienation of all rights including the right to self-defense, Hampton jettisons alienation theory and endorses a "fallback" position she reconstructs from previously neglected sections of Hobbes's writings.[1] Unlike alienation theory, this position purports to

---

1 Hampton claims the fallback theory can be found in Hobbes's *Leviathan*, though she recognizes that Hobbes's primary argument is clearly intended to support alienation theory. Agency theory, however, renders the creation and maintenance of a political sovereign consistent with individuals' possession of an inalienable right to self-defense. See Hampton, pp. 239–47. In addition, as I noted in Chapter 1 in the subsection "Hobbes and the Social Contract Tradition," it should be

justify a sovereign with only limited power and authority and invites us to understand the relationship between subject and sovereign as one of principal and agent, rather than slave and master. Hampton's chief objective, then, is to explicate and defend, on Hobbes's behalf, this modified Hobbesian fallback position, or "agency theory," a position which preserves the fundamental insights of Hobbes's approach, while discarding perhaps his most objectionable and infamous conclusion. In this and the following chapter, my objective is to present and assess Hampton's arguments for agency theory.[2]

OVERVIEW OF HAMPTON'S JUSTIFICATORY STRATEGY

The first stage of Hampton's argument postulates a hypothetical, prepolitical state of nature populated by individuals who, but for their circumstances, are supposed to be just like us. That is, they are supposed to be human beings with the same innate physiological and psychological characteristics we have. Most importantly for Hampton's purposes, they are supposed to be, as she supposes we are, predominantly rational. In the next section of this chapter, I introduce the defining elements of Hampton's state of nature in the course of presenting her second-stage analysis of conflict in the state of nature. According to this analysis, predominantly rational individuals in the state of nature would inevitably, because of their intrinsic human nature, be both unable to cooperate and embroiled in a war of all against all. Hampton discusses and rejects Hobbes's two accounts of the cause of such conflict and replaces them with her own

clear that Hampton's project is to defend Hobbes's theory for the sake of intellectual progress. She nowhere endorses Hobbes's theory, her modified version of Hobbes's theory, or any contractarian theory as representing her *own* views in political or moral theory.

2 Because the contractarian strategies underlying both agency and alienation theories are very similar, consideration of the former will necessarily overlap somewhat with analysis of the latter.

version. Hampton thus agrees, albeit on different grounds, with Hobbes's conclusion that human beings in the state of nature would be unable to cooperate and forced into perpetual conflict.

The bulk of Hampton's efforts in her stage-two analysis, however, are devoted to the task of demonstrating the existence of what in Chapter 1 I termed an "internal solution" to the problem of conflict in the state of nature. Recall that an internal solution to a problem in the state of nature is one which individuals in the state of nature could provide for themselves. Thus, Hampton argues that individuals living in the state of nature would be able ultimately to end (or perhaps avoid *ab initio*) the war-scale conflict they face. They would be able to do this, she claims, by selecting and empowering a sovereign, who will in turn deter conflict and insure cooperation. This stage-two analysis introduces and relies upon the fundamental distinction between the individual and collective rationality of political association. Political association is "individually rational" to create or maintain just in case its creation or maintenance can be achieved by individuals pursuing strategies which maximize their individual utility.[3] Political associations which are individually rational in this sense are "rationally feasible." Political association is "collectively rational" just in case individuals living in it are better off than they would be living without it. Political association is therefore collectively rational if and only if it is mutually advantageous. As we have seen, the pursuit of individually rational strategies sometimes results in collectively irrational outcomes, as in the case of the single-play prisoner's dilemma. Chapter 3 assesses Hampton's argument for the existence of an internal solution and emphasizes the distinction between individual and collective rationality in evaluating its normative implications.

One of the fundamental burdens of contractarianism is to

---

3 In Hampton's theory, individual rationality amounts to maximizing utility functions which range over purified or idealized preferences. See the section entitled "Conflict in the State of Nature" in this chapter.

explain the relevance of demonstrating the existence of an internal solution to the state-of-nature problem. "Why," one might ask, "should I care whether or not hypothetical individuals in a hypothetical state of nature would be able to create a political association? Whether they do it by consent, convention, or otherwise would seem to have no bearing on justifying the state to me, an actual person, living here and now." Given Hampton's extensive efforts to prove that an internal solution exists in her state-of-nature scenario, it will be useful to explain the role this solution plays in Hampton's overall contractarian argument. To provide this explanation, we must first complete the overview of Hampton's justificatory strategy by describing the third and final stage of the agency theory argument.

The linchpin of agency theory's final (i.e., stage-three) argument is what I will call "the inferential argument." The inferential argument claims that we can infer the individual and collective rationality of creating and maintaining a political association for actual individuals now living in actual societies, from the individual and collective rationality, respectively, of creating and maintaining a political association in the state of nature. The results of the interaction of hypothetical individuals in the state of nature are supposed to provide the basis for an inference concerning the consequences of abandoning political association in contemporary societies. Having shown in stage two that the state of nature is a state of war, that political association is collectively rational relative to the state of nature, and that political association can be created and maintained by persons pursuing individually rational strategies, Hampton argues that political association is individually and collectively rational to create and maintain for actual people now living in an actual society. Put succinctly, agency theory claims that (1) there is some form of political association which is individually rational for us to create and maintain, and (2) political association is individually rational for us to create or maintain if and only if it is collectively rational for us to create and maintain.

50

The inferential argument, therefore, is intended to support two descriptive claims. By itself, the argument seeks to demonstrate the individual and collective rationality of political association for us. Although it seeks to prove these descriptive claims by inferring them from the demonstrated rationality of creating (and then maintaining) political association in the state of nature, they might in principle be supported by other, more direct approaches. For example, one might attempt to demonstrate the collective rationality of political association now by conducting empirical studies designed to prove that the state provides individuals with services whose benefits to everyone exceed their costs to everyone, and whose production would not be possible without the state. Or one might attempt to demonstrate the individual rationality of maintaining political association by arguing that the choice individuals face now of whether to support the state can be accurately modeled as a game- or decision-theoretic problem in which the dominant strategy, or uniquely rational decision, is to support the state. Although the empirical and game- or decision-theoretic approaches might use the state of nature as a heuristic device, the state of nature is inessential to them. Their conclusions are based directly on analysis of current political association. In the inferential argument, however, the state-of-nature analysis serves as a fundamental premise, rather than a mere heuristic. Hobbes's argument relies on analysis of the hypothetical state of nature, rather than current political association, and derives conclusions about current political association only indirectly through an argument by analogy to the state of nature.

After examining Hampton's account of conflict in the state of nature, I present and assess the inferential argument. The first task will be to assess whether the inferential argument adequately supports the claim that there is some form of political association which is individually rational for us to create and maintain (i.e., claim (1) of stage three). But even if the inferential argument succeeds in demonstrating the rationality of political association for actual individuals living under political authority today, the question of the legitimacy of such political authority will still remain unanswered. For merely demonstrating the individual rationality of an institution does not, without more, suffice to demonstrate its moral legitimacy. The inferential argument, therefore, does not by itself purport to establish the moral legitimacy of the state; it purports only to establish the rationality of the state. In order to complete the task of justifying the state, Hobbes attempts a "reduction," or "redefinition," of morality to individual rationality. If morality should be understood as requiring no more than individual rationality, then a demonstration of the individual rationality of creating and maintaining a political sovereign suffices to prove its moral legitimacy. Thus, the third and final claim in stage three of Hobbes's argument is that (3) political association is morally legitimate if and only if it is individually rational. Hampton presents several arguments to motivate this reduction of morality to individual rationality, and in the last major section of this chapter, I critically assess them.

Put together, Hampton's third-stage claims constitute a formally valid argument for the conclusion that there is a legitimate political association available to us and that all and only collectively rational political associations are legitimate:

1. There is some form of political association which is individually rational for us to create and maintain.
2. Political association is individually rational for us to create and maintain if and only if it is collectively rational.
3. Political association is morally legitimate if and only if it is individually rational.

Therefore,

4. There is some form of political association for us which is both individually and collectively rational and thus morally legitimate.
5. Every form of political association which is collectively irrational is individually irrational and thus morally illegitimate.

This argument clarifies both the role and form of an internal solution in Hampton's theory. An internal solution has two roles. First, it provides one argument for stage three's first claim: that some political association is, for us, individually rational to create and maintain. To play this role, however, the internal solution has to take a particularly strong form. I have, until now, always noted in passing that an internal solution will demonstrate how individuals in the state of nature *could or would* independently solve the state-of-nature problem. Given the role an internal solution is to play in Hampton's theory, however, only one of these two possible forms of an internal solution will suffice. If the inferential argument works, then a demonstration that rational individuals living in a state of nature could create and maintain a political association would demonstrate at most that it could be individually rational for us to create and maintain one as well. But in order to establish the legitimacy of our political association, as well as any other possible political associations we might contemplate, we need to know that such associations are in fact individually rational for us to create and maintain. If the inferential argument is sound, then we can infer the individual rationality of our political association from the fact that predominantly rational individuals in the state of nature would be able to create and maintain a political association. But we cannot infer the individual rationality of our political association from the fact that predominantly rational individuals in the state of nature could (i.e., might) be able to create and maintain a political association. Such a proposition would support only the claim that our political association could be individually rational and thus could be legitimate, a claim which falls short of the contractarian mark. Thus, only a strong form of an internal solution will suffice to demonstrate, together with the inferential argument, the individual rationality of some form of political association for us.

The second role the internal solution plays is to establish stage three's second claim: that political association is individually rational for us to create and maintain if and only if it is collectively rational. Hampton's argument is that the same mechanism which explains how and why predominantly rational individuals in the state of nature would create a political authority also explains how and why such individuals living under political authority would succeed in dismantling a collectively irrational regime. The structure of interaction which makes possible an internal solution to the state-of-nature problem, in Hampton's view, also makes possible, indeed inevitable, an internal solution to the potential problem of political association – namely, the problem of disempowering a collectively irrational political regime. Put another way, an internal solution to the state-of-nature problem explains how predominantly rational individuals can and will successfully create a state, notwithstanding the apparent structural similarity between doing so and the single-play prisoner's dilemma. An internal solution to the potential problem of political association explains how predominantly rational individuals can and will successfully rebel against a collectively irrational state, notwithstanding the apparent structural similarity between doing so and the single-play prisoner's dilemma. On Hampton's view, both internal solutions admit of the same structural description.

Hence, by providing an internal solution to the state-of-nature problem, Hampton lays the foundation for providing an internal solution to the potential problem of political association. Given the existence of both internal solutions, it follows that the only political associations it will be individually rational to create and maintain will be those which are not collectively irrational. For the second internal solution entails that maintaining such a regime is individually irrational, and therefore, that creating it (at least intentionally) would be counterproductive and thus individually irrational. Combined with the inferential argument, the two internal solutions together prove stage three's second claim: that political association is individually rational for us to create or maintain if and only if it is collectively rational for us to create or maintain. Hampton, then, finds in Hobbes's theory a central role for the contractarian project of demonstrating the existence of an internal solution to the state-of-nature problem.

Having considered and rejected both the inferential argument and Hampton's arguments for a reduction of morality to rationality, I waive these objections in Chapter 3 and consider the details of Hampton's argument for her internal solution to the state-of-nature problem. I question Hampton's defense of two different scenarios explaining how predominantly rational individuals in the state of nature would be able to create a political sovereign. But more importantly, I contend that if Hampton's scenarios are correct, her contractarian theory, or at least the ethical reduction on which it is based, is subject to a *reductio ad absurdum*. In particular, I find that even those sympathetic to a reduction of morality to some form of rationality would not endorse Hobbes's identification of morality exclusively with individual rationality. For Hampton's own arguments entail that oppressive, collectively irrational institutions may be individually rational and thus legitimate. As we have seen, Hampton argues that while it can be shown that the creation and maintenance of collectively rational political institutions is individually rational, it likewise can be demonstrated that collectively irrational institutions will not be individually rational to create or maintain. She claims that her arguments for the individual rationality of maintaining collectively rational regimes establish the individual rationality of rebellion in a collectively irrational regime. In Chapter 3, I will disagree.

Summary

The overarching objective of agency theory is, as its name suggests, to liken both the descriptive and normative status of the state to that of an agent charged with the duty of acting in, and only in, its principal's best interests. Stage one of agency theory defines a state-of-nature scenario the details of which are provided in the following section's presentation of Hampton's account of conflict in the state of nature. Stage two argues that individuals in the state of nature will avoid an otherwise inevitable war of all against all by instituting and empowering a sovereign. The technical arguments explaining the feasibility of instituting and empowering a sovereign are presented and assessed in Chapter 3. Stage three argues that we can infer the individual and collective rationality of creating and maintaining a political sovereign in society today from the conclusions of stage two. Moreover, stage three argues that because morality can be reduced to individual rationality, the individual rationality of political authority establishes its legitimacy. Both stage-three claims are presented and assessed in this chapter.

The next section provides an introduction to some of the basic suppositions and arguments which form Hampton's case for agency theory, beginning with a summary of Hobbes's and Hampton's accounts of conflict in the state of nature. In the course of this summary, I present Hampton's stage-one definitions and stage-two account of interaction in the state of nature, each prerequisites for understanding the arguments that follow.

CONFLICT IN THE STATE OF NATURE

You will recall that the state of nature is supposed to serve as the basis for an inference concerning the rationality of political association for actual individuals. The fact that individuals living in the state of nature would all be better off living in some political association is supposed to show that individuals currently living under political regimes would all be worse off living in the state of nature. Thus, this inference requires a demonstration of the collective rationality of creating and maintaining a political authority in the state of nature. This, in turn, is done by providing an account of conflict in the state of nature.

Hobbes hopes to show the collective rationality of political authority by demonstrating it to be a solution to an intolerable problem shared by everyone in the state of nature. He claims that ordinary human beings interacting in the state of nature not only would be unable to cooperate, but in addition would be engaged in a perpetual "war" of all against all.[4] Hampton finds in *Leviathan* two distinct accounts of such conflict, both of which rely upon Hobbes's characterization of human psychology.

According to Hobbes, human beings are psychological egoists, who cannot help but act to satisfy their desires. As Hampton defines it, Hobbes's psychological egoism is the view that "all of my actions are caused by my desires and that my desires are produced in me by a 'self-interested' bodily mechanism" (Hampton, p. 23). The claim that our desires are produced by a "self-interested bodily mechanism" means that our desires are "generated by our inherent biological pursuit of pleasure" (Hampton, p. 22). Thus, it is supposed to be a necessary psychological truth that human beings seek to satisfy their desires. Rationality, for Hobbes, is derived from psychological egoism. At first blush, it appears that rationality merely requires that individuals seek to satisfy their desires. Or in the parlance of contemporary economics and game theory, rationality requires individuals to maximize their utility functions. But according to Hampton, Hobbes's notion of rationality is somewhat more complex than the simple maximization of utility functions. Hobbes endorses what Hampton calls the "healthy deliberation" conception of rationality:

> What each of us has reason to do is what will best achieve not what he actually wants, but what he would want, at the time of acting, if he had undergone a process of "ideal deliberation" in which a) he knew all the relevant facts (where he "could have" known these facts, in some relevant sense of that phrase), b) his reasoning was free from distorting influences, and c) he was not affected by desires produced in him by diseased physiological processes. (Hampton, p. 40)

4 For Hobbes, a state of war need not consist in perpetual, actual conflict, but instead constitutes an environment in which actual conflict is highly probable, always threatening personal, physical security and undermining the potential for reliable cooperation. See *Leviathan*, ch. XIII.

Hobbes claims that human beings are predominantly rational psychological egoists; that is, they are healthy deliberators most of the time.

Hobbes's first account of conflict in the state of nature begins by stipulating that resources in the state of nature are moderately scarce. The scarcity of resources necessitates competition. Individuals thus must compete cooperatively or uncooperatively. But Hobbes argues that cooperative behavior in the state of nature is irrational. As Hampton reconstructs the argument, the irrationality of cooperation is supposed to follow from the fact that cooperative agreements in the state of nature will have the structure of the single-play prisoner's dilemma. Thus, the predominantly rational individuals of the state of nature will be unable to cooperate. The resulting conflict will be deep and widespread. Hampton calls this "the rationality" account of conflict, and rejects it on two grounds. First, she claims that cooperative agreements in the state of nature would have the structure of iterated prisoner's dilemmas in which cooperation might be rational.[5] Second, she claims that if all cooperative agreements in the state of nature are single-play prisoner's dilemmas, then individuals will be unable to keep an agreement to adopt political authority to solve their problems, and at least Hobbes's existence proof for an internal solution in the state of nature (i.e., the explanation of the emergence of political authority) will be undermined.[6] This account of conflict in the state of nature, according to Hampton, either fails to demonstrate the existence of conflict, or succeeds at the price of undermining a central premise in the contractarian project.

Hobbes's second account of conflict in the state of nature proceeds from an additional psychological fact Hobbes postulates. Human beings, according to Hobbes, have certain

---

5 See Hampton, pp. 74–7, and Kavka, pp. 129–36.
6 Hampton's proof of the existence of an internal solution does not contemplate *per se* agreements to adopt a political sovereign. Nevertheless, even Hampton's internal solution would appear to be jeopardized by the rationality account. See Chapter 3.

"passions" which motivate them to act contrary to reason. In particular, Hobbes claims their passion for glory will be responsible for driving them to ignore the benefits of cooperation and irrationally risk their self-preservation. Passions are manifest irrationality, either because they are produced by a defective desire-producing mechanism, or because their presence distorts proper "means-ends" reasoning. Hampton calls this the "passions account" of conflict and rejects it on two grounds.[7] First, it seems to contradict Hobbes's psychological assumption that individuals are predominantly rational. And if the passions account is held to be consistent with the predominant rationality assumption, then whatever disruptive and distorting passions individuals possess arguably would be insufficient to cause enough conflict in the state of nature to justify the need for Hobbes's absolute sovereign. Second, if individuals are rendered sufficiently irrational by passions so as to generate widespread conflict in the state of nature (contrary to Hobbes's psychological assumption), then once again, the contractarian argument for the existence of an internal solution to the state-of-nature problem will be jeopardized.[8] For at least Hampton's argu-

---

7 In addition to the two grounds discussed in the text, Hampton also notes that the assumption of a widespread passion for glory in particular seems to be at odds with the assumption that the state of nature is not a community. Glory, or the desire for a favorable reputation or status among one's fellows, seems to be attainable only if one is living in something like a community. But this is inconsistent not only with Hobbes's individualism, but with his conclusion that all social interaction and development can take place only after the creation of an absolute sovereign. See Hampton, p. 74.

8 Hampton makes this point by arguing that the passions account is inconsistent with Hobbes's second law of nature directing individuals to seek peace for self-preservation:

The passions disrupting cooperative activities in general in the state of nature would also seem to disrupt the creation and completion of the contract to institute the sovereign. After all, creating the sovereign by surrendering one's right to all things is the content of Hobbes's second law of nature. And if the other laws of nature are rendered invalid by these passions, then why isn't the second law also made invalid by them? So if these passions

ment for the existence of an internal solution turns on the predominant rationality of individuals in the state of nature. Under the passions account, proving the existence of an internal solution would require a demonstration that pre- dominantly *ir*rational individuals can and should create and maintain a political authority, a task Hobbes apparently never attempted and Hampton is reluctant to undertake. More- over, by threatening Hampton's particular internal solution, the passions account seems to undermine the Hobbesian argument for the legitimacy of political authority as well. For the latter is supposed to follow from the individual rational- ity, not irrationality, of the genesis and maintenance of polit- ical authority.

We should note, however, that Hampton's reasons for rejecting the rationality and passions accounts stem from Hobbes's commitment to the strategy of inferring the indi- vidual rationality of contemporary political association from the individual rationality of political association in the state of nature. As the overview of Hampton's justificatory strat- egy has shown, Hobbes's strategy places a great deal of weight on the existence of an internal solution to the state- of-nature problem. Yet as I noted, one might embrace Hobbes's reduction of morality to individual rationality and yet abandon his commitment to the inferential argument. Such an approach would seek other strategies for demon- strating the individual rationality of political authority, such as the empirical or game- or decision-theoretic strategies discussed previously. The rationality and passions accounts, therefore, are not incompatible with the fundamental nor- mative premise underlying Hobbes's justification of the state (i.e., the reduction of morality to individual rationality).[9]

> are so deep-seated as to generate total war, it would seem that rational pursuit of self-preservation will not be powerful enough among enough of the population to bring about peace. (Hampton, p. 73)

9 In addition to its incompatibility with Hobbes's use of the inferential argument for justification, Hampton rejects the passions account on the ground that it is inconsistent with his attempt to justify an absolute

Rather, they are incompatible with his contractarian strategy of proving that contemporary political association is individually rational by an inference from the state-of-nature analysis.

Given the deficiencies of the rationality and passions accounts of conflict in the state of nature, Hampton replaces them with what she calls "the shortsightedness" account. Hampton's account of shortsightedness should not be confused with the view that individuals in the state of nature simply desire present benefits far more than future benefits. For as Hampton explains:

> Hobbes cannot simply condemn people for being shortsighted if it turns out that they want short-term benefits and do not care about the future. If I want to live for the moment, how am I wrong or irrational to do so, given that, according to Hobbes, what is good for me is what I desire? (Hampton, p. 82)

sovereign. But she admits that the passions account does not undermine attempts to justify a limited sovereign. She concedes that the passions account might be consistent with a Lockean argument for a limited sovereign:

> [If] the passions account is used to explain why certain contracts fail to be completed, Hobbes's state of nature will look remarkably similar to Locke's. In this state of nature, men and women are able to cooperate, make contracts, and thereby implicitly recognize private property. Why do these reasonable creatures need an absolute sovereign? Locke persuasively argues that they do not. . . . In such a situation . . . one does not need an absolute sovereign to *create* patterns of cooperation. (Hampton, p. 72)

Thus, Hampton's rejection of the passions account on the basis of its inadequacy as a premise in Hobbes's argument for an absolute sovereign does not explain why *she* rejects this account. Her project, after all, abandons the Hobbesian argument for an absolute sovereign and defends agency theory, the Hobbesian fallback position advocating a limited sovereign. However, in dismissing the passions account, Hampton is as much concerned with remaining true to Hobbes's original position, as she is with constructing a successful contractarian argument on his behalf. Given the purely exegetical concern to ascribe to Hobbes the position most consistent with *his* views (i.e., alienation theory), rejection of the passions account may well be necessary.

Instead, her claim is that shortsightedness results from mistaken reasoning which leads to the creation of false beliefs. Hampton's shortsighted individuals do not have desires which place atypical weight on present benefits. Rather, they have erroneous beliefs about the relationship between their behavior and future benefits. According to Hampton, one mistake individuals might make is simply to fail to perceive the advantage of cooperation in iterated prisoner's dilemmas. As she puts it, some of the "less intellectually talented inhabitants" of the state of nature might simply "not understand that the long-term advantages of cooperation would be much greater [than non-cooperation]" (Hampton, p. 82). Another, more widespread, mistake individuals might make is to conclude that their interactions with others are not sufficiently likely to repeat. In other words, individuals who understand the long-term benefits of cooperation in iterated prisoner's dilemmas might nonetheless regard all of their interaction in the state of nature to be a single-play prisoner's dilemma. An individual making this mistake in reasoning, according to Hampton, will wrongly believe

> that the chances of her interacting again with her fellows are independent of what she does; she does not appreciate that she can and should pursue cooperative interactions with her fellows that, if successfully completed, could benefit her and them substantially. (Hampton, p. 83)[10]

There are enough individuals who are shortsighted for either of these reasons that even those who do understand the rationality of cooperation will fear interaction with those

10 Hampton's view that shortsightedness results from intellectual shortcomings might be called a "cognitive" account. For a competing account of Hobbes's explanation for widespread shortsightedness, see Mark C. Murphy, "Hobbes's Shortsightedness Account of Conflict," *Southern Journal of Philosophy* 31, no. 2, (1993): 239–53. By arguing that shortsightedness is a direct and inevitable consequence of Hobbes's action theory, Murphy presents a "motivational" account of shortsightedness.

who do not. The result will be a combination of irrational and rational noncooperation and conflict. In addition, there will be enough individuals whose desire for glory will lead them to overestimate their superiority and ability to win confrontations that conflict will be further exacerbated.

Having located the source of conflict in the state of nature, Hampton then argues that political authority is collectively rational because it can transform what otherwise would effectively be a single-play prisoner's dilemma into a game in which cooperation is individually rational. By penalizing noncooperation (e.g., breach of contract) with coercion, political authority can provide even shortsighted individuals with incentives for complying in what otherwise would be a standard, single-play prisoner's dilemma in the absence of the state's sanction for breach. In addition, coercion can serve as a deterrent to those whose desire for glory disrupts and distorts their reasoning process. Even these individuals will no longer mistakenly estimate themselves to be better off not cooperating than cooperating. For a state sanction punishing noncooperation can dramatically increase the probability and magnitude of harm associated with it. Thus, the collective rationality of political authority is demonstrated by showing that political authority will prevent conflict and enable cooperation among individuals who, because of their shortsightedness, necessarily will experience conflict and noncooperation in its absence.

THE INFERENTIAL ARGUMENT

One reason for identifying the reasons individuals have for creating the state in Hobbes's state of nature with our reason for maintaining our political association is that the latter can be inferred from the former. According to this argument, the Hobbesian state of nature is supposed to reveal truths of humans in apolitical (i.e., anarchic) settings:

> [W]hat holds true of the people in the state of nature is also supposed to hold true of us. Indeed, they are meant to be us

stripped of our political clothing and much, if not all, of our social clothing. . . . Hence, their remedy for war is also our remedy, because our propensity to act wrongly, like theirs, has not been created or substantially affected by our society. (Hampton, p. 270)

The state of nature is supposed to provide the basis for two distinct inferences concerning the rationality of political association. First, from the fact that individuals in the state of nature are at war and deprived of the fruits of cooperation, it is supposed to follow that were we to abandon political association, we too would be at war and unable to cooperate. Second, from the fact that individuals in the state of nature can solve their conflict and cooperation problems with (and only with) political association, it is supposed to follow that our political association is already providing a solution to the problem we would have were we to abandon it. Thus, our reason for maintaining our political association is the same as the reason individuals in Hobbes's state of nature have for creating and maintaining their political association. Hampton's state of nature is thus defined according to the strategy of realistic constructionism. As such, assessment of the inferential argument requires an evaluation of the accuracy of that scenario as a predictive model applicable to our actual circumstances.

Now, with respect to the first inference, why should we think that anarchy in Hobbes's state of nature would be importantly similar to the anarchy which would ensue upon the abandonment of our political institutions? In other words, why should we think that Hobbes's state of nature provides an accurate model of what our condition, vis-a-vis conflict and cooperation, would be were we to abandon our political institutions? From Hampton's discussion of contractarian justification, we can construct an answer to this question. She claims that contractarianism endorses the view that human nature is defined outside of political interaction:

[T]he social contract theorist believes it makes sense to think of individuals as conceptually prior to the political systems in which they live, and to this extent the contractarian is an individualist. . . . [T]he contractarian presupposes that none of the intrinsic features of human beings (i.e., those features that establish us as human) are *politically* created. . . . In the traditional social contract argument, people's failure to behave cooperatively is presented as natural, rather than as socially created, and incurable through social manipulation. It is a given in the state of nature, a failure that people can hope to control and minimize (rather than cure) only through the institution of the state. (Hampton, p. 270)

The "intrinsic nature" of human beings is supposed to define human motivation and behavior outside of the state. And it is this intrinsic nature that is responsible for conflict and noncooperation in the state of nature.[11] In particular, the psychological egoism and shortsightedness of individuals, which work in tandem to cause conflict and noncooperation in the state of nature, must be attributable to intrinsic human nature. Without some coercive apparatus to introduce external incentives for cooperation, intrinsic human nature will continue to produce conflict and noncooperation. Thus, the problems in the state of nature represent the problems we would have without political coercion. But is the contractarian thesis concerning our "intrinsic nature" true?

It is difficult indeed to assess a claim concerning the true and ultimate nature of human beings. Whether or not such a claim is true would seem to be a matter for psychology, not philosophy. And we see that in Hobbes's contractarianism, this view of human nature is presupposed, not argued for. It is supposed to be the embodiment of an individualist assumption which is distinctive, even constitutive, of contractarianism:

11 Hampton denies that contractarianism need endorse the extreme, Hobbesian position according to which our real nature is not even partly socially created. Some intrinsic features, she admits, might be the product of social interaction.

Unless the contractarian takes this individualist position, his justification of the state is problematic. If, for example, our propensity to act wrongly can be remedied by our society, then why isn't the state justified only as a useful but temporary "tutor" – indeed, one we may already have outgrown? On the other hand, if our society is instrumental in making us selfish and violently competitive, whereas we would not be so "naturally," why shouldn't we create institutions to prevent that development (rather than deal with its results), keeping the state in the meantime only if it does not encourage what we are trying to prevent? On either view, we would want the state to "wither away." (Hampton, p. 271)

Here Hampton recognizes that contractarianism presupposes the individualist assumption according to which individuals are naturally and inevitably prone to conflict and noncooperation in the absence of political coercion. If it does not make such a presupposition, then the state may be at best temporarily needed, at worst never needed, even dreaded. Now we cannot, of course, merely endorse a presupposition because in its absence our theory will not work. We need to have some evidence that the presupposition is true. Hobbes simply stipulated his view of the immutable psychological nature of human beings, and Hampton likewise simply stipulates that human beings are by nature shortsighted. But psychological theses cannot be defended from an armchair. Here, then, is a clear objection to Hobbes's theory. His contractarian theory depends, for the ultimate justification of the state, and as we shall see, his motivation of the reduction of morality to individual rationality, on the truth of two psychological theses concerning the intrinsic nature of human beings: psychological egoism and shortsightedness. But these theses are never supported by psychological data and theory. However, though we would prefer a psychological theory which confirms Hobbes's psychological egoism, I shall grant its truth for the purposes of assessing Hobbes's contractarian justification. In doing so, then, I have already granted him his version of the contractarian's individualist assumption according to which humans are, by nature, shortsighted psychological egoists. And this assumption does appear to suffice to demonstrate that actual individuals, if interacting in a Hobbesian state of nature, would experience conflict and noncooperation.[12]

Let us briefly take stock. The inferential argument we are considering holds that Hobbes's state of nature provides the basis for an inference concerning the nature of apolitical interaction for actual individuals living in current political association. From the fact that individuals in Hobbes's state of nature are conflict prone and unable to cooperate, we are to infer that we would have the same problems without political association. This inference is based on a psychological assumption according to which human beings necessarily are conflict prone and unable to cooperate in apolitical settings. Hobbes's version of this assumption is psychological egoism, and Hampton supplements this assumption with that of shortsightedness. Though these crucial assumptions are unsupported, I am granting them for purposes of assessing Hampton's overall contractarian project. Toward that end, we now must consider the justificatory use to which this first inference is to be put.

The point of the first inference from the problems of the state of nature to our potential problems is to support the second inference previously mentioned: from the reason individuals in Hobbes's state of nature have for creating and maintaining their political association, we are to infer that our reason for maintaining our political association is the same. This second inference concerning the solution to our potential problem is based on the solution to the same problem faced by individuals in Hobbes's state of nature. Together, the first and second inferences establish an isomorphic causal relationship between the apolitical problems and political solutions in the state of nature and those which would and do obtain, respectively, in contemporary society.

---

12 See Chapter 5 for a discussion of Gauthier's argument that interaction in the state of nature, even if properly characterized as structured by single-play prisoner's dilemmas, would result not in conflict but in cooperation.

Therefore, because political association in the state of nature is individually and collectively rational, we can infer that our political association is individually and collectively rational. The state of nature is thus supposed to function as a reconstructed, causally accurate model of contemporary society were it to abandon its political institutions.

The first problem with the inferential argument is that it does not establish that actual individuals now living in contemporary societies would return to a *Hobbesian* state of nature were they suddenly deprived of their political institutions. Here, we must take care to observe the distinction between "apolitical" and "prepolitical" association. The state of nature is, as Hampton defines it, not only apolitical but *pre*political as well. That is, the state of nature is not only free from any political government but has never been subject to political government previously. But even if we grant that the intrinsic nature of individuals renders them conflict prone and uncooperative in Hobbes's prepolitical setting, it does not necessarily follow that individuals having already lived in society will be conflict prone and uncooperative in the postpolitical setting which would obtain were their society suddenly to plunge into anarchy. We can admit the contractarian's individualist claim that "it makes sense to think of individuals as conceptually prior to the political systems in which they live" (Hampton, p. 270), and grant that Hobbes's state of nature represents an accurate model of *pre*political human interaction, and yet deny that the *a*political, yet *post*political, interaction resulting from the sudden emergence of anarchy in contemporary societies would be identical to the interaction in Hobbes's prepolitical state of nature.

The relevant difference between individuals in Hobbes's state of nature and contemporary individuals thrust into an apolitical setting is that the former have never lived under political authority while the latter have never lived without it. It seems plausible that even psychological egoists might interact differently in a prepolitical state of nature than they would in a postpolitical anarchy. We would expect egoists that are the product of generations of political beings to have radically different desires than those who have never experienced political association and benefitted from the fruits of cooperation. A self-interested desire-producing mechanism would be expected to generate quite different desires for individuals living in political association for thousands of years than for individuals in Hobbes's state of nature. And we might expect the former to possess considerably more other-regarding desires than the latter. If they would possess more other-regarding desires, then what are otherwise prisoner's dilemma situations can be transformed into interactions where cooperation is dominant.[13] This possibility illustrates how we can hold that human nature is intrinsically egoistic and that in Hobbes's state of nature this egoism is responsible for conflict and noncooperation, but deny that in a postpolitical setting, the same intrinsic nature would continue to cause conflict and noncooperation. In Hampton's words, we can grant that "none of the intrinsic features of human beings are . . . *politically* created," and that individuals' "failure to behave cooperatively is . . . natural, rather than . . . socially created," but deny that the causal connection between this intrinsic nature and conflict and noncooperation is "incurable through social manipulation." Though "[i]t is a given in [*Hobbes's* prepolitical] state of nature," it might nonetheless not be a failure that people can hope "to control and minimize (rather than cure) only through the institution of the state" (Hampton, p. 270). We can admit that there is an immutable, intrinsic nature of human beings which causes conflict and noncooperation in Hobbes's state of nature and that this intrinsic nature cannot be changed or "cured" by political association, but claim that very same nature has different implications in the context of political and postpolitical association. Thus, though human nature remains the same in prepolitical, political, and postpolitical settings, harmonious and cooperative in-

---

13 For a clear explanation of how altruistic desires transform a prisoner's dilemma matrix into one in which cooperation is dominant, see Kavka's discussion of altruism and the state of nature in Kavka, pp. 154–6.

teraction might be impossible only in the first, although it remains possible in the second and third because of the likely effects these different environments would have on the content of individuals' desires.

We have reason, then, to question the inference from the problems in Hobbes's state of nature to the hypothetical problems of contemporary society because this inference presupposes not only that individuals are psychological egoists, but that their desires will remain primarily self-regarding in both pre- and postpolitical settings. If individuals in the postpolitical settings we are considering have significantly many other-regarding desires, then they will not suffer from the conflict and noncooperation endemic to Hobbes's state of nature. Thus, political association need not be rational in postpolitical settings as it is in Hobbes's state of nature. Whether or not individuals' desires would be substantially more other-regarding in political and postpolitical settings than in Hobbes's prepolitical state of nature is again a question for the empirical sciences to answer. But even though we have granted Hobbes's psychological egoism without their consultation, we would be ill-advised likewise to ignore their expertise when assessing environmental effects on the content of individuals' desires. And surely even common sense tells us that individuals with radically different heritages in radically different environments will have significantly different desires.

There is another problem with the inferential argument. Suppose individuals do have an intrinsic nature such that in any state of nature, any set of human beings, prepolitical or postpolitical, would be unable to cooperate. Suppose further that individuals in a contemporary political society refuse to obey their political authorities, and that their refusal results in the abandonment of those political institutions. What reason do we have for supposing that society would return to any state of nature, much less the state of nature Hobbes envisions? The inferential argument presupposes, first, that the abandonment of contemporary political institutions would result in a state of nature, and second, that the state of nature would resemble Hobbes's state of nature. For the inferential argument claims that conflict and noncooperation are the product of both intrinsic human nature and certain circumstances of Hobbes's state of nature. But even if contemporary society should reject its current political institutions, it does not follow that any state of nature would ensue. In fact, individuals might act to undermine one set of institutions so that another might replace it. Most rebellions have as their objective the institution of a new government to replace the old, not the achievement of a perpetual anarchy. The inferential argument is intended to establish that obedience to contemporary political authority is rational, and thus moral, because it constitutes our only alternative to anarchy, which is much worse. But even if anarchy necessarily would be much worse than virtually any political association (a claim I will later deny), current political institutions do not constitute a unique alternative to a state of nature. There are infinitely many possible political institutions under which individuals might live, all of which are collectively rational relative to a state of nature. So even if we grant that we can infer, on the basis of Hobbes's state-of-nature scenario, that contemporary life in the absence of political authority would be worse than contemporary life under political authority, it does not follow that obedience to whatever mutually advantageous political authority is in place is rational, and thus moral. It only follows that some political authority or other is collectively rational. The inferential argument must be supplemented with an argument according to which disobeying a political authority already in place is more likely to result in anarchy than in the institution of a new political authority – a political authority which is perhaps mutually advantageous relative to the old one.[14] Hampton provides no such argument.

14 Moreover, even if such an argument is provided, and we can conclude that a state of nature would ensue should current political institutions be abandoned, whether that state of nature would exhibit the environmental, as well as individual, characteristics of Hobbes's state of nature is an entirely contingent matter. For example, it might be that

But perhaps the most serious problem with the inferential argument is that it establishes, at best, the collective rationality of current political authority. But Hobbes's ethical reduction identifies morality with individual rationality, and so his contractarian theory must demonstrate not the collective but individual rationality of obedience to contemporary political institutions. For an individual might concede she is better off living under the current political authority than she would be living in any state of nature, and yet deny that it is rational for her to obey it. This is because, as is well known, not all collectively rational states of affairs are individually rational. As the prisoner's dilemma illustrates, it may be rational for individuals not to cooperate even when cooperation is mutually advantageous. Thus, we cannot simply infer the individual rationality of cooperation with contemporary political authority from its collective rationality. So far, the inferential argument seems to have shown, at most, that contemporary political authority is, relative to contemporary anarchy, collectively rational. But if contemporary political authority is to be morally justified it must be shown to be individually rational. Can the inferential argument demonstrate the individual rationality of compliance with contemporary political authority?

The inferential argument claims ultimately that contemporary individuals have the same reasons for creating *and maintaining* political authority as do individuals in Hobbes's state of nature. Thus, if it can be demonstrated that it is rational for individuals in Hobbes's state of nature to comply with the political authority they create, then it should be rational for contemporary individuals to comply with their political authority already in place. The inferential argument, then, will establish the individual rationality of contemporary political authority only if (1) it can demonstrate

essential resources are not scarce in the state of nature to which certain contemporary societies would return. At the very least, Hampton must concede that even egoistic, shortsighted humans might not fail to cooperate if they were in a state of nature, unlike Hobbes's, in which resources were abundant.

the individual rationality of compliance with political authority for individuals in Hobbes's state of nature, and (2) we have reason to infer the individual rationality of contemporary political authority from this demonstration. By considering Hampton's demonstration of the individual rationality of creating and maintaining political authority in the state of nature, we can assess the success not only of that demonstration, but whether that demonstration can provide the basis for an inference to the individual rationality of creating and maintaining current political authority. In Chapter 3, we will examine in detail Hampton's arguments for the individual rationality of creating and maintaining a political sovereign in the state of nature. There I will argue that Hampton's arguments for the existence of an internal solution to the state-of-nature problem fail. But I do concede that if they succeed, it is individually rational for us to obey a collectively rational political authority. However, I also contend that those same arguments, if successful, establish the individual rationality of maintaining a collectively irrational political authority. Thus, Hampton's arguments, at best, succeed in demonstrating the moral legitimacy of collectively rational political regimes at the expense of demonstrating the legitimacy of collectively irrational regimes as well. This, in turn, leads me to question the viability of Hobbes's reduction of morality to individual rationality. But before we consider Hampton's arguments for the individual rationality of creating and maintaining political authority, we will examine her reconstruction of Hobbes's motivations for endorsing the reduction of morality to individual rationality in the first place. That is the subject of the following section.

THE REDUCTION OF MORALITY TO RATIONALITY

Hobbes reduces morality to rationality by advocating a particular form of ethical subjectivism. According to Hampton, "Hobbes is an ethical subjectivist in the sense that he defines value as subjective preference" (Hampton, p. 49). Hobbes

73

defines " 'good' as 'what we desire', and 'bad' as 'what we are averse to' " (Hampton, p. 29). In other words, Hobbes understands " 'good' objects or states of affairs as defined by all or some of a person's desires, and 'right' or 'rational' actions are understood instrumentally, as those actions that are the most effective ways of attaining the good (i.e., desired) objects or states of affairs" (Hampton, p. 28). We can say that Hobbes defines morality in terms of rationality, so long as we bear in mind Hampton's "rational deliberation" conception of rationality introduced in the previous discussion of conflict in the state of nature. Recall that according to that account:

> What each of us has reason to do is what will best achieve not what he actually wants, but what he would want, at the time of acting, if he had undergone a process of "ideal deliberation" in which a) he knew all the relevant facts (where he "could have" known these facts, in some relevant sense of that phrase), b) his reasoning was free from distorting influences, and c) he was not affected by desires produced in him by diseased physiological processes. (Hampton, p. 40)

Thus, morality, according to Hampton's version of Hobbes, requires that individuals pursue the good using the most effective means possible, where "the good" is defined as their real desires (as defined by the healthy deliberation conception of rationality):

> [R]eason is to be considered the instrument of only real desires, not spurious desires. Or, to put it another way, an action is rational only if it is in pursuit of an object we really want, not one we want only because we are in some way sick, or physically damaged, such that this desire represents a biological mistake. (Hampton, p. 41)

But when Hampton says that "an action is rational only if it is in pursuit of an object we really want" does she mean that an action is rational only if it is in fact an effective means of

74

satisfying the desire the actor is seeking to satisfy, or only if it is believed by the actor to be an effective means of satisfying the desire? And if the latter is intended, does the rationality of the act turn on the mere possession of the requisite belief by the actor or must such a belief be epistemically justified?

When Hampton first begins to explicate Hobbes's definition of rational action, she explains Hobbes's position to be that "any act is rational if it is one an individual *would* determine he *should* take to fulfill his present desires *if* he had true beliefs" (Hampton, p. 36). This statement implies that the actual beliefs of an agent are irrelevant to the rationality of that agent's actions. Thus, I could unjustifiably, but nevertheless correctly, believe an act to be the most effective means to fulfill my real desire, yet be acting rationally and therefore morally. And someone else might justifiably, but nevertheless incorrectly, believe her act to be the most effective means to fulfilling her real desire, yet be acting irrationally and therefore immorally. As Hampton's exegesis of Hobbes's theory continues, she seems to confirm this view. She explains that Hobbes "was prepared to call wrong (and thus irrational) those actions in pursuit of an object that an individual mistakenly believes to be the best way to achieve a desired end" (Hampton, p. 36). The mere fact of being mistaken, irrespective of the justification of the mistaken belief, is dispositive of the rationality, and therefore, morality of an actor. Finally, when Hampton introduces the full-fledged "healthy deliberation conception" of rationality, she counts among the sources of a person's irrationality that he "reason[s] using incorrect beliefs and arrive[s] at an incorrect conclusion" (Hampton, p. 40). But such a view is very counterintuitive. It is at least questionable whether the rationality of an actor should even in part be a function of the truth of the actor's beliefs. But whether or not the truth of an actor's beliefs is relevant to determining the rationality of that actor's actions, the justification of the actor's beliefs, whether true or false, would seem to be at least equally, if not more, relevant.

Hampton does caution that Hobbes does not

> mean that one must have full information about how to pursue one's goals in order to be rational, but he does seem to believe that, at the very least, one cannot be rational if one pursues a goal incorrectly in circumstances in which one could have gained access to the information one needed about how to achieve that goal. (Hampton, p. 37)

Hampton's view here suggests that one could be rational even if she pursues a goal incorrectly if the goal is pursued in circumstances in which she could not have gained access to the information she needed about how best to achieve the goal. Presumably, in such circumstances, the beliefs upon which the actions were based are justified, even though false. But this view is clearly inconsistent with the previous characterizations of Hobbes's view. According to the latter, there is no room for imperfect information; either beliefs are correct or they are not. If the former, then the actor is rational (provided the other conditions for healthy deliberation are satisfied); if the latter, then the actor is irrational. Perhaps, though, this passage indicates that Hampton thinks Hobbes equivocates between requiring merely justified belief and requiring true, and not necessarily justified, belief. In any event, I will attribute to Hampton, and thus Hobbes, what I take to be the more plausible view that an act's rationality is in part a function of the beliefs of the actor. Thus, I will hold that, according to Hobbes's reduction of morality to individual rationality, one's actions are ethically permissible or required only if they are justifiably believed to constitute effective means of satisfying one's real desires. One's actions are morally prohibited if they are irrational and therefore not justifiably believed to be an effective means of satisfying one's real desires. This subjectivist ethics is the essence of Hobbes's reduction of morality to rationality.

Hobbes's subjectivist ethics is supposed to find support in his metaphysics and his psychology: "This sort of ethical view rests solidly on Hobbes's psychology and is clearly consistent with his materialist metaphysics. It presupposes no nonmaterial moral objects or qualities and no strange prescriptive powers associated with moral commands" (Hampton, p. 28). In fact, we find that Hobbes's view is that "moral philosophy can be 'derived' from Hobbes's psychology . . . that ethics is simply a branch of psychology, which is itself a branch of physics" (Hampton, p. 28). The task of the following section will be to determine whether or not Hobbes, as Hampton explicates his views, successfully motivates his ethical reduction.

The metaphysical arguments

One argument Hampton provides for Hobbes's subjectivist ethics is based on Hobbes's commitment to nominalism and materialism. Nominalism (as opposed to realism) is the view that there are no universals or properties. According to nominalists, only particulars exist. Although nominalists deny the existence of properties, they do not, of course, dismiss talk of properties as incoherent. Instead, they explain away the appearance of an ontological commitment to properties in sentences which appear to refer to them. They explain how such sentences can be true even though there are no properties. For example, nominalists concede that the sentence "Tomatoes and apples are red" might be logically equivalent to the sentence "Tomatoes and apples have the property of being red," but the use of the word "property" in this sentence is pleonastic – merely a *façon de parler* with no ontological commitment.[15] Materialism (as opposed to

15 The sentence "Tomatoes and apples are red" is also conceded by the nominalist to be logically equivalent to the sentence "There is a property of redness which tomatoes and apples have." However, the logical form of the latter sentence would be given by substitutional, not objectual, quantification. For the difference between substitutional and objectual quantification, see Stephen Schiffer, *Remnants of Meaning* (Cambridge, Mass.: MIT Press, 1988), pp. 234–9, 274, n.10, 285, n.1. Schiffer explains the nominalist's position by considering the sentence [a] "Mother Teresa is humble," and the sentence [b] "Mother Teresa has the property of being humble." In [a], the term "Mother Teresa" refers to a

selfless woman [who] is an objective, language-independent en-

dualism) is the view that there are no nonphysical entities (e.g., substances, states or events, or properties).[16] [17] Even entities which appear to be nonmaterial (e.g., mental states like beliefs and desires), on this view, are reducible to (i.e.,

> tity. Her existence in no way depends on language, let alone on there being a term that refers to her, and one may have knowledge of her that is prior to one's knowledge that 'Mother Teresa', or any other singular term, refers to her. (Schiffer, p. 234)
> But according to the nominalist, the term "humble" does *not* refer

to

> any language-independent entity humility, the property of being humble. . . . There is no entity, "the property of being humble" related to 'humble' in anything like the way that Mother Teresa is related to 'Mother Teresa.' Understanding [a] does require awareness of the woman Mother Teresa: to understand an utterance of [a] one would have to know that the speaker was talking about her. But there is no other thing awareness of which is required to understand [a]. There is not to be found among the things that *really exist* anything that may correctly be called 'the property of being humble'. . . . [But the nominalist] agree[s] with the Platonic Realist that [b] is a trivial, pleonastic paraphrase of [a]. His *disagreement* comes at the Realist's claim that 'the property of being humble' in [b] is *referential*; that ostensible singular term refers to nothing. (Schiffer, pp. 235–6)
> How can the sentence [c] "There is something that Mother Teresa has (viz., humility)" follow from [b], the sentence "Mother Teresa has the property of being humble" if the occurrence of 'the property of being humble' in [b] is nonreferential? As Schiffer puts it, "[T]he answer, of course, is that the existential quantification in [c] is a *substitutional* quantification" (Schiffer, p. 236).
> See also W. V. O. Quine's "On What There Is" in *From a Logical Point of View* (Cambridge, Mass.: Harvard University Press, 1953), pp. 1–19. Schiffer quotes and explains the essence of Quine's position: "One may admit that there are red houses, roses, and sunsets, but deny, *except as a popular and misleading manner of speaking*, that they have anything in common." (Quine, p. 10.) As Schiffer explains Quine,
> The "popular and misleading [to whom?] manner of speaking" in which one can say truly that there is something (viz., the color red) that red houses, roses, and sunsets have in common is the 'there is' of substitutional quantification. It is the same 'there is' to be found in 'There was lasciviousness in his grin' and 'There's a good chance that you'll win'; it is the quantifier that allows 'There

identical with) physical entities.[18] Materialism rejects the possibility that mental entities are irreducibly nonmaterial.[19] Hampton claims that nominalism and materialism logically entail a subjectivist ethics. Thus, Hobbes would be

are many things that don't exist – the Loch Ness Monster, God, Sherlock Holmes.' (Schiffer, p. 236, quoting William Lycan, "The Trouble with Possible Worlds," in M. Loux, ed., *The Possible and the Actual* [Ithaca, N.Y.: Cornell University Press, 1979].)

16 It would be more precise (i.e., conceptually symmetrical to the opposition of nominalism and realism) to oppose materialism to idealism, the view that there are no material entities. But the more common debate in the philosophy of mind is between materialists and dualists, who hold that there are both material and nonmaterial entities.

17 On the difference between substances, states or events, and properties, see S. Schiffer's *Remnants of Meaning*, p. 142.

18 Reductive materialism is not, of course, the only alternative to Cartesian (or interactive) dualism. Instead of arguing that nonmaterial (i.e., mental) events and material events can be causes for one another, as Cartesian dualism holds, or that there are no irreducibly nonmaterial events, as reductive materialism holds, some, following G. E. Moore, argue instead that nonmaterial entities merely "supervene" on material ones. The supervenience relations relied upon in supervenience theories are many, varied, and sometimes complex. David Brink describes a typical supervenience theory in which supervenience is construed as:

a nomological or lawlike relation between, say, properties such that one property F (the supervening property) supervenes on another property or configuration of properties G (the base property or properties) just in case it is a law that if something is G, it is F. One consequence of supervenience is that two things cannot differ in their supervening properties without differing in their base properties. Supervenience, so construed, does not imply naturalism . . . because supervening properties need be neither identical with nor constituted by base properties. Naturalists claim that moral properties supervene on natural properties *because* moral properties are constituted by natural properties. (Brink, p. 160)

Thus, supervenience theory provides an alternative to naturalism or what I have referred to as reductive materialism generally. For more on supervenience theory, see S. Schiffer, pp. 153–4, 165–6; Jaegwon Kim, "Supervenience and Supervenient Causation," *The Southern Journal of Philosophy* 22 (1983): 45–56, "Epiphenomenal and Supervenient Causation," *Midwest Studies in Philosophy* 9 (1984): 257–70, and "Cau-

committed, as both a nominalist and materialist, to ethical subjectivism. She claims that an objectivist ethics "is certainly inconsistent with Hobbes's materialist metaphysics." It is inconsistent because an objectivist ethics holds that a

> nonnatural and nonmaterial quality of 'rightness' is supposed to attach to certain actions . . . [and that this quality] is not reducible to any material object, certainly not to any physiological feature of human beings. . . . [T]his view would commit Hobbes – a philosopher with strong nominalist tendencies – to admit the reality not only of a certain property but also of a nonmaterial property. . . . [Hobbes] would be loath to do any such thing; consider, for example, his rejection of nonmaterial moral objects such as the summum bonum and the golden mean postulated by Aristotelian moral theorists. (Hampton, p. 31)

In a nutshell, Hampton's claim is that Hobbes's commitment to nominalism and materialism would be incompatible with any objectivist ethics. Hobbes, therefore, could adopt no position other than subjectivism. But nominalism and materialism are, in fact, compatible with any number of nonsub-

sality, Identity, and Supervenience in the Mind–Body Problem," *Midwest Studies in Philosophy* 4 (1979): 31–49; and Paul Teller, "A Poor Man's Guide to Supervenience and Determinism," *The Southern Journal of Philosophy* 22 (1983): 137–62.

19 Hampton (pp. 11–12) defines Hobbes's materialism as holding the following five claims to be true:

1. There is only one world, which various languages and styles of explanation characterize differently.
2. There is no change in the world without a physical change.
3. The materialist language has [or will have] in its domain all and only those fundamental objects that exist.
4. A materialist explanation of an event will always be in terms of the operation of the fundamental physical objects in accordance with laws [which for Hobbes are deterministic].
5. It is possible to reduce both ethical and psychological language to talk of matter, motion, and the laws of nature.

jectivist theories.[20] To see this, consider the details of Hampton's claim.

Hampton never defines "objectivism" and "subjectivism" outright. But she is at pains to distinguish the senses in which Hobbes is both an objectivist about the truth of moral principles and a subjectivist about value:

> Hobbes can even regard himself as a 'moral objectivist' of sorts, because he has shown that moral propositions can be understood to be objectively true and necessary if they are interpreted as assertions of a causal connection between certain actions and a desired common goal. . . . Hobbes is a

20 At times, Hampton's discussion seems fundamentally to confuse the relationship between materialism and realism. Consider the passage quoted in the text. Hampton says that objectivism holds that a "nonnatural and nonmaterial quality of 'rightness' is supposed to attach to certain actions . . . [and that this quality] is not reducible to any material object" (Hampton, p. 31). She then claims that "this view would commit Hobbes – a philosopher with strong nominalist tendencies – to admit the reality not only of a certain property but also of a nonmaterial property" (Hampton, p. 31). Although Hampton is right to worry that a nominalist would not concede the existence of any property, these passages might suggest that a materialist would not allow the existence of a property (i.e., "quality") which is not reducible to a material object. Though Hampton is correct that a materialist cannot allow for *nonmaterial* properties, it is the fact that such properties are properties of nonmaterial entities, not that they are properties *per se*, which accounts for their incompatibility with materialism. For materialism can countenance the existence of "irreducible" *material* properties (i.e., because they are material, there is no need to reduce them).

This is just to say that the rejection of nonmaterial entities does not entail a rejection of all *abstract* entities, like properties. In particular, materialism's rejection of purely mental entities, for example, does not extend to an aversion to purely abstract entities, like numbers and properties. Of course, materialists who countenance properties (i.e., realist materialists) will countenance only *material* properties. These are properties of material things. So a materialist can allow not only that there are such things as rocks, but that rocks have physical properties, like having a certain weight or mass. A materialist can consistently deny the existence of nonmaterial entities, yet insist that there exist all the properties associated with the physical sciences.

subjectivist in the sense that he defines value as subjective preference: For him, there is no objective good or right, but only, as he puts it, what is 'good for someone or other.' But he is an ethical objectivist in the sense that his moral propositions are statements of causal connections that purport to be true. . . . Hobbes [is] an ethical subjectivist in virtue of his subjectivist theory of value[,] but a subjectivist who nonetheless seeks to espouse objective moral principles. (Hampton, pp. 49–50)

Since Hampton asserts that Hobbes is an objectivist about moral principles, we must assume she regards this position as consistent with Hobbes's nominalism and materialism. Her claim, therefore, must be that nominalism and materialism are incompatible with value objectivism.

What, then, is "value objectivism"? Though Hampton does not directly say what an objectivist value theory consists in, we can discern two distinct objectivist positions from her discussion. At first blush, Hampton seems to define a version of value objectivism which is wed by definition to certain metaphysical positions. This definition holds both that a "nonmaterial quality of 'rightness' . . . attaches to certain actions," and that this quality "is not reducible to any material object" (Hampton, p. 31).[21] Here Hampton defines objectivism as entailing both the denial of nominalism (i.e., there is a property – what Hampton calls a 'quality' – of rightness) and the denial of materialism (i.e., there is an entity, the property of rightness, which is irreducibly nonmaterial).[22] We might call this version of objectivism

21 We might note that, strictly speaking, a quality or property would not, on anyone's view, be reduced to a material *object*, but would at most be reduced to a material *property*.

22 It is clear that Hampton intends to define objectivism as opposing nominalism and is here using the word "property" in its metaphysically significant, nonpleonastic, sense. She explains that this version of objectivism would force Hobbes "to admit the reality . . . of a certain property" (Hampton, p. 31). It is also clear that Hampton intends objectivism to be defined in opposition to materialism. In fact, Hampton claims that objectivism is exemplified by theories which

"complex objectivism" because it merges the definition of objectivism, a position usually addressing a purely meta-ethical question, with realism and dualism, positions addressing the metaphysical questions of whether there are properties and whether there are nonphysical entities.

But Hampton's claim must amount to more than the tautological assertion that nominalism and materialism are inconsistent with complex objectivism. For the latter is *defined* as affirming the existence of an irreducibly nonmaterial property, and therefore is inconsistent with nominalism and materialism by definition. If the question at issue is the relationship between meta-ethical positions like objectivism and metaphysical positions like nominalism and materialism, we cannot meaningfully answer it by defining the former in terms of the latter. Put differently, the claim that nominalism and materialism are inconsistent with complex objectivism only proves that a complex objectivist could not consistently assert nominalism and materialism. It does not prove that nominalism and materialism are incompatible with other forms of objectivism. And it is, of course, precisely these forms of objectivism, which do not beg any metaphysical questions at the outset, which must be used in any informative analysis of the relationship between objectivism and ontology.

Hampton's discussion does allow us to construct a metaphysically nontendentious definition of objectivism. She claims that Hobbes's subjectivist value theory "defines value as subjective preference. . . . There is no objective good or right, but, as [Hobbes] puts it, what is 'good for someone or other' " (Hampton, p. 49). If we define objectivism as the contradictory of this view of subjectivism, objectivism would consist in the view that (1) value is not defined merely as subjective preference and (2) there is an objective good or

posit "nonmaterial moral objects such as the *summum bonum* and the golden mean," entities which are "not reducible to any material object" (Hampton, p. 31).

right – something which is not merely relative to individuals (i.e., "good or right for someone or other"), but which is good or right nonrelatively. We might call this view "simple objectivism." Now we can meaningfully ask whether simple objectivism is compatible with nominalism and materialism.

Is there any reason why a simple objectivist cannot be a nominalist? Can a simple objectivist consistently maintain that there are no properties? Consider the general approach of classical, Aristotelian objectivist ethics. According to this view, "valuable life consists in the possession of certain character traits, the exercise of certain capacities, the development of certain relations with others and to the world," and so forth.[23] This view is clearly an objectivist value theory on Hampton's view: (1) value is not defined as subjective preference and (2) good and right are not relative – the traits and capacities constitutive or determinative of value are defined independently of the individuals and actions evaluated. Good and right, therefore, would not be relative to particular individuals, but would be "objective" facts true for everyone: an individual is good if and only if he or she possesses the specified character traits, capacities, and so on. The same act, for example, could not be both right *for me* but wrong *for you* at the same time. Either it does or does not consist in the exercise of certain capacities, the development of certain relations with others, and so forth.

Can a simple objectivist holding this view deny that there is the property of being morally right or good, not to mention the properties of having certain character traits, capacities, and relations? Of course she can. Her position on the existence of any of these properties would be no different than any nominalist's position on properties in general. She would hold that particular acts can be either right or wrong. The sentence "Lying and cheating are wrong," she would concede, is logically equivalent to the sentence "Lying and cheating have the property of being wrong." But the use of the word "property" in this sentence is pleonastic; it adds

23 Brink, p. 221.

84

no further meaning to the sentence "Lying and cheating are wrong." The sentence "Lying and cheating have the property of being wrong" is true if and only if the sentence "Lying and cheating are wrong" is true. But she would nonetheless deny that there are any such things as moral properties. Lying and cheating can be right or wrong without there being a property of rightness or wrongness which lying and cheating have in common. Or so the nominalist objectivist, like all nominalists, would maintain.

Is simple objectivism inconsistent with materialism? Simple objectivism requires only that value consist in something other than subjective preference and that moral truths are not relative to particular individuals. But surely a simple objectivist theory need not countenance irreducibly nonmaterial entities in order to define value in nonsubjective terms and to hold moral goodness or rightness to be nonrelative. Consider again the Aristotelian version of simple objectivism: that moral goodness consists in the possession of certain character traits, and so on. This objectivist view is in no way committed to irreducibly nonmaterial entities. It does require an ontology that countenances the existence of character traits, capacities, and relations. But just as the objectivist is free to understand traits, capacities, and relations either in nominalist or realist terms, she is likewise free to understand them in materialist or dualist terms. No matter of logic prevents this simple objectivist from being either a dualist or a reductive materialist about traits, capacities, or relations – or, for that matter, mental states. The fact is that even an objectivist who posits a *summum bonum* or golden mean might nonetheless maintain that such an entity is reducible to some physical entity.[24] In short, the compatibility of sim-

24 Thus, even a materialist like Hobbes might not "believe that moral objectivists like Aristotle use moral terms, such as *summum bonum*, that do not refer" (Hampton, p. 50), but might instead believe that such terms do refer, if only to entities which are reducible to material entities. Indeed, even a divine command theory positing God (a view Hampton claims A. E. Taylor and H. Warrender ascribe to Hobbes) might admit of a materialist reduction.

ple objectivism and reductive materialism is quite straight-forward.

Even the strongest objectivist position, one which affirms the existence of mind-independent moral facts, is logically independent of these metaphysical positions.[25] Although we might infer from such a view that moral truths are mind independent, we could not infer that there are any proper-ties at all, much less that there are moral ones. Nor could we infer that there are any irreducibly nonmaterial entities. It is logically possible that there are mind-independent moral facts even though there are no properties or irreducibly nonmaterial entities. There is no reason to think that any version of objectivism, which is not by definition committed to realism and dualism, would be logically contradicted by nominalism or materialism. There is no reason why an ob-jectivist is not free to choose between nominalism or realism and materialism or dualism. Hobbes's ethical egoism simply does not follow from his or any nominalist or materialist metaphysics.

The argument from psychological egoism and internalism

Another argument for Hobbes's subjectivist ethics is prem-ised on his commitment to psychological egoism and Hamp-ton's defense of a meta-ethical position called "internal-ism."[26] As Hampton explains it, internalism is the view which requires that individuals be capable of doing their duty for duty's sake. Or phrased more directly in Kantian terms, internalism holds that individuals should be capable of acting from duty, and not merely according to duty. Hampton's claim is that if Hobbes endorsed an objectivist ethics, his concomitant insistence on psychological egoism

25 This view is commonly referred to as moral realism, but should not be confused with the view that there are moral properties.

26 Hampton's discussion of internalism is based on the views expressed by Nagel in T. Nagel, "Hobbes's Concept of Obligation," *Philosophical Review* 68 (1959): 68–83. But internalism has a considerable tradition both before and after Nagel.

would entail that Hobbes's ethics violates the internalist principle. The resulting Hobbesian view, according to Hampton, would be one in which "morality can be only an intellectual activity . . . that can have no motivational effect on human action. Yet to strip morality of all its motivational power is to destroy in a fundamental way the essence of the concept of moral obligation" (Hampton, p. 32).

To understand Hampton's claim that psychological egoism and internalism entail a subjectivist ethics, let's first look to Hampton's discussion for a more refined definition of internalism. What precisely does Hampton mean by internalism? She claims that a morality which violates the internalist principle will "have no motivational effect on human action," and will be stripped "of all its motivational power" (Hampton, p. 32). What does Hampton mean when she says that morality should have a "motivational effect" or should have "motivational power"? If we are to be true to Hobbes's theory, human motivation must be explained ultimately in terms of desires. As Hampton explains, Hobbes's theory of human motivation traces the "origin of voluntary motion" to desires. Hobbes distinguishes between " 'vitall' motion, or the internal movements of our bodily parts (e.g., movement of the blood), and 'voluntary' or 'animal' motion, that is the external movements of the body (e.g., movement of a limb)" (Hampton, p. 13). According to Hampton's interpretation,

> either the vital motions that initiate an image in the brain increase, in which case one experiences pleasure and initiates voluntary motion toward the object, or else these vital motions decrease, in which case one experiences pain and begins voluntary motion away from the thing sensed. The former is called man's appetite, desire, or love for that object; the latter is man's hatred of or aversion to it. (Hampton, p. 13)

Hampton appropriately refers to this view as Hobbes's "desire-based theory of human motivation" (Hampton, p. 30). But of course, even Hobbes's theory must also provide

87

a role for beliefs in the explanation of human behavior. For it would seem that an action cannot, at least rationally, be motivated by a desire unless it is predicated as well on a belief that taking that action will serve to increase the chances of satisfying that desire.[27]

In light of Hobbes's psychological theory, how might morality have a motivational effect on human action? Given that, for every act, possession of a desire to commit the act is a necessary condition, in Hobbes's view, for the voluntary commission of that act, morality would have a motivational effect on human beings only if human beings desire to act morally.[28] But even if human beings desire to act morally, an act of a minimally rational person can be understood to be causally motivated by such a desire only if it is preceded by a belief that the act is a moral one. So a morality governing healthy and thus minimally rational Hobbesian individuals would satisfy Hampton's internalism only if such individuals at least potentially possessed the desire to act morally. They could be said to be motivated by morality only if they act, at least in part, because of a desire to act morally. And when they do so, they must therefore believe that their act is a moral act.

Now let's consider Hampton's argument. Her claim is that the truth of internalism and Hobbes's psychological egoism entail the truth of Hobbes's subjectivist ethics. According to Hampton, Hobbes's ethical egoism squares nicely with psychological egoism and internalism, but objectivism does not. Referring to any objectivist theory, Hampton states that:

27 In passing, Hobbes notes the unavoidable connection between beliefs and desires when he observes that: "For of things wee know not at all, or believe not to be, we can have no further Desire, than to tast and try" [*Lev*, 6, 4, 24] (Hampton, p. 14).

28 One might argue that morality itself somehow causes individuals to develop the desire to conform to morality, and so guarantees that individuals will act morally. But it is difficult to understand how "morality itself" or "the concept of morality," and the like, can have independent causal powers.

> Any such moral theory, if it is made consistent with Hobbes-
> ian psychology, will be without motivational force . . . and if
> it is given motivational force, it will be inconsistent with that
> psychology. . . . In the end Hobbes's insistence on espousing
> a largely egoistic psychology is, as Nagel appreciated, the ruin
> of any attempt to incorporate a moral theory into his argu-
> ment in which moral action is both objective and opposed to
> self-interest. (Hampton, p. 33)

And the only alternative to objectivist ethics, according to
Hampton, is Hobbesian subjectivist ethics. She argues that
by redefining terms like "good" to mean "what we desire"
and "right" to mean "instrumentally valuable as means to
what is good," Hobbes guarantees that psychological egoists
will be capable of being motivated by morality. And should
morality be defined apart from self-interest, Hampton claims
that individuals will be incapable of being motivated at all to
conform with morality. In Hobbes's political argument, for
example, Hampton claims that he

> is concerned with getting people to act in certain ways; in
> particular, he wants them to institute and maintain an abso-
> lute power. Given his psychological theory, people will do
> this *only if they believe it is in their self-interest.* Hence, *self-
> interest is all that can yield obedience to the laws of nature and
> political obedience to the sovereign.* (Hampton, p. 32; emphasis
> added)

Hampton holds that according to Hobbes's psychology, individuals will commit only acts they believe to be in their
self-interest. She then concludes that if morality is not defined in terms of self-interest, individuals will therefore be
incapable of being motivated to conform with morality. But
is it true that Hobbesian psychological egoists will be incapable of being motivated to conform with an objective morality? As we have seen, internalism requires that agents be
capable of being motivated by a desire to do the moral thing.
Does it follow, as Hampton argues, that psychological ego-

ists could have such a desire only if morality is defined, as Hobbesian subjectivism would have it, in terms of self-interest? Clearly not.

Hampton's argument fails to maintain the crucial distinctions between the origin and content of desires, and between the role of beliefs and desires, in Hobbes's psychology. Hobbes's psychology does not, as Hampton's argument maintains, entail that individuals will do only what they believe to be in their self-interest. Rather, Hobbes's psychological egoism entails that individuals' acts are causally motivated by their desires, and that their desires are produced by a self-interested, desire-producing mechanism. Of course, everything such individuals do is, in one (analytic) sense, self-interested. But the point of explicating this sense of self-interest in terms of desires which are produced by a self-interested, desire-producing mechanism is to allow individuals to have all sorts of desires, some of which may not be selfish.[29] The virtue of this formulation of Hobbes's psychological egoism is that it reconciles the fundamental claim that individuals are self-interested with the possibility that such individuals can nonetheless possess non-self-regarding interests. As Hampton puts it, the advantage of explicating Hobbes's psychological egoism in this way is that "he can maintain simultaneously that people are able to pursue other-regarding objects for their own sake . . . but do so because these objects are pleasure-producing or pain-avoiding. . . . I may or may not be conscious of the physiological sources of desire, but I do know what I desire, and this is the distinction Hobbes's psychology respects" (Hampton, pp. 23–4). The "physiological source" of such other-regarding desires is the self-interested, desire-producing mechanism which explains why individuals have the desires, self- or other-regarding, that they have.

---

29 See the section in this chapter on conflict in the state of nature for Hampton's discussion of Hobbes's view of the relationship between self-interest and desire formation.

Given that psychological egoists, according to Hampton, can possess non-self-regarding desires, there is no reason why a healthy deliberator could not possess a desire to do what is morally right, even if, as would be possible under an objectivist ethics, what is morally right to do is to act contrary to one's self-interest. Psychological egoists are perfectly capable of desiring to commit non-self-regarding acts. Consider, for example, a straightforward objectivist ethics, like the classical Aristotelian ethics considered earlier. Psychological egoism states that individuals will always act to satisfy their desires. Aristotle's virtue ethics, let us say, states that individuals ought to strive to attain certain traits of character, capacities, and so on, some of which require the commission of other-regarding acts. An internalist Aristotelian ethics, then, would require that individuals be capable of desiring to do what promotes, achieves, develops or exemplifies such traits and capacities. Are psychological egoists somehow prevented from having such a desire? Certainly not.

Because psychological egoists can possess non-self-interested desires, they can possess a desire to comply with a morality which requires committing non-self-interested acts. Psychological egoism allows that individuals might have and act upon a desire to promote, achieve, develop or exemplify the virtues espoused by an Aristotelian ethics. And in the event a psychological egoist does possess such a desire and acts on it, he will do so when he believes the act to be required by such a morality. Such a psychological egoist will, therefore, at least in some instances, commit an act he believes to be contrary to his interests. Psychological egoism simply does not entail that individuals will be incapable of being motivated to act in accordance with an objective morality, even in the event that morality requires the commission of non-self-regarding acts.

Similarly, defining morality in terms of self-interest, as Hobbes's subjectivist ethics does, cannot guarantee that individuals will satisfy the internalist requirement and therefore be motivated to conform with morality. To be sure, such a definition of morality insures that every act each individual commits will be in accordance with morality. Psychological egoists will, by definition, do what is in their self-interest, even if they are acting to satisfy non-self-regarding desires. (They are nonetheless doing what is in their self-interest in the sense that all of their desires, even non-self-regarding ones, are produced by a self-interested desire-producing mechanism.) However, internalism requires that when individuals act in accordance with morality, such actions are, at least in part, causally motivated by a desire to act in accordance with morality. But even psychological egoists, as Hampton has defined them, will not necessarily do what is in their self-interest *because morality requires that they do so.* This is just to say that psychological egoists need not desire to conform to morality – even a Hobbesian, subjectivist, self-interested morality – despite the fact that they are constitutionally incapable of committing acts contrary to such a morality. Thus, defining morality subjectively in terms of self-interest can no more guarantee the satisfaction of the internalist's requirement than defining morality objectively in terms of other-interests can guarantee the violation of the internalist requirement. If Hobbes's objective is to guarantee satisfaction of the internalist requirement that individuals be capable of being morally motivated, Hampton's ethical egoism falls short of the mark for Hobbes's psychological egoists.

Thus, as a matter of logic, Hobbes's psychological egoism and internalism are equally consistent with subjectivist and objectivist ethics. We might wonder, of course, whether a desire to commit other-regarding acts – the desire contemplated by a potential internalist-objectivist ethics – could in fact rather than merely in principle be produced by a self-interested desire-forming mechanism. But there is no *a priori* reason to think that a self-interested desire-forming mechanism will not produce other-regarding desires. To the contrary, there is ample scientific theory to support the view that such a mechanism would in fact produce a significant quantity of precisely such desires.[30] Nevertheless, all that needs to be shown here is that such desires are in fact possible, and so long as they are, objectivism, psychological egoism, and internalism are rendered consistent.

But suppose we reinterpret and strengthen Hampton's internalist thesis to hold that individuals not only be capable of being morally motivated, but that such moral motivation is necessarily sufficient and overriding in all cases in which it is present. This stronger version of internalism recognizes that individuals, even granting Hobbes's reduction of morality to individual rationality, need not always be morally motivated (i.e., they need not always be motivated by a desire to conform even to a subjective morality), but insists that when a moral agent is morally motivated, such motivation is necessarily sufficient to compel him to do what is morally required. It seems clear that Hobbesian egoists will satisfy this internalist thesis given Hobbes's subjectivist reduction of morality to individual rationality, but that objectivist theories of morality will not. Psychological egoists who

30 And if we consider other non-egoistic ethical theories, we find even more compelling reasons to suppose such desires might be produced by a self-interested desire-producing mechanism. Consider a naive utilitarian view according to which rightness and goodness consist in the maximization of net aggregate utility. According to an internalist utilitarian, then, individuals must have the desire to maximize general utility. In fact, recent evolutionary research indicates that the latter sorts of desires not only can be explained but should be expected to be generated by a "self-interested" desire-producing mechanism. See, for example, Scott Boorman and Paul Levitt, *The Genetics of Altruism* (New York: Academic Press, 1980); Richard Dawkins, *The Selfish Gene* (New York: Oxford University Press, 1976); W. D. Hamilton, "The Evolution of Altruistic Behavior," *American Naturalist* 97 (1963): 354–6; J. Maynard Smith, "Group Selection," in *Readings in Sociobiology*, edited by T. H. Clutton-Brock and Paul Harvey (San Francisco: W. H. Freeman, 1978), pp. 20–31; R. L. Trivers, "The Evolution of Reciprocal Altruism," in *Quarterly Review of Biology* 46 (1971): 35–57; George Williams, *Adaptation and Natural Selection* (Princeton: Princeton University Press, 1966); and E. O. Wilson, *Sociobiology: The New Synthesis* (Cambridge, Mass.: Harvard University Press, 1975).

are healthy deliberators *necessarily* conform to Hobbesian morality. They are constitutionally incapable of voluntarily committing acts contrary to their self-interest even if they believe they are acting contrary to their self-interest because they are committing an act causally motivated by an other-regarding desire. Healthy deliberators thus conform to morality whether or not they are morally motivated: *a fortiori*, they necessarily comply with morality every time their actions happen to be causally motivated by a desire to act morally. But Hobbesian egoists do not necessarily conform to objective moral constraints because such constraints need not coincide with the satisfaction of their desires. Here, then, is a version of internalism which, given psychological egoism, is satisfied by Hobbes's subjectivist ethics but not by objectivist ethics.

But there seems to be something peculiar about the manner in which Hobbes's ethics satisfies the internalist principle. Notice that when Hobbesian egoists are motivated to do the moral thing, it is not the fact that they possess such a motivation that is guaranteed ultimately to compel them to conform to morality. Rather, it is the fact that they are psychologically "hard-wired" to satisfy their desires, irrespective of whether they have a desire to conform to morality, that accounts for their complying with moral requirements when they are morally motivated. In other words, the reason that possession of a moral motivation is a sufficient condition for the moral conformity of Hobbesian egoists is *not* that the Hobbesian egoists' desire to conform to morality is always overriding when weighed against competing motivations. Rather, Hobbesian egoists conform to morality because they are psychologically compelled to do what is moral, whether they have such a desire or not. Given Hobbes's subjectivism, morality always requires individuals to do what is in their self-interest. And healthy Hobbesian individuals necessarily do what is in their self-interest by virtue of the fact that all of their actions necessarily are believed and intended by them to be a reasonable means for satisfying their desires, and the fact that their desires are produced by a self-interested desire-producing mechanism. Whatever their desires, they *will* act to satisfy their desires no matter what. But is this the sort of connection between motivation and action internalists want to isolate? I think not.

Strong internalists want the fact that an agent is morally motivated to be the overriding reason why that agent conforms to morality. But the only fact which explains conformance to Hobbesian morality by Hobbesian egoists is psychological egoism, not possession of moral motivation. Put another way, it is a causal, not logical, connection between moral conformity and moral motivation, not psychological egoism, which internalism demands. The idea behind strong internalism is that possession of a moral motivation should be causally sufficient, not necessarily logically sufficient, to bring about conformance with moral norms. Hobbesian subjectivism insures that possession of moral motivation will be a *logically* sufficient condition for Hobbesian egoists to comply with morality, but it does no more to demonstrate that possession of moral motivation will provide a *causally* sufficient condition for Hobbesian agents to comply with morality than does an objectivist ethics which does not define morality in terms of self-interest. Even Hobbes's ethics does nothing to guarantee that agents who possess a desire to act morally will do the moral thing in virtue of possessing such motivation. Rather, it guarantees only that such agents will do the moral thing because they are psychological egoists. For neither an objectivist nor subjectivist ethics can insure that moral motivation will provide a sufficient condition for moral compliance. And this fact should be unsurprising. Whether or not moral motivation will override other motivations is a matter of contingent psychological fact, not meta-ethical definition.

In the final analysis, Hobbes's psychological egoism and the truth of either a weak or strong internalist thesis does not entail his subjectivist reduction of morality to rationality. Weak internalism requires that individuals be capable of possessing moral motivation, and Hobbesian egoists can possess such motivation whether we adopt an objectivist or subjectivist ethics. Strong internalism requires that when individuals do possess moral motivation, such motivation be a causally sufficient condition for their acting in accordance with morality. But Hobbesian subjectivist ethics can no more guarantee such a causal connection between moral motivation and moral action than can an objectivist ethics.

The "ought implies can" argument for Hobbes's ethical reduction

There is, however, another argument for the reduction or redefinition of morality to rationality that demands our attention. Gregory Kavka has pointed out that the standard meta-ethical thesis of "ought implies can," when combined with psychological egoism, seems to generate an argument for a reduction of morality to rationality:

> When conjoined with Psychological Egoism – at least in the form that says we are, by nature, purely self-interested creatures – this doctrine implies that moral ought-principles can require of an individual only conduct consistent with his self-interest (or believed by him to be so consistent). For the individual would be motivationally incapable of performing acts known to be against his interests. (Kavka, p. 310)

We must consider whether the "ought implies can" principle, together with Hampton's psychological egoism, provides a sound argument for Hobbes's subjectivist ethics.

Let us begin by supposing the "ought implies can" principle and Hampton's psychological egoism are both true. Now if morality requires of a psychological egoist that he commit some act known by him to be contrary to his self-interest, does it follow that the psychological egoist will be unable to commit that act? This would certainly be the case if psychological egoism entailed that individuals commit only those acts they believe to be in their self-interest. But as we are now well aware, Hampton's psychological egoism requires no such thing. It requires only that healthy deliberators' desires be produced by a self-interested desire-producing mechanism, and that healthy deliberators believe their actions to be a reasonable means of satisfying their desires. Psychological egoists need not have exclusively self-regarding desires. They may have genuinely other-regarding desires, and they may have a desire to conform to morality. Should a psychological egoist possess either of these desires, he would be perfectly capable of committing non-self-interested acts which an objective morality might require. Thus, the truth of psychological egoism, as Hampton defines it, and the "ought implies can" principle does not logically entail the truth of Hobbes's subjectivist ethics. Hobbes's subjectivist ethics requires only that individuals commit those acts believed by them to constitute an effective means of satisfying their rational desires. And while there is no guarantee that individuals will be capable of acting according to an objectivist ethics, it is clearly possible that they will be.

Nonetheless, it might be argued that while psychological egoists might not be capable of conforming to an objectivist ethics, thus proving a violation of the "ought implies can" principle, Hobbes's subjectivist ethics guarantees that psychological egoists will have the capability of doing what morality requires. But is this true? Hobbes's subjectivist ethics requires healthy deliberators to commit acts which they believe to be reasonable means of satisfying their desires. But notice that Hobbes, as Hampton reconstructs his views, does not say that morality requires all individuals, healthy and unhealthy deliberators alike, to do whatever they desire to do *simpliciter*. If it did, and we grant that psychological egoists will necessarily act on their desires, then of course psychological egoists could not help but do what morality, so defined, requires of them. But in fact Hobbes's subjectivist ethics requires individuals to do what is rational according to the healthy deliberation theory of rationality. And that theory defines rational action in terms of full knowledge, undistorted reasoning, and real desires (i.e., desires produced by a healthy desire-producing mechanism). Thus,

there will be individuals who are incapable of acting morally, even on Hobbes's subjective ethical view, because they
have not fully informed themselves, have distorted reasoning processes (e.g., distorted by a desire for glory), or mal-
functioning desire-producing mechanisms, and thus are not
acting on their real desires. Although Hobbes's subjectivist
ethics does seem to guarantee that the "ought implies can"
principle will be satisfied by healthy deliberators, he admits
that some individuals are irrational, and so must admit that
even his subjectivist ethics violates the "ought implies can"
principle with respect to these individuals. And we have no
more reason for supposing that most people will be healthy
deliberators than we have for supposing that individuals
will have other-regarding desires compatible with actions
required by an objectivist ethics. Whether or not psychological egoists are rational deliberators and have non-self-
regarding desires is an entirely contingent fact. And whether
or not either Hobbes's subjectivist ethics or an objectivist
ethics will violate the "ought implies can" principle will
depend on this contingent fact. Neither view guarantees
that the "ought implies can" principle will not be violated
given the truth of psychological egoism.

There is, however, a version of the "ought implies can"
principle that does seem to motivate Hobbes's subjectivist
ethics. Suppose the "ought implies can" principle is taken
to require only that well-functioning human beings be capable of acting morally. The principle, we might say, is intended to make moral behavior physically and psychologically attainable for human beings. The "ought implies can"
principle thus constitutes a criterion of adequacy for all moral
theories: if healthy deliberators are incapable of conforming
to morality, then that morality is unacceptable. Hobbes claims
that if people are healthy, and thus healthy deliberators,
they will be able to conform to morality. Moreover, he claims
that most people are healthy deliberators. An acceptable
morality will simply not apply to individuals who are not
healthy, and who are thus incapable of conforming to morality. But if morality is defined objectively, it is possible that

both unhealthy and healthy deliberators are incapable of acting morally. An objectivist ethics might require actions that, in principle, are not possible even for healthy psychological egoists. The healthiest deliberator in the world might nonetheless lack non-self-regarding desires and thus be incapable of conforming to an objectivist ethics which requires an other-regarding act. If this were the case, we could not reconcile the "ought implies can" principle with such an objectivist ethics merely by saying that some individuals are not bound by morality, but must instead pronounce the entire objectivist ethics unacceptable.

This version of the "ought implies can" argument holds that, if psychological egoism is true, Hobbes's subjectivist ethics guarantees that healthy human beings will be able to conform to morality, while an objectivist ethics can make no such guarantee. Thus, Hobbes's subjectivist ethics should be adopted to guarantee that the "ought implies can" principle is not, even in principle, violable. Unfortunately, Hobbes's ethical subjectivism constitutes a "cure" that is worse than the "disease." Hobbes purchases conformity to this version of the "ought implies can" principle at the price of rendering morality tautological: all and only those individuals who cannot help but act morally are bound by morality. This is because Hobbes's psychology and ethics seem to entail a deterministic view of moral choice and action.

Psychological egoists who are healthy deliberators cannot help but choose those actions they believe to be most likely to lead to the satisfaction of their real desires. And psychological egoists who are not healthy deliberators cannot help it if their actions are not rational, or if the desires they act on are not their real desires. Hobbes's psychology and ethics cannot allow for the possibility that an individual might be a healthy deliberator and yet choose freely not to act morally. For moral action is rational action, and healthy deliberators are, by definition, rational actors. Yet even internalism admits that individuals capable of doing and being morally motivated to do the moral thing may nonetheless choose not to do the moral thing. Moral motivation need not always be overriding. But if we grant the present version of the "ought implies can" principle, Hobbes's psychology and ethics lead to the consequence that only those individuals who necessarily act morally are bound by morality. On Hobbes's ethical view, immorality becomes a conceptual impossibility because only healthy deliberators are bound by morality. Unhealthy deliberators, because they are unhealthy, are not bound by morality. But healthy deliberators will, by definition, act rationally. And since this is all morality requires, healthy deliberators will, by definition, act morally. It turns out that the only individuals bound by morality are individuals who necessarily act morally. Those individuals capable of acting immorally are not bound by morality. No one bound by morality can be immoral. Immorality is impossible. Surely, the "ought implies can" principle cannot require us to adopt a morality according to which immorality is impossible. This would render morality otiose.

The only way Hobbes might avoid this consequence is to reinterpret his psychological egoism to hold that individuals have control over their desires. If individuals have control over their desires, then even healthy deliberators might decide not to act morally. But this would seem impossible on Hampton's interpretation of his psychological egoism. Healthy individuals can act only to satisfy their desires, and even if they were capable of causing their desire-forming mechanism to form particular desires, they would first have to possess a desire to do so. And in principle, this latter desire can be in their power to produce only if it is in turn preceded by a third-order desire to produce it, and so forth *ad infinitum*. Postulating the power to produce the second-order desire to satisfy one's desires leads to the postulation of a psychologically impossible infinite regress of desires. The fact is that desires will be produced only contingently by the desire-producing mechanism, and individuals cannot in principle have ultimate control over what desires it produces. Thus, we cannot say that individuals genuinely choose their actions, for they can act only on their desires which they can choose only if they happen to have a desire to make such a choice. But they cannot, in any ultimate sense, choose to have such a desire. Their desire-producing mechanism must produce in them a desire to have certain desires.[31] Thus, Hobbes's psychological views appear to entail a rather strong determinism which, together with his ethics, blocks attribution of moral responsibility to all but those individuals who cannot help but behave morally. Moreover, if unhealthy deliberators are not to be morally blamed for their irrational acts, it is unclear why healthy deliberators are to be given moral credit for their equally determined rational acts. Hobbes's psychology and subjectivist ethics together render morality tautological at best and vacuous at worst.

On the other hand, it is quite possible that an objectivist ethics will be consistent with the "ought implies can" principle, so long as individuals happen to have non-self-regarding desires. And we have good reason to believe that most individuals do have such desires, and are certainly capable of acquiring them if they do not. Moreover, an objectivist ethics does not lead to the absurd consequences yielded by Hobbes's subjectivist ethics. An objectivist can hold that individuals are bound by morality and yet recognize that individuals may weigh their various desires and decide to act contrary to morality, even though they are capable of acting morally. In this respect, objectivist ethics seem preferable to Hobbes's subjectivist ethics. The only advantage of Hobbes's subjectivist ethics is that it guarantees that no matter what desires individuals have, they will, if healthy, be capable of acting morally. But it simultaneously guarantees that healthy individuals are not only capable, but psychologically compelled to act morally. And the version of the "ought implies can" principle which motivates Hobbes's extreme ethical position also entails that the only individuals capable of acting immorally (i.e., unhealthy

31 Moreover, because desires can be overridden by other desires, what desires they act upon will be a function of the strength of their desires, and they cannot choose what strength their desires will have any more than they can choose what desires they will have.

individuals) are not bound by morality. If we are to preserve the possibility of immoral action, and thus the relevance of morality, we must reject the version of the "ought implies can" principle which necessitates Hobbes's subjectivism.

So we have seen that the first version of the "ought implies can" argument does not motivate a Hobbesian reduction of morality to rationality any more than it motivates an objectivist ethics. And if the second version motivates the reduction, and thus motivates Hobbes's subjectivism, it should be rejected. For the latter carries with it a more serious problem than it solves.

Summary

I have considered Hampton's arguments for the Hobbesian reduction of morality to rationality and found them wanting. Neither nominalism, physicalism, weak internalism, nor strong internalism requires such a reduction. All of these views are no more or less consistent with Hobbes's subjectivist ethics than standard objectivist ethics. In addition, I considered an argument from the "ought implies can" principle, explicitly mentioned by Kavka, and found that a reduction of morality to rationality does not render Hampton's egoism any more consistent with a plausible version of the "ought implies can" principle than does an objectivist ethics. And though a different version of this principle does seem to motivate Hobbes's subjectivism, it seems more plausible to reject the principle than to adopt Hobbes's subjectivism and the tautological morality it entails. In the end, even though I have granted *arguendo* Hampton's psychological egoism, I have been unable to find a compelling argument in support of Hobbes's reduction of morality to individual rationality.

If, however, we grant the reduction of morality to individual rationality, then the justification of the state will depend on the success of the inferential argument. But we have seen that the inferential argument not only rests on dubious empirical claims concerning the intrinsic nature of humankind, but also incorrectly presupposes that human beings in a prepolitical state of nature will have the same self-regarding interests as those in any postpolitical state of nature would have. And even if we waive these objections to the inferential argument, it will have established at best the collective rationality (e.g., mutual advantage) of the state. Given the Hobbesian reduction of morality to individual rationality, the argument's success in demonstrating the legitimacy of political authority, however, depends on it demonstrating not the collective but the individual rationality of the state. In the following chapter, we turn to Hampton's arguments for the individual rationality of creating and maintaining the state.

Chapter 3

Hampton's internal solution: a dilemma

Hampton's theory provides a prominent role for the demonstration of the existence of an internal solution to the state-of-nature problem. As we have seen in Chapter 2, two central claims turn on this demonstration. When combined with the inferential argument, it is supposed to prove that (1) some political association is, for us, individually rational to create and maintain, and (2) political association is individually rational for us to create and maintain if and only if it is collectively rational. In this chapter, my aim is to show that Hampton's contractarian argument either fails by its own terms to justify political authority, or succeeds at the cost of legitimizing regimes which are clearly pretheoretically illegitimate, even by the lights of those who advocate a reduction of morality to rationality. I waive the previous criticisms of Hobbes's motivation for the reduction of morality to rationality and the objections to the inferential argument. The central problem with Hampton's contractarianism, I will argue, is that it presupposes a reduction of morality to individual rationality and takes into account collective rationality only indirectly when collective and individual rationality merge. The reduction of morality to individual rationality has led contractarians to focus their energy on the problem of demonstrating the individual rationality of creating political institutions in the state of nature. This problem has vexed philosophers who blame the prisoner's dilemma for the conflict and noncooperation of the state of nature. The problem has been to show that despite the fact that the individual rationality of agents in the state of nature prevents them from engaging in collectively rational cooperation, such individuals could nevertheless cooperate to create a state which functions, *inter alia*, to enforce contracts and obviate the prisoner's dilemma. The question has been "How can individuals whose rationality prevents them from keeping cooperative agreements among themselves engage in the cooperation necessary to create a political sovereign?" Thus, contractarians have appreciated for some time the problem posed by the divergence between individual and collective rationality in the state of nature. But contractarians have also appreciated that a solution to the problem of creating a political sovereign in the state of nature may create more problems than it solves. In fact, it may turn out that life in political association is worse than life in the state of nature. Moreover, once a political sovereign is in place, it may be individually rational to maintain the sovereign even if doing so is collectively irrational. Just as rational individuals might not be able to create a collectively rational political sovereign in the state of nature, we might also doubt whether rational individuals could depose a political sovereign even when doing so is collectively rational. Should it be individually rational to maintain a collectively irrational regime, a contractarian view endorsing the Hobbesian reduction of morality to individual rationality would have to conclude that such a regime is legitimate. This, I will argue, constitutes a *reductio ad absurdum* of such a contractarian theory.

Hobbes confronts the problem of a collectively irrational sovereign directly. He claims that even a malicious sovereign could not make life worse than it would be in the state of nature, and so denies that political association can be collectively irrational when compared to the state of nature. Locke, of course, in his now famous passage in the *Second Treatise*, was the first of many to doubt this claim:

> As if when Men quitting the State of Nature entered into Society, they agreed that all of them but one, should be under the restraint of Laws, but that he should still retain all the

Liberty of the State of Nature, increased with Power, and made licentious by Impunity. This is to think that Men are foolish that they take care to avoid what Mischiefs may be done them by *Pole-cats* or *Foxes*, but are content, nay think it Safety, to be devoured by Lions. (Locke, 2T, 93, 372)

Hobbes is forced to deny that life under a sovereign could be worse than life in the state of nature because he is convinced that only an absolute sovereign can solve the problems of the state of nature, and he recognizes that absolute sovereigns may not be deposable.

Hampton, however, claims that Hobbes's psychological and ethical views are inconsistent with the institution and maintenance of an absolute sovereign and argues that a limited sovereign can and rationally should be instituted in the state of nature. Hampton argues that such a sovereign could be removed by the same process by which she is instituted, whenever the sovereign's rule is no longer collectively rational. I will be considering this process in detail later, but for now we should note that both Hobbes and Hampton seem to concede that a theory which has the consequence of condoning a collectively irrational political authority should be rejected. Hobbes hopes to avoid this consequence by embracing a dubious empirical claim, while Hampton argues that whenever sovereign rule is collectively irrational, it will thereby become individually rational to act with others to depose the sovereign. At worst, sovereigns will be deposed when their rule is collectively irrational. At best, sovereigns will understand their vulnerability to revolt should their rule become collectively irrational, and will, because they are rational, insure that their rule remains collectively rational. Thus, for Hampton, the key to avoiding the *reductio ad absurdum* of contractarianism is a successful theory of individually and collectively rational rebellion.

Hampton claims that the same process whereby individuals in the state of nature institute and maintain a political sovereign will serve to bring about the individual rationality of rebellion when rebellion is collectively rational as well. So in order to assess Hampton's arguments for the individual rationality of collectively rational rebellion, we must first consider her arguments for the individual rationality of acting to institute a sovereign in the state of nature.

THE RATIONAL EMERGENCE OF A SOVEREIGN IN THE STATE OF NATURE: A DILEMMA

Hampton presents a three-step argument to demonstrate the individual rationality of instituting a sovereign in the state of nature. The first step is to demonstrate the individual rationality of having a political sovereign. This is provided by the account of conflict and noncooperation in the state of nature considered in Chapter 2. That account was supposed to demonstrate that everyone in the state of nature would be better off if there were a sovereign who was able and willing to enforce cooperative agreements and prevent conflict. Given that account, every rational individual in the state of nature will prefer to have a political sovereign. The second step is to solve the sovereign-selection problem. Even if it is clear that having a political sovereign would make everyone in the state of nature better off, individuals in the state of nature still must be able collectively to solve the problem of determining who that sovereign will be. The third stage of instituting a sovereign is the demonstration that rational individuals in the state of nature can empower the sovereign they select in the previous stage. Even if individuals in the state of nature have managed to select one individual to become sovereign, to become an effective sovereign that individual must not only be selected but empowered as well.

The problem of empowering the sovereign constitutes the central obstacle to demonstrating the individual rationality of instituting a political sovereign in a state of nature. Moreover, Hampton's solution to this problem also serves as her solution to the problem of demonstrating the individual rationality of collectively rational revolution. The structure of my criticism of her solution will be dilemmatic. I will argue that either her solution to the empowerment problem of instituting a political sovereign in the state of nature fails, or it succeeds at the price of rendering some collectively irrational regimes individually rational to maintain, and thus morally legitimate. The latter horn of the dilemma, I will argue, should signal the likely failure of reductions of morality to individual rationality alone – reductions which therefore do not directly take account of collective rationality – and thus the failure of any contractarian theories which rely upon such a reduction.

Before beginning the critique of Hampton's internal solution, however, we should pause to clarify the criterion of evaluation which should guide such a critique. Recall that in Chapter 2, I distinguished between two forms an internal solution might take. While the weaker form would demonstrate only that individuals in the state of nature *could* (i.e., might) be able independently to solve their problem, the stronger form would demonstrate that such individuals *would* be able to solve their problem. As I noted, Hampton's theory requires the strong form of an internal solution, because, when combined with the inferential argument, the weak form would suffice to establish only that our political association might be individually rational to create and maintain. In turn, this proposition would suffice to establish only that political association for us might be legitimate, a far less powerful conclusion than Hampton's theory promises. Thus, my critique of Hampton's arguments for the existence of an internal solution will attempt to measure their success at proving the stronger claim. The guiding inquiry will be to assess whether or not Hampton's arguments succeed in proving that individuals in the state of nature would be able to solve their problem and create a state. In presenting the first horn of the dilemma facing Hampton's theory, I will argue they do not.

Hampton's solution to the problem of empowering a sovereign rests, at crucial junctures, on game-theoretic notions and arguments explicated in her discussion of the leadership-selection problem. Consideration of her argument will thus begin with an analysis of Hampton's game-theoretic solution to the leadership-selection problem.

THE PROBLEM OF SELECTING A SOVEREIGN

The second step in demonstrating the individual rationality of instituting a sovereign in the state of nature is to provide an account of how individuals in the state of nature will be able to select a prospective sovereign. Hampton argues that the problem of selecting the individual who will become sovereign should be modeled as a coordination game. Her argument rests on her general discussion of coordination games and their solutions. A presentation of this discussion and the objections to its analysis will lay the foundation for a critique of her particular argument applying her general analysis to the problems of selecting and empowering a sovereign.

Coordination games and their solutions

Game theory distinguishes between two types of coordination games. Following David Lewis, Hampton defines coordination games as "situations of interdependent decision by two or more agents in which coincidence of interest predominates and in which there are two or more coordination equilibria" (Hampton, p. 138, quoting Lewis, 1969). For each individual in a pure coordination game, the payoffs associated with each alternative are the same. The player who chooses an alternative which others have not chosen will lose the same amount as he would have lost had he chosen any other alternative which others did not choose. Similarly, the player who chooses an alternative which all others have chosen will gain the same amount as he would have gained had he chosen any other alternative which all others chose. In a "pure coordination game," each player cares only that he choose the same alternative as everyone else, and is indifferent to which alternative that turns out to be. Hume's example of a pure coordination problem is rowing a boat. If two people both desire to cross a lake, but are in a rowboat which requires them to row simultaneously in order to go straight, these individuals must somehow coordinate their actions so that the boat is effectively rowed. The various possible solutions to coordination games – ways in which everyone might coordinate their actions to achieve a mutually desired result – are called "coordination equilibria": "situations in which the combination of the players' actions is such that no one would be better off if any single player, either oneself or another, acted differently" (Hampton, p. 138, citing Lewis, 1969). Unilateral defection from a coordination equilibrium in a pure coordination game is irrational; it would ruin the desired coordination and everyone, including the individual who changes his behavior, would be worse off than before the defection. In pure coordination games, deviance from an alternative which has achieved coordination offers no possible gain. As in the coordination achieved in the convention of driving on the right side of the road (in the United States), all have an interest in coordinating their behavior and driving on either the right or left side of the road, and (let us assume) no one has any preference for one alternative over the other. Once everyone begins to drive on the right side, deviance from this alternative would increase the probability of loss to everyone without increasing the probability of gain for any individual, including the defector. Once everyone has fixed on the same alternative in a pure coordination game, no one has any incentive to deviate from it. Deviance from an alternative which has achieved coordination in a pure coordination game has a "downside without an upside." Hence, such alternatives, once selected, are stable. Solutions to pure coordination games are "stable equilibria."

There is no conflict among players in a pure coordination game because each player is indifferent between the particular alternatives available. Every player's interest converges on the goal of achieving coordination on any alternative. But how do players in pure coordination games coordinate their behavior and solve their problem of choosing the same alternative? How, in other words, can players solve a pure coordination problem? There are two possibilities. First, someone – the players or someone else – might be able to change the structure of the game from a pure coordination game into one in which the same alternative is best for everyone. A change in the structure of the game is effected by changing the payoffs associated with each alternative. Such a change might be achieved by introducing additional incentives or punishments for choosing particular alternatives. Hampton calls this approach the selective incentive strategy.

By changing the structure of a game, selective incentive strategies don't really "solve" a game; rather, they *redefine* it. Thus, the possibility of a successful incentive strategy is consistent with the claim, made earlier in Chapter 2, that the single-play PD has no solution.[1] Nonetheless, the use of incentives and punishments might transform what would otherwise have been a single-play PD into a different game in which cooperation is individually rational. The introduction of a mechanism to enforce agreements can, of course, transform a single-play PD into a game in which cooperation rather than defection is dominant. Still, it would be, strictly speaking, incorrect to say that the introduction of additional incentives can *solve* a single-play PD, for the single-play PD is, by definition, a game in which the suboptimal equilibrium is dominant. If a situation *really* has the structure of a single-play PD, then the single-play PD matrix defines the only possible range of outcomes and entails that rational players will be unable to cooperate to secure the optimal equilibrium. From a game-theoretic perspective, if a real-life situation appears to have the structure of a single-play PD but is one in which the introduction of incentives and punishments sufficient to make cooperation rational is possible, then the situation does not in fact have the structure of a single-play PD. For the latter is one in which, incentives and punishment possibilities notwithstanding, the utilities associated with all possible outcomes entail that rational utility-

---

1 But see Gauthier's claim to the contrary in Chapter 5.

maximizers necessarily will not cooperate and will therefore secure a suboptimal equilibrium. Thus, we might say that selective incentive strategies solve a problem by changing, rather than solving, the underlying game which in the first instance appears to generate the problem.

A problem with the apparent underlying structure of a pure coordination game thus can be solved by changing its game-theoretic structure to one in which individuals are no longer indifferent between the alternatives. Selective incentives can insure that every individual will find it rational to select the same alternative and that therefore coordination will be achieved. Suppose, for example, that individuals are trying to coordinate on driving on one side of the road or the other, and in the midst of their deliberations, someone announces that he will pay one thousand dollars to every individual who drives on the right side (or he will fine every individual who drives on the left one thousand dollars). If his promise is credible, every individual will now have a reason – the same reason – to choose driving on the right side. The incentives will insure coordination. And because pure coordination equilibria are stable, once coordination is achieved, removing the incentives will not affect the equilibrium. No one has incentive to change his behavior.

The second way coordination problems are solved is through what Hampton calls a "salience strategy." Lewis, following Thomas Schelling, suggests that most pure coordination problems are solved "through the agency of a system of suitably concordant mutual expectations" (Lewis, p. 25). Concordant mutual expectations are created by the "salience" of one particular alternative over the others – a salience that each will expect the others to notice and use as a basis for choosing that alternative over the others. A salient alternative is "one that stands out from the rest by its uniqueness in some conspicuous respect. . . . It merely has to be unique in some way the subjects will notice, expect each other to notice, and so on" (Lewis, p. 35). The salience of one alternative over the others can provide the basis for concordant mutual expectations. Lewis explains how salience has the potential to create concordant mutual expectations:

> [Players] might all tend to pick the salient as a last resort, when they have no stronger ground for choice. Or they might expect each other to have that tendency, and act accordingly; or they might expect each other to expect each other to have that tendency and act accordingly, and act accordingly; and so on. Or – more likely – there might be a mixture of these. Their first- and higher-order expectations of a tendency to pick the salient as a last resort would be a system of concordant expectations capable of producing coordination at the salient equilibrium. (Lewis, pp. 35–6)

There are at least three ways an alternative might achieve salience. First, an alternative might become salient as a result of a preexisting convention or practice. Consider the convention governing cut-off telephone conversations. Ordinarily, the person who initiated the call will call back the other party if the line is disconnected midconversation. The preexisting convention according to which the initiating caller routinely recalls the other party if disconnected serves to make that solution salient. Second, an alternative might become salient as the result of an explicit or implicit agreement resulting from negotiations or other procedures like coin-tossing or lotteries. In Hume's rowboat example, both players might simply agree to row forward in tandem at a designated time. Because both players want the same result, neither has incentive to defect from the agreement. Third, an alternative might become salient as a result of some peculiar or distinctive property it has uniquely and which therefore makes it somehow obvious. As a matter of contingent psychological fact, that alternative will stand out in the minds of every other player. Provided each believes that others will notice the same alternative as distinctive, each will expect the others to choose that alternative for lack of any other reason to choose among the alternatives. The salience of an alternative, whether produced by convention, agreement, or otherwise, can create concordant mutual expectations which in turn serve as reasons for every individual to choose the same alternative. Salience, in other words, can turn one alternative in a pure coordination game into a coordination equilibrium. And, as in the problem of deciding which side of the road to drive on, once coordination is achieved, no one has incentive to deviate from the alternative on which everyone's choice has converged. Thus, whether achieved by a selective incentive strategy or by a salience strategy based on preexisting convention, explicit agreement, or contingent psychological fact, solutions to pure coordination games are individually and collectively rational to keep.

"Mixed coordination games," like pure coordination games, are ones in which each player prefers that all players coordinate their action to achieve a mutually desired result. But unlike pure coordination games, the coordination equilibria of mixed coordination games distribute the gains of coordination unequally among the possible alternatives. Individuals playing a mixed coordination game are not indifferent between the various alternatives on which everyone's choices might converge to achieve coordination. Instead, each player has a favored alternative which she prefers to become the coordination solution. Thus, although everyone prefers some coordination equilibrium to no equilibrium at all, each individual most prefers that particular coordination equilibrium which accords him or her the greatest share of the gains of coordination. The classic, but unfortunately sexist, example of a mixed coordination game is the "Battle-of-the-Sexes" game in which a husband and wife each prefer (1) going out to staying home, (2) being with the other to being alone, and (3) going to different events (a prize fight and a ballet, respectively). This game is a coordination game because each prefers to be with the other more than going to his or her most preferred event. Both would be worse off at their preferred event without their partner than at their least preferred event with their partner. But the game is a mixed coordination game because each prefers to coordinate with the other on their own preferred equilibrium (i.e., their preferred event). Mixed coordination games combine the motivation to cooperate, as in pure coordination games, with the noncooperative motivation to compete, as in the single-play PD. Mixed coordination games like the Battle-of-the-Sexes thus incorporate elements of cooperation and conflict.

How are mixed coordination problems solved? Just as problems with the structure of a pure coordination game can be solved by incentive strategies, problems with the underlying structure of a mixed coordination game can be solved similarly: by changing their underlying game-theoretic structure. An incentive strategy might be used to transform a problem with the structure of a mixed coordination game into a problem with the structure of a game, unlike a mixed coordination game, in which the same alternative is the best for every player. In such a game, because there is only one coordination equilibrium, coordination will be achieved. But unlike problems with the structure of pure coordination games, those with the structure of a mixed coordination game might not be solvable through the use of salience strategies because of the conflicting motivations embedded within the game. The mere salience of an alternative may not suffice to insure that every individual will choose it. For once an alternative in a mixed coordination game becomes salient, there are by definition some players who would be better off if some other alternative became salient and ultimately became the coordination equilibrium. These individuals, unlike individuals in pure coordination games, will therefore have an incentive to refuse to choose the salient alternative and to seek instead to make their most preferred alternative the salient one. Or, if we imagine the mixed coordination game to require sustained or repeated action over time (as many real-life situations require), once coordination is achieved by everyone's having chosen the same alternative, all have incentive to change their concordant behavior and ruin the coordination in order to attempt to change everyone's choice to their most favored alternative. The equilibria in mixed coordination games are for this reason not stable. Hampton contends, however, that upon analysis, salience strategies can solve mixed coordination games. Her solutions to the leadership-selection and sovereign-empowerment problems turn in part on her defense of this position.

Hampton's solution to the sovereign-selection problem

Hampton claims that the sovereign-selection problem is a mixed coordination game because although each individual prefers some sovereign to be selected rather than no sovereign, each also prefers that he or she be the sovereign selected. She claims that this mixed coordination problem can be solved either by introducing incentives to change individuals' preferences, or by making a certain equilibrium salient. Hampton focuses on the latter, presumably because it is unclear how individuals in the state of nature could introduce incentives to change individuals' preferences for being the sovereign. The solution to the sovereign-selection problem lies, according to Hampton, in making one individual the salient choice for all to choose. Ultimately, Hampton endorses voting in successive elections as the preferred method for making a particular coordination equilibrium in the sovereign-selection problem salient. Once this equilibrium is salient, Hampton claims, a sovereign will have been selected and the sovereign-selection problem will be solved.

But why don't the individuals participating in the sovereign-selection process simply refuse to accept the results of the elections which make someone else the salient choice? Why should we think that merely making one equilibrium salient should provide a solution to *any* mixed coordination game? The response Hampton offers promises to explain the rationality not only of accepting the sovereign selected by elections in the state of nature, but, as we will see later, of empowering this sovereign as well.

Hampton recognizes that individuals deciding whether to accept the sovereign selected in the state of nature will be faced with a decision whether to "hold out" for their most favored alternative (namely, to be selected as sovereign themselves) or to "give in" to a less favored alternative (namely, the sovereign already selected as the outcome of successive elections). She reasons through the various possible strategies individuals facing this choice might use.

The first strategy is to bluff. According to this strategy, each individual will "try to convince the others that she will *never* give in, either because she is irrational or because (she says) her preferences are not as they appear" (Hampton, p. 156). Bluffers hope to convince others that their only choice is between no agreement or agreement on their terms. But as Hampton observes, if everyone uses the bluff strategy, "and everyone suspects that each of the others is bluffing, there will be complete deadlock" (Hampton, p. 156). Hampton claims that group members therefore "will be rational to use other strategies to break that deadlock and finally coordinate on a solution to their problem" (p. 156).

Hampton's analysis of the bluff strategy is, however, too quick. It is not clear that bluffers will always find it rational to pursue other strategies in order to avoid potential deadlock. The rationality of abandoning the bluff strategy and turning to other strategies will depend, of course, on what those other strategies are. An alternative strategy will be rational to pursue only if it has a greater expected value (probability of success times magnitude of benefit to the individual deciding whether to choose that strategy) than the bluffing strategy has. The expected value of the alternative strategy has to be compared to the expected value of continuing the bluffing strategy. Even in the face of apparent deadlock, there is a positive, nonzero probability that others will break the deadlock, thereby advantaging the remaining bluffers. Just as the bluffing strategy itself is premised on the hope that holding out will compel others to give in, individuals using the bluffing strategy will likewise hope that holding out, even in the face of apparent deadlock, will induce others to give in. The collective action problem which individuals might attempt to solve by bluffing reoccurs again at the level of deciding whether to break a deadlock in favor of an alternative strategy. The fundamental incentive structure of the problem which creates the bluffing in the first place does not change as a result of the prospect or existence of a deadlock. The rationality, therefore, of pursuing an alternative strategy does not follow as a matter of logic from the possibility or existence of a deadlock. Rather, it will turn on the relative expected values of the bluff strategy and alternative strategies.

The alternative strategy Hampton endorses recommends that any player with a disproportionately large stake in achieving coordination should give in before the deadline for bargaining is reached. Her argument for the rationality of this strategy has two premises.[2] The first premise is that there is a "deadline effect." This premise claims that as a deadline for achieving agreement approaches, the probability of achieving agreement decreases: "The closer she gets to the deadline, the more likely it is that agreement on some outcome will not be reached" (Hampton, p. 156). The second premise is that it will be rational for players with greater stakes in the game to give in to the holdouts before it will be rational for those with lesser stakes to give in. These large stakeholders will give in by agreeing conditionally to choose the holdouts' alternative so long as everyone else will do the same (otherwise, they risk wasting their efforts): "the [relatively] bigger her stake in reaching an agreement, the sooner it will be rational for *her,* as opposed to those with lesser stakes, to be willing to give in conditional on enough others doing so, rather than continue to hold out and risk no solution at all" (Hampton, p. 156).

Evaluation of Hampton's solution to the sovereign-selection problem, thus, would involve an evaluation of both of the above claims. Why should the approach of a deadline effect a decrease in the probability of achieving agreement? Why should a difference in relative stakes make larger stake-

---

2 As Hampton puts it, this argument for the rationality of this strategy is premised on the assumptions that (1) "people have stakes of unequal sizes in coordination being reached," and (2) "there is a fairly clear deadline to their bargaining" (Hampton, p. 156).

holders less likely to hold out than smaller stakeholders? But because the central concern of this chapter is to evaluate Hampton's solution to the sovereign-empowerment problem, these questions will not be pursued here. However, Hampton builds her solution to the sovereign-empowerment problem in part on this argument for the rationality of accepting a second-choice solution to the mixed coordination game of selecting a sovereign. We will therefore have occasion to consider portions of the sovereign-selection solution below, where it is applied to the problem of empowering a sovereign.

THE INDIVIDUAL IRRATIONALITY OF EMPOWERING A SOVEREIGN: THE FIRST HORN OF THE DILEMMA

The third and final step to demonstrating the individual rationality of instituting a sovereign in the state of nature is to provide an account of how a prospective sovereign could be empowered in the state of nature. Hampton argues that there are two methods by which a political sovereign might be empowered by rational agents in a state of nature. The first purports to show that the game-theoretic structure of the problem of empowerment proves that the actions required to empower a sovereign are individually rational to take. According to this scenario, the structure of the problem renders voluntary empowerment, and thus institution, of the sovereign rational. Hampton calls this method of empowering a sovereign "the creation of a commonwealth by institution." The second recognizes that not only the empowerment of a sovereign, but the sovereign-selection process as well, might take place via an "invisible hand" device. According to this scenario, a collective demand for protection and contract regulation will set in motion market-like mechanisms which ultimately will produce a political sovereign. Because the sovereign which results from the market-like mechanisms in the state of nature is not an intended result of voluntary action, Hampton calls this method of instituting a sovereign "the creation of a commonwealth by acquisition."

The key to understanding both of Hampton's arguments for the rational emergence of a political sovereign in the state of nature lies first in understanding what actions individuals are required to do in order to empower a sovereign. According to Hampton, "[a] person is a ruler only when his subjects do what he says; so people presumably make someone a sovereign (i.e., their master) when they (or at least most of them) obey his commands" (Hampton, p. 173). However, one of the primary purposes of instituting a sovereign in the first place is to enable a sovereign to solve prisoner's dilemmas by punishing individuals who violate cooperative agreements. "Instituting an individual as sovereign therefore means *doing whatever is required to give the sovereign punishment power. . . . [C]omplying with the agreement to create a sovereign means obeying his order to punish others*" (Hampton, pp. 173–4). In order to demonstrate the rationality of empowering a sovereign, either by institution or acquisition, Hampton must explain why enough individuals will find it rational to obey the sovereign's punishment commands so that she can rule effectively. Following Hampton, we might say that the sovereign needs to have an effective "punishment cadre" to enforce her commands. Such a cadre is necessary to make each individual's expected utility of compliance with the sovereign's commands greater than that of disobedience of her commands. Only then will the sovereign's attempts to enforce contracts change the payoffs to parties in what otherwise would be prisoner's dilemma contracts so that compliance with such contracts will be rational.

Hampton has two distinct accounts of the individual rationality of the institution of a sovereign in the state of nature. The first turns on a distinction between different game-theoretic models for the provision of different types of collective good problems. The second relies on the rationality of cooperation in an iterated prisoner's dilemma. I consider each in turn.

Individual irrationality of empowering a sovereign

Mixed coordination games and the argument for the individual rationality of empowerment

One reason why we might doubt that individuals in the state of nature could create a punishment cadre is that such a cadre constitutes a collective good. As I noted in Chapter 1, the two defining characteristics of collective goods are their nonexcludability and jointness of supply. A collective good provides benefits from which it is either impossible or impractical to exclude those who did not contribute to its production or do not contribute to its maintenance. It has been argued that the provision of collective goods, so defined, has the structure of a single-play prisoner's dilemma.[3] Hampton therefore anticipates the objection that the provision of an effective punishment cadre, like the provision of many other collective goods, will be subject to the free rider problem. In particular, she considers the objection that rational individuals commanded by the prospective sovereign to enforce the sovereign's commands (i.e., individuals the sovereign chooses to be in her punishment cadre) will refuse to do so and will instead attempt to free ride on a punishment cadre formed by others:

> Wouldn't the structure of the situation and their preferences be such that it would be more rational to *refuse*, given that what would be produced by obeying the sovereign (i.e., peace) would be a collective good from which nonproducers could not be excluded? Indeed, in this situation, wouldn't each find it rational to ride free, benefitting from the enforcement but refusing to carry it out? And if each found it rational to refuse to obey the sovereign's enforcement commands, wouldn't this mean that no one would do so, thus leaving the sovereign without sufficient power to be a sovereign? It certainly appears as if empowering the ruler involves creating a collective good, and thus performing collectively rational but individually irrational actions – in this case, punishment actions. And if people are unable to produce collective goods of this

3 See Hardin, 1982.

sort in the state of nature, inasmuch as their production involves them in a problem analogous to a prisoner's dilemma, how are they suddenly able to produce *this* good? From what Hobbes has told us about the nature and motivations of these people, they will have no way of doing so. (Hampton, p. 175)

The logic of Hampton's argument may appear to fly in the face of common sense. A natural response is to point out that rational actors would realize that, given the symmetrical reasoning of most other actors in the state of nature, their attempting to free ride will be futile. For everyone else will attempt to free ride and in the end no collective good will be provided. Each party will realize this, and therefore, this response concludes, the rational individual will opt to contribute. Unfortunately, even if rational actors realize that the reasoning leading them to free ride will similarly lead others to free ride, it simply does not follow that they will therefore contribute, realizing that attempting to free ride is futile. This is just to say that collective action problems might have the structure of a single-play prisoner's dilemma in which noncooperation (noncontribution) is a dominant strategy, utility-maximizing irrespective of what actions others take. In the single-play PD, even if the prisoners know they are in a PD, they are unable to escape their dilemma: no matter what the other does, the best strategy for each is not to cooperate.

Hampton's response is to argue that while the free rider problem does potentially attend collective action problems, free riding is a dominant strategy only in those collective action problems which have the structure of a single-play PD. There are other sorts of collective action problems which have a different underlying game-theoretic structure. In these problems, free riding is not a dominant strategy because its rationality is dependent upon, rather than independent of, the behavior of others. Hampton's strategy, then, is to argue that the collective action problem of creating an effective punishment cadre does not have the game-theoretic structure of a single-play PD. Instead, she argues it is properly modeled as having the structure of a mixed coordination game: namely, a multiparty version of the Battle of the Sexes. Although free riding is the most preferred outcome for each participant in this game, it is not a dominant strategy. Hampton illustrates her point by using a three player version of Hume's example of the problem of draining a meadow:

> [E]ach player's favorite situation is that in which the other two players drain the meadow and she languishes at home, eventually enjoying the good produced at no cost to her. Next best is the situation in which the three of them share the work to be done, which is better than the situation in which she and only one other player split the work between them (doing half of the work is worse than doing a third of it). But this option is substantially better than the situation in which the meadow is not drained because none of them or only one of them is willing to do it, and of course the worst situation is that in which she puts in work almost equal to the benefit to be received from the good to be produced, but is never assisted by anyone else, so that the good never gets produced and she loses whatever resources she put into the attempt to produce it. (Hampton, pp. 179–80)

Unlike a single-play PD, in which noncooperation is rational irrespective of how the others behave, the rationality of not cooperating (i.e., attempting to free ride) in this meadow-draining game depends on what others will do:

> [I]n this [game], it is *not* rational for her to refuse to drain the meadow *whatever the others do*. She should refuse if she thinks that the other two people will do it [i.e., she should attempt to free ride], but she should *not* refuse (i.e., she should pay the cost of draining the meadow) if she thinks that only one, and not the other, is willing to drain the meadow. It is better for her (indeed, *much* better for her) to help the one other person do the work to get the meadow drained than to let the meadow go undrained. And, of course, she knows that the others' preferences are symmetric with hers. (Hampton, p. 180)

Thus, while free riding is the most preferred outcome for each individual in the meadow-draining game, it nevertheless will be rational, under certain circumstances, for players to choose instead to contribute to the draining of the meadow, rather than to attempt to free ride. In particular, when a player believes that the good will be provided if and only if she contributes, she should contribute. For example, in the meadow-draining game, the player should contribute "if she thinks that only one, and not the other, is willing to drain the meadow" (Hampton, p. 180). Under these circumstances, attempting to free ride is, of course, irrational. Hampton's strategy, then, is to show that the game-theoretic structure of the problem of creating an effective punishment cadre is not one in which free riding is a dominant strategy, but is instead one in which free riding is, or can be made by the sovereign-elect to be, irrational. She thus hopes to show not only that it has the structure of a mixed coordination game, like the meadow-draining game, but that the circumstances under which the sovereign will attempt to form her cadre are structurally analogous to those conditions under which free riding is irrational in the meadow-draining game. She therefore argues that the sovereign-elect will be able to insure that the individuals deciding whether to join the punishment cadre will believe their participation in the cadre to be necessary for its formation, and thus will find it irrational to attempt to free ride.

We should note that although Hampton's strategy is designed to address the free rider problem which attends many collective action problems, collective action problems are also plagued by the assurance problem. Even if potential contributors to a collective good were not inclined to free ride, they nonetheless might be rational not to contribute if their contribution is not refundable should the good not be provided. If they do not have sufficient assurance that the good will be produced once they have contributed, then they risk incurring the cost of their contribution without receiving the benefit of the good, provided their contribution is not refundable. The assurance problem is illustrated in the meadow-draining game as the third possible outcome. But, as we will see, there is some reason to think that the conditions under which the free rider problem would be solved would suffice to solve the assurance problem as well.

We already know that the meadow-draining game (and thus the sovereign-selection problem) does not have the structure of a single-play PD. However, this fact alone explains only why free riding would not be a dominant strategy. Even in mixed coordination games, like the meadow-draining game, free riding might sometimes be rational. But, as I have noted, Hampton must argue that the sovereign-empowerment problem is not only a mixed coordination game (like the meadow-draining game), but that it is one in which free riding is irrational. Because the latter does not follow from the former, Hampton needs to explain the conditions under which free riding will be irrational in a mixed coordination game, and then demonstrate that these conditions would be met in the sovereign-empowerment scenario. Hampton's discussion of collective action problems in general helps reveal the conditions under which free riding might be irrational in a mixed coordination game.

Hampton begins by distinguishing between two different types of collective goods. "Incremental" collective goods are ones which come into existence gradually and only in degrees. National defense, clean air, and clean water are examples of incremental goods. Individual contributions increase, if only slightly, the degree of provision of incremental goods. Although it is possible to specify levels of funding which are either necessary or sufficient for the provision of an incremental good (five hundred dollars is insufficient and five hundred billion dollars is probably sufficient for an effective U.S. national defense to exist), there is no precise level of funding which is both necessary and sufficient for the provision of an incremental good. In contrast, "pure step" collective goods are ones which do not admit of degrees. A "step good" is one "whose magnitude is not a linear function of the contributions made to produce it, [but] one that comes into existence only after a very large contribution 'step' " (Hampton, p. 177). Pure step goods come into existence immediately after a certain threshold is met, and then cannot be increased in magnitude by further contributions. Hampton uses the examples of a bridge and the election of a political candidate as illustrations. Ninety percent of a bridge is no bridge at all, and once a bridge is connected from end to end, it is complete. It makes no sense to say that an individual contribution to an uncompleted bridge increases the magnitude of a collective good. Until the bridge is complete, no benefits can be derived from it *qua* functioning bridge. Similarly, electing a public official is an all-or-nothing proposition: either the candidate is elected, in which case further votes don't increase the "electedness" of the candidate, or she is not elected, in which case the votes received don't create a "less-elected" official.

In her discussion of collective goods, Hampton suggests that incremental goods have the underlying structure of a single-play PD and thus will be subject to the free rider problem, while step goods have the underlying structure of a mixed coordination game and thus will not necessarily be subject to the free rider problem. This difference helps to explain why Hampton believes that a solution to the sovereign-empowerment problem will consist in demonstrating the empowerment of the sovereign to constitute a step good rather than an incremental good. She believes that once she proves this proposition, she has explained why individuals attempting to empower the sovereign will not face the free rider or assurance problems. Consideration of the differences between incremental and step goods, however, at most suggests that only the former necessarily have the structure of a single-play PD in which free riding is necessarily rational.[4] The fact that a collective good is incremental is

---

4 However, even this proposition overstates the relationship between incremental goods and the free rider problem. As Hampton herself notes, there are some "incremental good[s] whose structure is such that at some levels of the good[s'] production, the incremental benefit to an individual exceeds her cost of providing that increment" (Hampton, Free Rider, p. 267). In that case, "if there are some levels of the

at best a sufficient, but not necessary, condition for the rationality of free riding on efforts to produce it. It is not the case that step goods are ones in which free riding is necessarily irrational. As we have seen, free riding on a step good – especially one with the structure of a mixed coordination game like the good of empowering a sovereign – is irrational only under certain circumstances. Therefore, in the final analysis, a demonstration that the collective good of empowering a sovereign is a step good will not suffice to explain the irrationality of free riding on others' efforts to empower a sovereign. The problem of empowering a sovereign has the structure of a mixed coordination game, and as such, is one in which free riding might, but need not, be rational. Our efforts, therefore, must be directed at uncovering the conditions under which free riding will be irrational, even in the case of the production of a step good. In order to discover these conditions, let's carefully examine those arguments which purport to explain why a step good would be less amenable to the free rider and assurance problems than an incremental good.

Hampton considers one argument which might explain why incremental goods will be likely to have the structure of a PD, while step goods will be more likely to have the structure of a mixed coordination game. This argument will help us to define the conditions under which the problem of providing collective goods in general, whether incremental or step, will be attended by the free rider problem. This, in turn, should help us understand when collective action problems which have the structure of a multi-person mixed coordination game, like the sovereign-selection problem, will

good's production in which the benefit to [the contributor] from an increment exceeds the cost [to that contributor] of providing it, [the contributor] is rational to produce it – as long as others find it rational to produce the good up to the level of that increment, and as long as the solutions have been found for any of the . . . game-theoretic problems (e.g., battle of the sexes, assurance or chicken problems) involved either in selecting producers for the good or in getting them to produce that level of the good" (Hampton, Free Rider, p. 270).

be subject to or free from the free rider and assurance problems.

Since there is no discrete quantity of an incremental good before which it is no good at all and after which it is a good, incremental goods have the property of being vague. Thus, using reasoning associated with the "Sorites" paradox, "[e]ach possible contributor may reason, 'My contribution to the heap is unnecessary; either the pile that exists already qualifies as a heap, in which case my stone doesn't contribute anything to the heap's production; or the pile is not a heap, in which case my adding one stone to it won't suddenly cause it to be a heap, meaning that, once again, my stone doesn't contribute anything to the heap's production'" (Hampton, Free Rider, p. 257). Now Hampton claims this reasoning is somehow fallacious, but admits there are no satisfactory demonstrations to that effect. And in fact, many incremental goods, like national defense, are ones to which any ordinary individual's contribution would make an imperceptible difference to its quantity or quality. In these cases, an individual's contribution would cost him more than he would benefit from the incremental improvement his contribution would effect in the good's production. It would therefore be rational not to contribute to such a good. Thus, while incremental goods might, because of the essential vagueness of their existence, lead individuals to attempt to free ride, we might think that step goods will not be susceptible to Sorites-like reasoning because they are, by definition, not vague. There is no question when they come into existence, and thereby return a benefit, *inter alia,* to their contributors.

This difference between step and incremental goods also forms the basis of an independent argument which purports to explain why production of step goods might overcome the free rider problem. Because a step good has the characteristic of coming into existence at a discrete point in time, a contribution to a step good arguably increases the probability of the good's being provided, whereas a contribution to an incremental good may not. To see this, imagine a step collective good that requires exactly one thousand units of contribution in order to be created. Now consider the individual who is in the position of deciding whether to make the one thousandth contribution to the good. His contribution will obviously change the probability of the good's being provided from less than one to exactly one; that is, his contribution is, at that point, sufficient to bring the good into existence. So long as there is some point at which one individual's decision to contribute will by itself bring the good into existence, then each prior decision to contribute will increase the probability of the good's being created by decreasing the number of contributions necessary to put the final potential contributor in the position of guaranteeing the good's creation by contributing. In this way, each prospective contributor's ability to affect the probability of the good's being provided can be derived from the last prospective contributor's ability to bring the good into existence by himself. This analysis in principle provides some explanation for why an individual's decision to contribute to a step good should cause a positive change in the probability of that good's being provided. It cannot, however, explain how an individual's contribution to an incremental good could affect the probability of its being provided. For, by definition, no individual will be in the position to bring an incremental good into existence by making a particular contribution. There is no discrete point at which the good will begin to exist. Thus, in the case of an incremental good, there is no "final contributor" whose contribution will bring the good into existence. Therefore, there is no final contribution to serve as the basis for a "reverse inference" to the positive effect of prior contributions on the likelihood of the good's being provided.

This analysis suggests two general conditions either of which must hold in order for free riding to be irrational. The first we might call "the causal effect condition." The causal effect condition requires that each individual's contributing to the project will have at least a positive effect on the probability that the good will be provided. Presumably, this would be the case only if an individual's making a contribution caused others to be more likely to make contributions themselves. The second we might call "the essentiality condition." The essentiality condition requires that each individual's contribution to the good is necessary for its production. How do these conditions affect the rationality of the free rider strategy? If the causal effect condition is satisfied, then each individual's making a contribution has a positive effect on the probability of others contributing. If this causal effect holds, then attempting to free ride might be irrational. In particular, if the probability of the good's being provided conditional on an individual's contributing is sufficiently higher than the probability of the good's being provided conditional on that individual's not contributing, it is possible that, for that individual, the expected value of attempting to free ride will be exceeded by the expected value of contributing. That is, because his contribution positively affects the probability of the good's being provided, the potential gain from free riding discounted by the relatively lower probability of the good's being provided might be exceeded by the potential gain from contributing discounted by the relatively higher probability of the good's being provided. Alternatively, if the essentiality condition is satisfied, and thus each individual's contribution to the good is necessary for its provision (e.g., each has an irreplaceable and essential part of the good), then there simply is no possibility of free riding: unless each individual contributes his essential part of the good, the good cannot be provided. Obviously, free riding will be an irrational strategy.

If the causal effect or essentiality conditions are satisfied, would the assurance problem be solved as well? Whether or not the assurance problem is surmountable will depend on whether, given the satisfaction of either the essentiality or causal effect conditions, individual contributors will have reason to fear that sufficiently many others will fail to contribute to the good's production that the good will not be provided. We might think, for example, that if the essentiality condition is satisfied, then given that collective goods are, by definition, ones whose benefits to each contributor exceed the contributor's costs, every individual will have sufficient incentive to contribute. If every contributor knows this fact, then there will be no assurance problem. Similarly, if an individual's contributing to a good sufficiently increases the probability of others contributing to the good, that increase in probability, if sufficient to make contribution rational, seems already to solve the assurance problem. For, by assumption, the individual's contributing, because of its effect on the likelihood of others contributing, increases the probability of the good's being provided. And this increase will provide the contributor enough assurance that the good will be provided that he will find it rational to contribute. Thus, satisfaction of the essentiality or causal effect conditions seems to alleviate both the free rider and assurance problems.

In order to demonstrate that individuals in the state of nature could create a punishment cadre, then, Hampton has to show that the collective action problem of creating such a cadre would satisfy either the essentiality or causal effect conditions. But at first blush, the problem hardly seems to satisfy such conditions. It is surely unrealistic to suppose that any single individual's decision to participate in a punishment cadre will be necessary in order to create it. If the population of the state of nature is even moderately large, the success of a punishment cadre will hardly depend on the membership of any one person. Similarly, it is implausible to suppose that any one individual's decision to join a cadre will have a significant positive effect on the likelihood of others' decision to join; since the latter would depend, in large measure, on the risks and potential benefits associated with joining the cadre – risks and benefits which, as we just noted, are unlikely to be affected by the decision of any one individual to join the cadre. And if no particular individual's membership is necessary for an effective cadre, and no individual's decision to join has an appreciable effect on the probability of the cadre's being created, each individual will properly conclude that his best strategy is to attempt to free ride. For his decision to join the cadre occasions a cost without a benefit. If he joins and the cadre is successfully created, his joining was, *ex hypothesi,* unnecessary. He would have been better off not joining and free riding instead. Moreover, even if he has no desire to free ride, if he joins and the cadre is not successfully created, he will have wasted his effort and perhaps exposed himself to danger. And he lacks any assurance that the cadre will be successfully created once he joins it. Thus, the creation of a punishment cadre initially appears to have the classic characteristics of collective goods plagued by the free rider and assurance problems.

Hampton's solution is to reconceptualize the problem. Instead of considering the creation of an effective punishment cadre, Hampton recasts the problem as one of creating a *minimally effective* punishment cadre. For the reasons just rehearsed, the problem of creating a more-than-minimally effective punishment cadre is unlikely to satisfy either the essentiality or causal effect conditions. But Hampton argues that the problem of creating a minimally effective punishment cadre will satisfy the essentiality condition. In Hampton's scenario, the sovereign-elect will calculate the exact number of members a punishment cadre must have in order to be minimally effective, but no more than minimally effective. Once this number is calculated, the sovereign will then single out and command precisely that number of individuals to carry out her punishment orders. But why would these individuals obey the sovereign's commands? Hampton's answer is that the sovereign's calculation of the number of individuals required to form a minimally effective cadre will be designed to insure that it is utility-maximizing for them to do so. According to Hampton, the sovereign will calculate the expected utility for any given prospective member should that member and all other prospective members join the cadre. This expected utility would be a function of his increased risk as a member of the punishment cadre and his increased utility from creating a sovereign whose punishment cadre would include him. The former would contemplate the dangers inherent in direct policing. The latter would include not only the benefits of being a member of a society effectively regulated by a sovereign (e.g., the fruits of cooperation), but would also include particular benefits potentially accruing only to the members of the sovereign's punishment cadre. Next, the sovereign calculates the individual's expected utility should he decide not to join the cadre. It is at this point that the conceptualization of the punishment cadre as minimally effective becomes crucial. A minimally effective cadre will be, according to Hampton, one in which each individual's contribution to it is necessary for its creation. Because it is minimally effective, it cannot succeed without at least the number of individuals the sovereign commands to join it. No member's joining is gratuitous. Thus, the expected utility for each prospective member who decides not to join the cadre is that of life in the state of nature. For without each person's membership, the cadre will not be provided and a sovereign will not be empowered. Each individual knows that his failure to obey the sovereign's punishment commands will be certain to result in the failure of the cadre to be created and a failure to replace the state of nature with a sovereign-commanded state. The sovereign thus determines the number of members in a minimally effective cadre by finding the unique number of members required in order to make the expected utility of each individual she commands to join the cadre, should he join the cadre, greater than the expected utility should he not join. In contrast to a minimally effective cadre, it would be impossible to make the expected utility of prospective contributors to the provision of a more-than-minimally effective cadre exceed that of not contributing because no single individual's contribution is necessary for its creation or appreciably changes the probability of its being provided. In a minimally effective cadre, however, each individual is in the position of Atlas, who is the unintentional "volunteer" holding up the world and who continues to hold the world up only because no one will take his place. Although Atlas prefers that someone else take his place, he so strongly prefers that the world be held up that he still prefers holding up the world to letting it fall. The job falls to Atlas not because he is the only one capable of holding the world up, but because his expected utility of continuing to hold the world up exceeds that of letting it drop. Although Atlas was tricked into holding up the world in the first place, individuals in the state of nature find themselves in a similar position vis-à-vis membership in a punishment cadre. The sovereign simply commands them to join the cadre. And even though each might prefer that someone else take his place in the cadre, he is nonetheless in the position of being a necessary member of the prospective cadre the sovereign has designed. Just as Atlas prefers holding up the world to letting it fall, so each individual prospective cadre member prefers joining the cadre to no cadre being created at all.

Hampton summarizes this argument for the individual rationality of joining a punishment cadre by asserting the truth of a simple expected utility inequality:

$$EU_g > EU_h$$

or,

$$p'(u_1) + (1\text{-}p')(u_3) > p(u_2) + (1-p)(u_3)$$

where EU_g is the expected utility to a salient individual, i, who "gives in" and joins the cadre, EU_h is the expected utility to i if i "holds out" and refuses to join the cadre, u_1 is the utility to i of the cadre's being provided with him as a member, u_2 is the utility to i of the cadre's being provided without him as a member, u_3 is the utility to i if no cadre is provided, p' is the probability of u_1, $1-p'$ is the probability of u_3 if i joins the cadre, p is the probability of u_2, and $1-p$ is the probability of u_3 if i does not join the cadre. Thus, Hampton's inequality claims that, for each prospective member of the cadre, the probability of the cadre's being provided if he joins it multiplied by the utility of having such a cadre, plus the probability of the cadre's not being provided if he joins it multiplied by the utility of not having such a cadre exceeds that of the probability of the cadre's being provided if he does not join it multiplied by the utility of having such a cadre, plus the probability of the cadre's not being provided if he does not join it multiplied by the utility of the cadre's not being provided.

This rather cumbersome and technical argument for the individual rationality of creating a punishment cadre boils down to two empirical issues which will determine whether the above inequality holds true. First, Hampton claims that p' is significantly greater than p. That is, the probability of the cadre being provided is greater if an individual joins it than if that individual does not. This is because a minimally effective cadre is one in which each individual's contribution is necessary for its creation. Second, she claims that u_1 greatly exceeds u_3. That is, the utility of having a cadre greatly exceeds that of not having one. Life under a sovereign is tremendously better than life in the state of nature.

Let's consider Hampton's first claim. She claims that the probability of a particular minimally effective cadre being formed with a given individual will be greater than the probability of its being formed without him. As we have seen, this claim is supposed to follow from the fact that each individual's contribution to the minimally effective punishment cadre is necessary for its provision. And it is clear enough that the probability of successfully creating *the particular prospective cadre the sovereign has chosen* would be zero if any individual selected to join the cadre chooses not to join. Given that each individual, by joining the cadre, eliminates one possible cause of the cadre's not being created, each individual's decision to join does in some sense seem to increase the probability of the cadre being formed. This is just to say that satisfaction of the essentiality condition seems to imply that individuals' contributions will increase the probability of a collective good's being provided. Thus, if we accept Hampton's claim that a minimally effective cadre is one which cannot exist without the prospective members she has commanded to join it, then each potential member's decision to join it would increase the probability of its being created. Moreover, because a minimally effective punishment cadre is, by definition, a step good, we can use precisely the same reasoning we used previously when considering why contributions to a step good would increase the probability of its being provided: Imagine, for example, that the minimally effective cadre consists in exactly one thousand members. The one thousandth individual to join the cadre will obviously change the probability of the cadre's being created from less than one to exactly one. That is, his contribution is, at that point, sufficient to create the cadre. So long as there is some point at which one individual's decision to join will by itself bring the cadre into existence, then each prior decision to join will increase the probability of the cadre being created by decreasing the number of contributions necessary to put the final potential member in the position of guaranteeing the cadre's creation by joining. In this way, each prospective cadre member's ability to affect the probability of the cadre's being provided is derivative from the last prospective cadre member's ability to bring the cadre into existence by joining it. This analysis provides, at least in principle, some explanation for why an individual's decision to join a minimally effective punishment cadre should cause a positive change in the probability of that cadre's being provided. We might therefore grant that Hampton's first claim – that $p' > p$ – is correct.

Hampton's second claim is that the utility of having a cadre greatly exceeds the utility of not having a cadre. This is just the claim individuals fare far worse when living in the state of nature than they would if they could empower a sovereign to end the violence and noncooperation in the state of nature. This much we have already established when we analyzed the state of nature. Hampton's second claim – that $u_1 > u_2$ – seems to be correct as well. What, then, is the problem with her argument?

The problem is that Hampton's analysis depends on the crucial and highly artificial supposition that the punishment cadre designed by the sovereign is the only cadre each indi-

vidual takes into account when calculating his expected utility. Hampton is right to claim that each individual's contribution is essential for the creation of a cadre which by
definition must include him. And if we further suppose that
any minimally effective cadre will be one whose minimal
effectiveness will depend on each individual's participation,
then each individual's contribution clearly does increase the
probability of that cadre's being provided. Thus, Hampton
is correct in concluding that an individual commanded by
the sovereign to join her minimally effective punishment
cadre would find it rational to join *if that particular cadre were
the only cadre possible.* But of course, every individual knows
that should the particular cadre which he was ordered to
join not be created, the sovereign is free to choose another
cadre composed of different individuals. Even though the
sovereign commands only the exact number of individuals
required for a minimally effective punishment cadre, each of
those individuals knows that should he refuse to join, the
sovereign can command someone else to take his place.
Indeed, the sovereign not only could but should do so if an
individual simply refuses to obey. Each individual knows
this and thus has incentive to force the sovereign to choose
someone else. When analyzed carefully, Hampton's argument only proves the unsurprising result that individuals
cannot free ride on a collective good which includes them by
definition. Once we abandon the unrealistic constraints of
Hampton's analysis, and allow for the possibility of the
sovereign's commanding another set of individuals to join a
cadre should her first attempt fail, then every prospective
member of the first cadre faces a very different decision.
Hampton's analysis establishes that the probability of a particular punishment cadre's being created should a chosen
individual join the cadre, will exceed the probability *of that
particular* cadre's being provided without that individual.
But my analysis has shown that the probability that some
effective cadre or other will be provided is not likely to be
affected by any one individual's decision to join a cadre. For
if an individual refuses to join a cadre he is commanded to

join by the sovereign, the sovereign is free simply to command someone else to join. Both the prospective sovereigns and prospective subjects alike will know this. Because individuals can expect the sovereign to choose others to take their place should they refuse to join the cadre, they have an incentive to free ride. Even though no individual wants to risk return to the state of nature, no one individual's holding out, on its own, creates such a risk.

Thus, if we redefine p' and p to stand for the probabilities that u_1 and u_2, respectively, will be realized, where u_1 is the utility to i if *some effective cadre or other* is provided with him as a member, and u_2 is the utility to i if *some effective cadre or other* is provided without him as a member, then it is not the case that $p' > p$. In fact, it appears that $p' = p$. The incentive for free riding therefore is not mitigated by an incentive not to risk return to the state of nature and it will not be the case that $EU_g > EU_h$. And given that there is an incentive to free ride, even those who wish to join will face an assurance problem. For they will know that others have an incentive to free ride and therefore must doubt whether enough others will join to create a cadre. If a cadre is not created, their efforts will be wasted. Thus, the problem of creating even a minimally effective punishment cadre still appears to present a classic collective action problem, plagued by the free rider and assurance problems. The individually rational behavior of prospective cadre members brings about a collectively irrational result.

Hampton does not directly respond to this criticism. But her discussion of the sovereign-selection problem suggests the response she would give. Hampton would argue that her model of each prospective cadre member's utility calculation is accurate. Although she would concede that in principle, the sovereign could simply choose replacements for individuals who refuse to join the cadre, in practice, the first individuals chosen would have to dismiss that possibility as too risky. Hampton would argue that once the original attempt to form a cadre fails, the risk associated with waiting until a different cadre is formed is so grave that practically any other alternative to waiting will have a greater expected utility. Hampton would argue that for this reason, the first individuals commanded to join a minimally effective punishment cadre would regard themselves as effectively facing a deadline. And, Hampton would contend, the introduction of a deadline into a situation with the structure of a mixed coordination game – the game-theoretic structure of the cadre formation problem – suffices to solve the problem.

In order to assess this argument, let's first consider it in the context in which Hampton presents it: as a solution to the sovereign-selection problem. Though Hampton never specifically claims that individuals facing the mixed coordination problem of empowering a sovereign (or more specifically, joining a punishment cadre) face a deadline, she does claim that individuals facing the coordination problem of selecting a sovereign face a deadline. And the reason individuals facing the latter problem are supposed to face a deadline, as we shall see, would suffice, if correct, to demonstrate that individuals facing the former problem similarly face a deadline.

As we have seen, Hampton argues that voting in successive elections is an effective device for solving the sovereign-selection problem in the state of nature. But she realizes that once the results of the final election are known, individuals will have an incentive to try to force new elections or to renegotiate who should be sovereign. Each individual most prefers himself to be sovereign, and will likely have different preferences regarding other potential sovereigns. But, Hampton claims, these individuals will not find it rational to seek renegotiation because they face the functional equivalent of a deadline which forces them to accept the first possible solution to their sovereign-selection problem. In this case, it forces them to accept the results of the first series of elections:

> Either they accept the results of the election and subjugate themselves to the winner of the election, whom they did not support, or they hold out for a better deal and risk no solution

to the problem and thus a return to the state of war. However, people's fear of this state would be so substantial, according to Hobbes, that no matter who was chosen, they would be rational to subordinate themselves to him, rather than risk a return to the hellish state. In other words, the state of war would be so awful for almost all of them that it would act in place of a time deadline. (Hampton, p. 163)

This argument suggests that individuals facing the mixed coordination problem of empowering a sovereign also must regard themselves as facing a deadline requiring them to accept the first possible solution to their empowerment problem. For the same reason that individuals should regard themselves as facing a deadline when trying to solve the sovereign-selection problem remains after a sovereign has been selected and individuals seek to empower her. Both problems are part of the problem of instituting a sovereign, and until a sovereign is successfully instituted, which requires not only selection but empowerment as well, individuals will still face the choice of giving in to the salient coordination solution (accepting the elected sovereign or joining a punishment cadre) or risking return to the state of nature. Because the latter is so terrible, most individuals cannot afford to risk it, and will therefore regard any coordination solution as a "bird in the hand" not worth risking for a better "bird in the bush." The excessive risk of seeking renegotiation and upsetting a salient coordination solution is supposed to create a deadline effect which forces individuals to regard the first possible solution to the problem of instituting a sovereign as the last possible solution. In effect, they reason that they are lucky to have survived long enough to have in their hands any solution to their problem, and therefore that the probability of surviving long enough to bring about a different solution is minute. Hampton's graphic illustration of this point is provided by her "American soldier" story:

Compare the situation of people in this Hobbesian world to the situation of the ten American soldiers being pursued by

140

Nazis and trying to escape across a lake in a boat with only
two oars. The best situation for each of the them would be to
huddle in the bottom of the boat; the worst situation would
be to remain on shore and face certain death at the hands of
the Nazis. Being a rower would be better than remaining on
shore – one would be only *risking* death, not *expecting* it. But,
of course, rowing is inferior to not rowing. Given the nature
of the options, we think it highly unlikely that this group of
ten would fail to agree on which two of them would do the
rowing. (Hampton, p. 181)

Now Hampton's deadline argument, along with the
American soldier illustration of it, raises two questions. The
first is whether individuals in the state of nature in fact are
in a situation analogous to the American soldiers in Hampton's tale. Life in the state of nature might be "solitary, poor,
nasty, brutish, and short." But is death so imminent to most
people that a few seconds – say the few seconds it would
take the sovereign to command someone else to join a cadre
once one person refuses – will likely make the difference
between life and death? An answer to such a question does
not readily admit of proof, but the proposition that a matter
of seconds will make a profound difference to every individual's expected welfare, even in the state of nature, appears
to be at best hyperbolic. The second question is whether,
even if the analogy holds, Hampton's insistence that the
American soldiers would solve their Battle-of-the-Sexes game
is unproblematic. We should note at the outset that if their
ability to solve their problem relies on a chain of command
backed by threat of governmental sanction, the analogy is
obviously inapposite. For no sanction-backed chain of command would be available in the state of nature. So we must
assume that their being soldiers is supposed to be irrelevant
to their ability to solve their problem. We might imagine ten
soap salesmen who don't even know each other in the place
of the soldiers. Is it clear these salesmen would have no
difficulty solving their problem? If we imagine the Nazis on
a hill above the shore with sharpshooters aiming at the boat,
is it clear that this group will be overflowing with volunteers

to sit upright and row? If there is considerable risk associated with an individual "giving in" and letting others free ride on his efforts, there is a significant risk that no one will volunteer or accept anyone else's order to volunteer. Despite the fact that each is certain to die if no one rows, each might hold out in the hope the others will row out of desperation. The incentives to free ride in this situation are palpable. Moreover, even if one individual is prepared to take the risk himself, he must worry that no others are prepared to take it. By sitting up and beginning to row he takes not only the risk of being shot while rowing, but also risks rowing one oar by himself and going nowhere, thus increasing the risk to his life in return for no potential gain. The assurance problem in this situation is thus clear as well. The tragic possibility of no one rowing only illustrates the potential suboptimality of the results of collective action problems. The fact that each actor is painfully aware of the suboptimality does not, by itself, serve to make giving in, or cooperating a rational act. Thus, even if the risks associated with remaining in the state of nature are very high, the potential benefits of free riding on others' joining a punishment cadre, and reaping the benefits without taking the risks, will likely be quite high as well. I suspect the expected utility of joining such a cadre, particularly a minimally effective cadre, would not be outweighed by the expected utility of refusing to join and waiting the several seconds necessary for the sovereign to put someone else on the spot by commanding them to join the cadre instead. Thus, to return to Hampton's initial inequality, while we might grant that u_1 greatly exceeds u_3, u_2 might well greatly exceed u_1. Once we allow, as I have just argued, that the sovereign might command another to take the place of a recalcitrant prospective cadre member, the free rider and assurance problems return. Thus, even though the utility of producing a cadre may greatly exceed the utility of life in the state of nature, the utility of having a cadre without being a member of it may greatly exceed the utility of having a cadre while being a member of it. The increased risk to oneself by joining a punishment cadre may make $p \times u_2$ much greater than $p' \times u_1$. Free riding on a punishment cadre might be *very* profitable because not attempting to free ride might well be extremely risky. Thus, it might be that $EU_h > EU_g$.

But suppose that Hampton is right that $EU_g > EU_h$, and that I am wrong that (1) u_2 is sufficiently greater than u_1 to make $EU_h > EU_g$ or that (2) p' is equal to p and therefore $EU_h > EU_g$. Her analysis still depends on two quite dubious propositions. The first is that the sovereign could perform the calculations required to determine the exact number of individuals required to form a minimally effective punishment cadre. Such a calculation would have to take into account not only innumerable empirical factors, but subjective utility estimates as well. The margin of error on the calculation of the number required for a minimally effective cadre would surely exceed one member. And if it did, then the cadre would not be known to be minimally effective. Individuals thus would be justified in doubting whether their membership would make a difference to the provision of the cadre. But even if the sovereign could, by some miracle, make a perfectly accurate calculation of the number of members required for a minimally effective cadre, she would surely be unable to convince every individual she chooses for the cadre that her calculation is accurate within a margin of error of less than one person. Surely even rational individuals will be reluctant to accept a potential sovereign's estimates of their expected utilities. Rational individuals, instead, would likely make different estimates of what constitutes a minimally effective cadre and might reject the sovereign's calculations. Individually rational agents will not automatically defer to a potential sovereign's estimates of their expected utilities.

The second dubious proposition is that a minimally effective punishment cadre even in principle exists. It seems implausible to suppose that the minimal effectiveness of a punishment cadre for a population of thousands could ever turn on the membership of one individual. Thus it is implausible to suppose that there is one number of members of a punishment cadre less than which it is irrational to join and at which it is rational to join for a salient individual. Only a Hercules could significantly affect the expected utility of members of a punishment cadre by joining it. A punishment cadre, in other words, is not a step good like a bridge, which comes into existence at one unique point, before which the bridge is no use at all, and after which the bridge is complete and fully functional. Rather, it is more like the incremental good of national defense. Just as a minimally effective national defense will not turn on the enlistment of one soldier or the purchase of one plane, a minimally effective cadre will not turn on the membership of one individual. Rather, the effectiveness of a real punishment cadre will necessarily admit of degrees. No group of human beings will ever be able to form a minimally effective punishment cadre, as Hampton defines it. Punishment cadres will be more or less effective, but never minimally effective in Hampton's terms. If this is so, then the problem of creating a punishment cadre will never satisfy the essentiality condition discussed above. It will never be the case that any one individual is necessary for the creation of an effective punishment cadre. And since all cadres admit of degrees of effectiveness, it is unlikely that any one individual's decision to join a cadre will significantly increase the probability of others joining it. Thus, the problem of creating a punishment cadre is unlikely to satisfy the causal effect condition either. In the final analysis, a real punishment cadre is therefore likely to be subject to the free rider and assurance problems which attend the provision of most collective goods.

The iterated PD argument for the individual rationality of empowering a sovereign

The argument for the individual rationality of joining a punishment cadre we just considered holds that that problem should be modeled as a mixed coordination game, one in which individuals will find it rational to join a punishment cadre once the sovereign so commands them. But Hampton recognizes that the bad reasoning and shortsightedness plaguing individuals in the state of nature may lead to them to refuse, irrationally in her view, to participate in a punishment cadre. She thus concedes that individuals in the state of nature are likely mistakenly to regard the empowerment problem as a prisoner's dilemma in which attempting to free ride is the dominant strategy. She therefore supplements her mixed coordination game account of the empowerment of a sovereign with an "incentive solution." According to Hampton, individuals can be induced to join a punishment cadre either by providing them with positive incentives for joining or threatening them with negative incentives for not joining.

Hampton then considers nonsovereign- and sovereign-provided positive incentives that might be used to induce individuals to join a punishment cadre. An example of the former is a good reputation. Hampton illustrates how joining a punishment cadre might enhance an individual's reputation in her discussion of the rationality of obeying a sovereign-elect's command to join a posse which will pursue a dangerous "outlaw": "A person might believe that he will be highly regarded by the rest of the community and thus will be better able to get what he wants if he participates in the posse, such that a good reputation is the pay he will receive for his cooperation" (Hampton, p. 182). But why would this incentive be sufficient to persuade individuals to join a punishment cadre? It remains to be shown that a good reputation is a good at all. If it is a good, then it is a good in either the state of nature or in political society, for individuals who volunteer to be members of the punishment cadre will enjoy their good reputation in either the former or the latter, depending on whether the cadre is provided. If the cadre is not provided, and individuals remain in the state of nature, why should their willingness to join the cadre benefit them?

Hobbes sometimes argues that reputations for keeping agreements may be beneficial in the state of nature because various individuals and groups may cooperate under certain circumstances with individuals who have reputations for keeping their agreements. The specific arguments for the benefits and thus individual rationality of securing such a reputation are complex, and as such, would take us far afield to consider. But in the present context, the reputation Hampton claims would be beneficial is not one for keeping agreements, but rather one for being willing to join a punishment cadre. The explanation of why a demonstrated willingness to join a cadre would result in a positive reputation, even if the cadre is not provided, must be found elsewhere.

Perhaps others would out of gratitude admire an individual for being willing to take a risk in order to benefit society, despite the fact that if such gratitude were predictable, it would be more difficult to ascribe to those who would join a cadre the non-self-regarding motive of benefiting society. If prospective cadre members valued such a reputation intrinsically, perhaps this gratitude would provide them with an incentive to join the cadre. But we have no reason to suppose that individuals in the state of nature would value such a reputation as an intrinsic good. And there is no apparent instrumental value to such a reputation. In fact, others might even attempt to exploit the perceived willingness of an individual to take other-regarding risks, by attempting to exploit such individuals in future interaction. It is quite unclear how such a reputation could be beneficial in the state of nature. Moreover, should the cadre be provided, it is unclear how even a reputation for keeping agreements would benefit an individual in the political society that results. For in such a society, *ex hypothesi*, the sovereign enforces contracts, and even reputations for keeping agreements are less relevant to determining the rationality of cooperative interaction. Political coercion, if justified, is supposed to make cooperation, or compliance with agreements, rational, at least most of the time. And if it is unclear how a reputation for keeping agreements would be beneficial in a political society, it is surely unclear how a reputation for joining a punishment cadre would be beneficial. Nor will it do once again to reinvoke the gratitude account of a good reputation, for the instrumental value of such a reputation is no clearer in political society than in the state of nature. And, once again, whether prospective cadre members will value such a reputation intrinsically is an entirely contingent matter.

But Hampton does not put much stock in the nonsovereign-provided incentive solution to the problem of empowering a sovereign. She argues instead that the sovereign could secure a punishment cadre by promising to provide prospective members with benefits (e.g., money and goods gained by, for example, taxation) once the cadre is provided and she obtains power. Hampton claims that such an agreement has the structure of an iterated PD, for the sovereign "would have to pay them if she wanted their services again, and they would have to keep rendering those services if they wanted this pay" (Hampton, p. 182). But as we have seen, the shortsightedness account of conflict and noncooperation in the state of nature prevents individuals in the state of nature from cooperating in iterated PD's. Thus, Hampton must explain why prospective cadre members would not be shortsighted in this case, and thus would understand the positive incentives for joining the cadre. She must drive a wedge between the shortsightedness account of conflict and noncooperation in the state of nature, and the present account of the individual rationality of joining a punishment cadre in the state of nature. The former holds that the rationality of complying in iterated PD's will be mistakenly overlooked by individuals in the state of nature, while the latter contends that at least with respect to the provision of a punishment cadre, individuals will not overlook the iterated nature of their interaction, and thus will find it rational to join the cadre.

Hampton provides us with two reasons for thinking that, despite the shortsightedness account of conflict, individuals in the state of nature will recognize the iterated nature of their interaction with a potential sovereign, and thus will find it rational to join her punishment cadre. First, she notes that the shortsightedness account renders cooperation in an iterated PD irrational, even for those who understand its rationality, because they must fear interacting with others who do not. She claims, however, that because "there are plenty of rational people in the state of nature who can be expected to understand the structure of this situation, she would be likely to succeed in getting enough people to create that posse" (Hampton, p. 182). Second, Hampton explains that, according to the shortsightedness account, individuals in the state of nature will mistakenly believe their future interactions with the same individuals to be very limited, and so will mistakenly regard iterated PD's as single-play PD's. But, she argues that

> the nature of the relationship between a sovereign and posse members should make it clear even to those prone to taking a shortsighted perspective in the state of nature that they will be in an iterated PD situation with her and that both parties have a lot to gain if they cooperate. (Hampton, p. 182)

It is supposed to be more obvious to prospective cadre members that their interactions with a prospective sovereign will take the form of an iterated PD than it is to them that they are already in the same situation vis-à-vis other individuals in the state of nature. Thus, once we grant Hampton's short-sightedness account of conflict and noncooperation in the state of nature, the success of her iterated PD account of the rationality of joining a punishment cadre depends on the above two explanations of the difference between individuals' understanding of the iterated nature of their interaction with each other and with a prospective sovereign in the state of nature. However, we needn't ask whether prospective cadre members would regard themselves as players in an iterated PD with the sovereign-elect until we first ask whether their interaction with the sovereign-elect who asks them to join her punishment cadre necessarily will iterate at all. The answer is no.

Hampton's claim that prospective cadre members would regard themselves as in an iterated PD with the sovereign-elect presupposes that prospective cadre members would believe that the sovereign-elect will become empowered and will then give them special benefits in return for their cooperation. But individuals will have iterated interaction with a prospective sovereign only if the prospective, unempowered sovereign becomes an actual, empowered sovereign. For if the prospective sovereign does not become an empowered sovereign, the prospective sovereign will be unable to reward those who carry out her punishment commands. Because there will be no sovereign-provided payoff for joining her cadre, there will be no further interaction between prospective cadre members and the sovereign-elect, at least none in which the sovereign-elect is able to provide positive incentives to prospective cadre members. Their interaction therefore will not iterate. Thus, whether Hampton is correct in claiming that prospective cadre members will regard themselves as entering into an iterated PD with the sovereign-elect will depend on whether they have reason to believe the sovereign will be empowered.

We have already considered and rejected Hampton's previous explanation of why individuals would join a punishment cadre. Hampton's explanation depended on prospective cadre members viewing themselves as players in a mixed coordination game. If that account were successful, then we could now infer that prospective cadre members would expect the cadre to be formed for the reasons that account provides. On this assumption, prospective members would indeed then be facing iterated interaction with the sovereign-elect; and, if Hampton is right that their shortsightedness would not apply in this context, they would therefore stand to gain from positive incentives the sovereign-elect might offer. There would be no question whether the sovereign-elect would become an empowered sovereign. If this were true, the positive incentives would serve merely as collateral reinforcement for the already rational strategy of joining a punishment cadre. But, of course, we are here assuming, as Hampton does, that the mixed coordination game account of the rationality of joining a punishment cadre fails because of the bad reasoning and shortsightedness of prospective cadre members, or for the reasons which I earlier argued serve to undermine the mixed coordination game account. Thus, the mixed coordination game account would not provide even those prospective cadre members who are not bad reasoners or shortsighted with reason to expect the sovereign-elect's cadre to be provided. If prospective cadre members are to expect the sovereign to become empowered, their expectation must be grounded on some alternative explanation of why enough individuals will join the sovereign-elect's cadre to empower her.

The positive incentive account we are presently considering is supposed to provide just such an account. But it appears instead to presuppose it, for without some account of why the sovereign-elect will succeed in creating an effective cadre, prospective cadre members will not have reason to expect the sovereign-elect to succeed in becoming empowered, and therefore will not have reason to expect the sovereign-elect will be able to reward them for their willingness to join the cadre. The mere prospect of potential rewards from an empowered sovereign, without more, will not provide rational individuals with sufficient reason to join a cadre. The probability of the sovereign becoming empowered must be sufficiently high to make the risk of joining the cadre worthwhile. But given the free rider and assurance problems discussed earlier, the probability of forming the cadre would not be high. And because the cadre-formation problem is, as I have argued earlier, unlikely to satisfy the causal effect or essentiality conditions, a prospective cadre member's joining the cadre will not, by itself, increase the probability of the cadre's creation. Prospective cadre members' estimates of the probability that the cadre will be created will therefore be very low. As a result, the effect of the prospect of rewards from iterated interaction with an empowered sovereign will likely be severely discounted by the low probability of the sovereign becoming empowered. Therefore, the positive incentive account is likely to help the individual rationality of joining a punishment cadre only if an independent explanation of the individual rationality of joining a punishment cadre already exists. The positive incentive account is thus either unsuccessful or unnecessary.

There is yet another objection to the positive incentive strategy for solving the empowerment problem. Even if we concede individuals in the state of nature would understand themselves to be in an iterated PD with a prospective sovereign, we might reject the claim that it is rational to cooperate in an iterated PD. If this is true, then we would at least amend Hampton's shortsighted account of conflict and non-cooperation in the state of nature, and instead endorse the rationality account she rejects. For if it is irrational to cooperate in an iterated PD, then the rationality of parties in the state of nature is sufficient to generate the conflict and non-cooperation contractarianism postulates in the state of nature.

Cooperation is, however, rational in the infinitely iterated PD, as Hampton claims. But interaction in the state of nature is not infinitely iterated. In fact, it is indefinitely iterated. Individuals do not live forever, nor do they interact forever with every individual with whom they might interact cooperatively. When this fact is taken into account, and a realistic discount parameter is invoked in calculating future, expected utilities, we find that there are no equilibria at all in the state of nature. Thus, in indefinitely iterated PD's, with realistic mechanisms for discounting future utilities, cooperation is neither an equilibrium nor dominant strategy and thus will not be forthcoming from rational individuals in the state of nature.[5] In the end, the positive incentive argument for the rationality of joining a punishment cadre must fail.

But Hampton also argues that joining a punishment cadre can be rendered individually rational by the sovereign-elect's providing negative incentives, instead of the positive ones facilitated by the iterated PD. She imagines a conversation between a prospective sovereign and someone who tells the

---

5 See J. Carroll, "Indefinite Terminating Points in the Iterated Prisoners' Dilemma," *Theory and Decision* 22 (1987). The author proves that there are no cooperative equilibria in the indefinitely iterated PD.

sovereign he will refuse to join the punishment cadre or posse. The sovereign responds:

> "If that is true, then I will order the punishment cadre to punish *you* . . ." Suppose you said to her: "Ha! I don't believe you'll be able to get a posse!" The sovereign can reply: "Then, if you're right, you'll have to remain in the state of nature, which is *worse* for you than participating in the punishment cadre, and because everyone else is in the same position, it is likely that I will get my posse, which means it is likely you will suffer future harm. Moreover, note that even if I don't field a posse, you will be worse off than if you had participated in it." (Hampton, p. 183)

Hampton's claim is that the prospect of the sovereign's succeeding enables the sovereign to provide individuals with a negative incentive for joining the cadre: If they do not, they will be punished in the event the sovereign does get her cadre. Her argument seems to be:

1. For every individual, remaining in the state of nature is worse than joining the punishment cadre, whether or not the cadre succeeds in empowering the sovereign-elect.
2. *Therefore*, it is rational to join the cadre and the cadre will be provided.

But why is remaining in the state of nature worse than joining a punishment cadre? Remember, joining the punishment cadre does not guarantee that the cadre will be provided. Hampton's claim is that, for every individual, remaining in the state of nature is worse than joining the punishment cadre, irrespective of whether the cadre ultimately is provided. But suppose we grant that remaining in the state of nature is worse than having political society, and that having a punishment cadre is a necessary, if not sufficient condition, for the latter. Even then it does not follow that every individual is better off joining a punishment cadre than he is in the state of nature. For if the cadre is not provided, the individual will have received no gain in joining. At best, such an individual will be no worse off than he is in the state of nature. However, if there are costs associated with joining a cadre that ultimately does not succeed, then an individual would be better off in the state of nature without having joined an unsuccessful punishment cadre. Such costs might take the form of increased personal risk by participating in a cadre that lacks sufficient membership to be effective. It may take some time to tell whether, in fact, a cadre is sufficiently large to be even minimally effective. And during that time, members of the cadre may be exposed to considerable risk. The only proposition we have reason to affirm is that individuals will be better off joining the cadre if the cadre will be provided. Then, they will be better off, first, for the same reason that even non-cadre members will be better off: they will no longer be in the state of nature. Second, they will be better off because they will not suffer the sovereign's *ex post* punishment for not joining the cadre, and they may benefit from positive incentives the sovereign might provide for them. There is only potential loss, and no potential benefit, however, for those who join an unsuccessful punishment cadre. Thus, remaining in the state of nature is not necessarily worse than joining an unsuccessful punishment cadre. Moreover, if it were, then whatever reason explained this fact would account for the rationality of joining a punishment cadre, and negative incentives would be unnecessary to render joining the cadre individually rational.

So whether or not it is rational to join a cadre given a negative incentive to do so will depend on whether the sovereign's threat to punish those who refuse to join the cadre is credible. This threat is credible under the same circumstances as those under which we found it reasonable for individuals to regard themselves as in an iterated PD with the sovereign: only if it is reasonable to believe the prospective sovereign will become a real sovereign, which requires that a cadre successfully be created. But as we have seen, individuals who (irrationally, according to Hampton) regard the punishment cadre as an incremental good would regard their contributing to its production as not affecting the likelihood of its being provided. Moreover, I argued earlier that the collective good of empowering a sovereign *is* an incremental good and that even if it were a step good, it would still be subject to the free rider and assurance problems. Thus, the negative incentives would be credible only if the sovereign already had enough individuals to make creation of the cadre probable in the first instance, in which case she wouldn't need negative or positive incentives in order to create her cadre. Presumably, whatever reason is supposed to make it rational to join even a cadre which does not succeed would account for the existence of this cadre. But whatever this reason is, it is not that individuals have either positive or negative incentives to join the punishment cadre. Those incentives presuppose, for their effectiveness, that the creation of the cadre is already probable, and this fact of course must be established by an independent argument not based on incentives.

Summary

We have considered Hampton's arguments for the individual rationality of empowering a sovereign by joining her punishment cadre and found them wanting. Neither the mixed coordination game argument nor the incentive argument demonstrates the individual rationality of joining a punishment cadre. The former fails because it incorrectly models a minimally effective punishment cadre as a step good, rather than an incremental good. And even granting the step good model, it fails to satisfy the essentiality or causal effect conditions and is thus likely to be subject to the free rider and assurance problems. Thus, even if considered a step good, a punishment cadre would not enjoy rational enlistment from individuals commanded by the sovereign to carry out her punishment commands because those individuals would merely refuse to obey, thus forcing the sovereign to command another individual to carry out her punishment commands. The latter argument fails ultimately because the effectiveness of both positive and negative incentives in motivating individuals to join a cadre presupposes the likelihood of a cadre being produced. But given that the free rider and assurance problems are likely to undermine the formation of a cadre, individuals will not assign a high probability to the prospect of the sovereign becoming empowered. Incentives therefore are unlikely to provide a satisfactory explanation of the individual rationality of joining a punishment cadre. Moreover, were there reason to assign a high probability to the prospect of an effective cadre being formed, both the positive and negative incentive arguments would be unnecessary to demonstrate the individual rationality of joining a punishment cadre.

The acquisition scenario and the individual rationality of empowerment

If my objections in the previous section are correct, then Hampton has failed to demonstrate that rational individuals would voluntarily institute a sovereign in the state of nature. But from *Leviathan*, Hampton reconstructs another account of the empowerment of a sovereign. And this account, she claims, will suffice to demonstrate that a political sovereign would emerge from the state of nature. According to this alternative scenario, individuals do not institute, but rather acquire a political sovereign. In effect, a political sovereign is forced upon them, not by a foreign power, but by the power of the "free market" system which would evolve in the state of nature.

The acquisition scenario of the emergence of a sovereign in the state of nature takes as its first premise the realistic inequalities of individuals in the state of nature. Although Hobbes assumes that individuals are equal enough in the state of nature so that none regard themselves as better off in it than in political society, he nonetheless concedes that some will be better warriors than others, and thus better able to attack and to defend themselves in the state of nature. In fact, Hampton argues that some individuals will consider themselves at such a disadvantage because they are relatively weak warriors that they will find it rational to accept an offer from a superior warrior for protection in exchange for obedience. Hampton refers to this arrangement as a "confederacy agreement" and calls a superior warrior who might offer this deal a "sovereign-entrepreneur" (an "SE" for short). The acquisition scenario of a sovereign claims that SE's and inferior warriors will make and keep such agreements in the state of nature. The acquisition scenario then provides an account of the emergence of many confederacies each of which begins with a confederacy agreement. According to the acquisition scenario, one dominant confederacy ultimately will emerge as the result of competition among the various confederacies.

But shouldn't we be suspicious of an argument which relies on the claim that individuals in the state of nature will make and keep cooperative agreements? Hampton responds to this concern first by distinguishing confederacy agreements from the single-play PD's:

> [T]he arrangement between the sovereign-entrepreneur and the weak warrior is not contractual. Out of fear and out of desire to receive future benefits, the weak warrior's *best* move is submission, and as long as he submits, the sovereign-entrepreneur's best move vis-à-vis him is to continue protecting him. . . . [C]learly it is not a prisoner's dilemma requiring the completion of a contract, because it is individually rational for each party to do what is required to create and maintain this confederacy. (Hampton, p. 168)

In single-play PD's, the parties cannot cooperate because it is individually irrational to make and keep any cooperative agreement.[6] Hampton argues, however, that it is individually rational to comply with confederacy agreements. But even if we agree with Hampton that cooperation is individually rational in confederacy agreements, and that such

---

6 As Hampton puts the point, in a single-play PD cooperation requires "the completion of a contract" (Hampton, p. 168).

agreements therefore cannot have the structure of the single-play PD, this fact alone cannot explain why individuals in the state of nature would cooperate in confederacy agreements. For the individual rationality of cooperation in confederacy agreements might be explained by their having the structure of an iterated PD. Yet shortsighted individuals in the state of nature by definition fail to appreciate the rationality of compliance in iterated PD's and therefore would not comply with confederacy agreements having that structure. And because Hampton's account of conflict in the state of nature requires a population of shortsighted individuals so large that even longsighted individuals would find cooperation in iterated PD's irrational for fear of mistakenly interacting with a shortsighted individual, compliance with confederacy agreements in the state of nature would not be likely. Thus, no power bases would be created in the state of nature and no ultimate SE would emerge as a unique sovereign. The acquisition scenario of a sovereign in the state of nature would fail. Therefore, assuming that compliance with confederacy agreements is, in principle, individually rational, Hampton's challenge is to provide an account of the individual rationality of compliance in confederacy agreements which does not depend on modeling them as iterated PD's. She attempts to meet this challenge by providing a game-theoretic model of confederacy agreements unlike any we have so far considered.

Hampton's analysis of the game-theoretic structure of confederacy agreements is premised on her analysis of the rationality of compliance. She argues that there are both positive and negative incentives for an inferior warrior to enter into and comply with a confederacy agreement. The inferior warrior's positive incentive for entering into a confederacy agreement is that he will fare better with the protection of the SE, who will provide such protection only if the weak warrior complies with the agreement and obeys the SE. The inferior warrior's negative incentive can be provided by the SE as well. The SE can threaten to attack the inferior warrior if he does not accept and comply with the confederacy agreement. These incentives, Hampton argues, are sufficient to render compliance with the agreement rational for the inferior warrior so long as the SE complies with her end of the agreement, provides protection, and withholds punishment. Furthermore, Hampton claims, the SE has a positive incentive to keep her end of the bargain contingent upon the inferior warrior keeping his end. By doing so, she will gain power and be better able to attack and defend herself. She will be on her way to building a "power base," and will gain the greatest share of the benefits created by the cooperative agreements on which her confederacy is founded.

Hampton provides a game-theoretic model of confederacy agreements which reflect these incentives for cooperation. She begins her discussion by distinguishing between different types of games. Hampton claims that among the various possible structures of agreements in the state of nature, there are not only single-play and iterated PD's, and pure and mixed coordination games, but "contingent-move" games as well. Hampton discusses two sorts of contingent-move games, one which embeds a PD and one which does not. The contingent-move game which embeds a PD is similar to an ordinary noncontingent-move PD, except the players do not move independently of one another. In an ordinary single-play PD, as Hampton puts it, "neither party's action is contingent on the other party's action" (Hampton, p. 277). Actions are "independent," for example, "in a situation in which the actions of the parties have to be made simultaneously, or are made out of sight of one another such that neither will know how the other acted until after they have performed their actions" (Hampton, p. 277). In contingent-move games with the structure of a single-play PD, one player must perform before the other performs. Hampton calls these "contingent-move PD-like games" ("PD-like games" for short). A PD-like game is simply a prisoner's dilemma in which one prisoner acts before the other does, knowing that the second prisoner will take his actions into account before he decides whether to confess. However, despite the fact that one player moves before the other, cooperation in the PD-like game is nonetheless irrational: Irrespective of whether the first party confesses, the second party will maximize his utility by confessing. Likewise, the first party's best move is to confess, regardless of whether the second party confesses. The difference between ordinary single-play PD's and PD-like games will likely have no bearing on the individual rationality of cooperation.[7]

However, cooperation can be rational in both iterated PD's and iterated PD-like games. These games are

> one[s] in which the cooperative action is individually rational for both parties. Suppose, for example, that either a simple PD game or a two-move contingent PD-like situation is iterated indefinitely. Because of the iteration, each player always believes that he has the prospect of moving after the other player's move, so that his move will be made contingent on what the other player has done previously. . . . [The] threat of punishment makes the completion of an agreement to cooperate. . . . *individually* rational, because each party knows he can be deprived of future benefits by the other party if he does not behave cooperatively on any given play. (Hampton, p. 229)

Compliance in both PD's and PD-like games can be individually rational if those games are iterated indefinitely.

Thus, cooperation is irrational in the single-play PD and the single-play contingent-move PD-like game, but may be rational in either of these games if they are iterated indefinitely. But Hampton identifies another type of contingent-move game, what she calls a "contingent-move agency game" ("agency game" for short), in which cooperation is individually rational for both parties, even though the game does not iterate. In the agency game, as with PD-like games, one party performs before the other performs. But the players'

7 Hampton does note that some PD-like games, unlike single-play PD's, might be ones in which cooperation is individually rational. See Hampton, p. 228, n. 8.

preferences in agency games are different from the players' preferences in PD-like games. As a result, in an agency game it is individually rational for the party performing second to comply with the agreement so long as the first party complies with it. And because the first party will be better off if the agreement is kept rather than breached, and he knows the second party will comply only if he complies, the first party will find compliance rational.

Hampton's example of an agreement with the structure of an agency game is an agreement between a people and their ruler. According to the agreement, the people will empower the ruler so long as the ruler governs in their best interests. Thus, the agreement at a minimum prohibits the ruler from governing in a fashion intended to make the people worse off than they would be in the state of nature. Hampton provides the following graphic representation of the actions and preferences over outcomes created following the people's response to the ruler's move in the Ruler-People example of the agency game:

Ruler	People	Ruler	People
Govern according to terms of empowerment	Keep in power	2	1
	Depose	4	3
Ignore terms of empowerment	Depose	3	2
	Keep in power	1	4

Figure 3.1. Ruler-People agreement as an agency game

Hampton's description of the Ruler-People game indicates that the ruler must move first and that this move precedes her empowerment. In order to move first, she must govern either "according to the terms of her empowerment" or not. We might wonder how she could govern at all, much less according to the terms of her empowerment, when she is not yet empowered to govern. Although Hampton does not elaborate, it might help to imagine an unempowered ruler issuing an edict without force, and then the people responding either by enforcing or not enforcing the edict, depending on whether the edict is consistent with the terms of her empowerment. We can think of the issuing of the edict as the first move, and the enforcement of the edict as the second move in a single-play agency game. The people, we might imagine, benefit from having the issuance and enforcement of the edict because they have, among other things, collective action problems which such edicts help to solve. The ruler benefits by having her edict enforced, either because she intrinsically values issuing enforced edicts or because there are other gains from being a ruler whose edicts are enforced, even if those edicts must conform to the terms of empowerment. But although the people prefer most the outcome in which the ruler governs according to the terms of her empowerment and they empower the ruler, the ruler prefers most the outcome in which she issues whatever edicts she pleases, contrary to the terms of empowerment, but her edicts are nonetheless enforced. Thus, the ruler fares best if the people cooperate while she defects, but the people fare best if both the ruler and they cooperate, for it would be contrary to their interests not to cooperate in the event the ruler issues edicts whose enforcement will make them better off. The people, thus, have no incentive to play the ruler for a sucker by responding to her cooperative first move by defecting with an uncooperative second move. The ruler does have an incentive to play the people for suckers and would do so if given the opportunity to move second, after the people have cooperated with the agreement by empowering her. But since the people have more power than the unempowered ruler, they can force her to move first. If the ruler issues a nonconforming edict, the people have no incentive to empower the ruler by enforcing the edict. But given that the ruler has to move first and knows her edicts will be enforced only if they are in the people's interests, she will issue conforming edicts and settle for her second-best outcome. Thus, in contrast to the PD-like game in which each party must settle for the third-best outcome in which neither complies, in the agency game, the party moving first secures her second-best outcome while the party moving second secures his most preferred outcome.

The account of individually rational cooperation in the iterated PD might also explain why cooperation is individually rational in an iterated agency game. But Hampton is here arguing that cooperation is rational in the single-play agency game, in which the structure of the parties' preferences and the order of the parties' performance alone account for the rationality of cooperation. Unlike an account of the rationality of cooperating in iterated games, expectations of long-term benefits stemming from future cooperation can play no role in explaining the individual rationality of cooperation in the single-play agency game. Indeed, the central purpose of Hampton's analysis of the agency game is, as we shall see, to prove that the individual rationality of cooperation need not depend on the parties' appreciation of the prospect of long-term benefits present only in iterated games. Instead, Hampton argues that the key to cooperation in the single-play agency game is that the party performing second prefers most the outcome in which both parties cooperate, unlike the single-play PD, in which each party prefers most the sucker strategy in which he defects from the cooperative agreement but the other player complies. Compliance in the agency game is supposed to be rational even if played only once.

We can now ask whether confederacy agreements have the structure of the single-play PD, the PD-like game, the iterated PD, or the single-play agency game. If we proceed on the assumption that confederacy agreements are individually rational to keep, we can rule out the single-play PD, in which keeping a cooperative agreement is not individually rational. Similarly, compliance with a cooperative agreement in a PD-like game is not likely to be individually rational either. However, compliance with a cooperative agreement is individually rational in both the iterated PD and the single-play agency game. Both are potential candidates for explaining the individual rationality of compliance with confederacy agreements. But the iterated PD cannot explain why shortsighted individuals in the state of nature would be able to comply with confederacy agreements. For Hampton is committed to the view that such individuals would not understand the rationality of compliance in an iterated PD. If they would, there need not arise a war of all against all in the state of nature. Therefore, if her account of the viability of the acquisition scenario is to be consistent with her account of conflict in the state of nature, Hampton must argue that confederacy agreements have the structure of the single-play agency game.[8]

In order to evaluate Hampton's claim, we have to test whether confederacy agreements actually have the structure of a single-play agency game rather than an iterated PD. The structure of the confederacy agreement is given by the preferences of the parties in it. Do these preferences match the preferences of the players in an agency game? If they do match, then it must be the case that in confederacy agreements the party performing second prefers to comply so long as the first party complies, and the first party prefers to defect, but complies because he knows the second party's compliance is contingent upon his. How are we to determine which party performs first in the confederacy game? Hampton claims that in an agency game, the player who is "significantly more powerful than the other player . . . can (a) move second in the game, where this move can be made contingent on how the other player has moved, and (b)

---

8 When Hampton first discusses the individual rationality of confederacy agreements, she does not give their precise game-theoretic structure, but rather refers us to a later discussion in which she introduces contingent-move games. The implication seems to be that confederacy agreements have the structure of contingent-move games, and not PD's of any sort. The analysis in the text justifies my assumption that Hampton views confederacy agreements as having the structure of a non-PD contingent-move game, and in particular, the structure of an agency game. For the other non-PD contingent-move game is the iterated PD-like game in which shortsighted individuals would improperly conclude cooperation is individually irrational.

secure her *most preferred outcome*" (Hampton, p. 229). As between the weak warrior and the SE, the SE is by definition the more powerful player. According to Hampton, that means the SE can force the weak warrior to move first and then base her responsive move on the weak warrior's prior move. Given this order of performance, if confederacy agreements have the structure of a single-play agency game, the weak warrior's and SE's preference rankings should match the rankings of the ruler and the people, respectively, in the Ruler-People game. For it is the people, and not the ruler, that have the power of empowerment in the Ruler-People game. Therefore, if confederacy agreements are single-play agency games, the "confederacy game" could be illustrated by the following graphic representation (the preferences are over outcomes created after the SE's response to the weak warrior's prior move):

Weak warrior ("WW")	Sovereign-entrepreneur ("SE")	WW	SE
Follow SE's commands	Protect weak warrior	2	1
	Don't protect weak warrior	4	3
Disobey SE's commands	Don't protect weak warrior	3	2
	Protect weak warrior	1	4

Figure 3.2. Confederacy agreement as an agency game

If confederacy agreements have the structure of a single-play agency game, then Figure 3.2 must constitute an accurate representation of the preferences of weak warriors and SE's in a confederacy agreement. But Hampton has defended the assignment of these preferences only in her Ruler-People example of an agency game. The rationale for those preferences in that context, however, will not suffice to explain the parties' preferences in a confederacy agreement. Recall Hampton's argument that the people will comply with the empowerment agreement by enforcing the sovereign's commands so long as those commands fall within the terms of their agreement. Those terms specify that the sovereign issue edicts whose enforcement would make the people better off. Whenever the sovereign's commands comply with the terms of her empowerment, the people therefore benefit by enforcing them. For example, if enforcement of the sovereign's command would solve a collective action problem, the people will benefit from enforcement. The people, therefore, have no incentive to defect from their agreement provided the sovereign, who moves first, complies with the agreement. The people have no incentive to play the sovereign for a sucker.

Would an SE have a similar incentive to comply with a confederacy agreement provided that the weak warrior has followed her command? Remember that we cannot explain the SE's incentive to comply in the single-play confederacy game by adverting to her incentive to secure future cooperation with the weak warrior. Such an explanation would be possible were confederacy agreements modeled as iterated agency games. But Hampton's strategy is to demonstrate that cooperation in the confederacy agreement does not depend on the parties appreciating the possibility of long-term benefits. Instead, she argues that cooperation is individually rational even in the single-play agency game, and that confederacy agreements can be modeled as single-play agency games. The rationality of the SE's compliance with a confederacy agreement once the weak warrior has followed her commands must therefore be explained by demonstrating that, even if the weak warrior and SE will never meet again, the SE is better off protecting the weak warrior than not. But why would this be the case? Since this is a single-play game, once the weak warrior has complied with the SE's command (say, to scratch her back), what short-term incentive does the SE have to comply with her promise to protect the weak warrior should the need arise? Her back has been scratched and she only stands to lose by risking harm in coming to the weak warrior's defense. And because the weak warrior will realize that the SE has no incentive to comply after the weak warrior complies, the weak warrior will not find compliance rational either. The crucial difference between the single-play Ruler-People game and the single-play model of a confederacy agreement is that the people have a short-term incentive to enforce an edict which complies with the empowerment agreement: By enforcing the edict, they are better off. But the SE has no short-term incentive to protect a weak warrior who has complied with the agreement by following the SE's orders. Once the orders have been followed, the SE has nothing to gain by complying with the agreement and protecting the weak warrior (ignoring, as we must, her interest in long-term cooperation).

Thus, there is no rationale for modeling the confederacy agreement as a single-play agency game. Although the people in the Ruler-People game will rank compliance above defection following the ruler's compliance, the SE in the confederacy agreement will rank defection above compliance following the weak warrior's compliance. Instead of Figure 3.2, the accurate model of a confederacy agreement is the following PD-like game in which the SE's best move is always to defect following the weak warrior's first move; the weak warrior's best move is to defect as well:

Weak warrior ("WW")	Sovereign-entrepreneur ("SE")	WW	SE
Follow SE's commands	Protect weak warrior	2	2
	Don't protect weak warrior	4	1
Disobey SE's commands	Don't protect weak warrior	3	3
	Protect weak warrior	1	4

Figure 3.3. Confederacy agreement as a PD-like game

I have argued, contrary to Hampton, that a confederacy agreement should be modeled as a PD-like game and not as a single-play agency game because the SE's preferences do not match those of the people in the Ruler-People game. But Hampton's model of the Ruler-People game, as well as confederacy agreements, is even more deeply flawed. It is obviously unrealistic to analyze the relationships between ruler and people, or weak warrior and sovereign-entrepreneur, as single-play games of any kind. In fact, even the examples I have used to illustrate these relationships as single-play games are strained. It is implausible to suppose that the people could act on a case-by-case basis, enforcing the ruler's commands one by one.[9] The ruler-people relationship is almost by definition a long-term one in which the sovereign is empowered over a long period of time. The overriding incentives of both ruler and people are long-term and the rationality of each cooperating depends on these incentives. Any analysis of that relationship which treats the actions of the parties as temporally discrete and their consequences as short-term is simply unsound. Likewise, it defies common sense to model a confederacy agreement between a weak warrior and an SE as a one-time, temporally sequenced exchange of services. Although we can conceive of such a discrete exchange, it is hard to imagine a case in which the SE would have a short-term incentive to comply following the weak warrior's compliance. Instead, a confederacy agreement, as the name suggests, is one in which a confederacy is created – a relationship in which the weak warrior undertakes to follow the SE's orders on a regular, long-term basis in exchange for the SE's agreement to protect the weak warrior on a regular, long-term basis. The overriding incentives of both weak warrior and SE are long-term and the rationality of each cooperating depends on these incentives. Hampton's characterization of the Ruler-People game and confederacy agreements as examples of agency relationships is insightful. But agency relationships, like all relationships, are not simple, one-time, temporally sequenced exchanges. They are mutually dependent, long-term undertakings in which parties simultaneously perform their duties to one another over time. To be sure, they are characterized by tit-

---

9 I will later have occasion to expose the fundamental flaw in the Ruler-People game: the fallacy of treating "the people" as a single unit and thus ignoring the obvious collective action problems confronting "the people's" enforcement of the ruler's commands. See the section in this chapter entitled "The Individual Irrationality of Deposing a Sovereign: The Second Horn of the Dilemma."

for-tat, reward-punishment strategies, but that mutually responsive dynamic reflects the iterated nature of the relationship and not a one-time response to a single first move by the ruler or the weak warrior, as the agency game model of those respective relationships would have it.

In sum, if we model the confederacy agreement as a single-play game, it should be modeled as a PD-like game in which cooperation will not be rational for either party. Moreover, neither the relationship between ruler and people nor weak warrior and SE should be modeled as single-play games of any sort. These are ongoing relationships in which each party's chief incentive for cooperation is to secure the long-term gains of cooperation. In the relationship between ruler and people, the ruler will gain over the long run either intrinsically or instrumentally from being ruler; the people will benefit over the long run from collectively rational rule. In the relationship between weak warrior and SE, the weak warrior gains personal security; the SE gains a servant and a chance to build a larger confederacy which might lead to her becoming sovereign.

Perhaps, though, Hampton could argue that confederacy agreements should be modeled as iterated PD-like games, and that confederacy agreements are nonetheless sufficiently different from ordinary iterated PD's that individuals in the state of nature will comply with them. Recall that Hampton earlier offered two reasons for supposing that the shortsightedness of individuals in the state of nature will not undermine compliance with an agreement to join a cadre, even though the rationality of compliance will depend on long-term incentives. She claimed that despite her assumption of general, widespread shortsightedness in the state of nature, prospective cadre members would nonetheless understand the iterated nature of their interaction with a sovereign-elect. Her first argument begins by noting that on her account of the state of nature, not all individuals are shortsighted. She then claims that the sovereign-elect would be able to form a posse consisting of members of the minority of longsighted individuals. Second, she argued that there is something special about

> the nature of the relationship between a sovereign and posse members [that] should make it clear even to those prone to taking a shortsighted perspective in the state of nature that they will be in an iterated PD situation with her and that both parties have a lot to gain if they cooperate. (Hampton, p. 182)

Could these arguments explain how confederacies could be created in the state of nature?

Hampton's first argument is based on the premise that there are longsighted individuals in the state of nature who will appreciate the long-term benefits of confederacy agreements. Given Hampton's description of the state of nature, this claim is true. In fact, by calling a strong warrior who enters into a confederacy agreement with a weak warrior a "sovereign-entrepreneur," Hampton implies that any strong warrior entering into such agreements is longsighted: The strong warrior intends to use this agreement to further her long-term goal of becoming sovereign. Similarly, there might be some weak warriors who are longsighted and therefore would desire to cooperate with a strong warrior in a confederacy agreement for their long-term benefit. But of course, there might be some shortsighted strong or weak warriors who enter into such agreements with the intent of playing the weak or strong warrior, respectively, for a sucker. Shortsighted warriors will defect from long-term iterated PD-like games whenever doing so is in their short-term interest. A strong warrior simply will refuse to defend the weak warrior once the weak warrior has followed her orders (say, scratched the strong warrior's back). Weak warriors will follow commands in return for protection until defecting by refusing to follow the strong warrior's orders is in the weak warrior's short-term interest (say, when the trusting strong warrior turns her back and the weak warrior can strike a fatal blow). Even if there are longsighted strong and weak warriors in the state of nature, they must be able to identify each other reliably before they will find cooperation in iterated PD-like games rational. But one of the central premises of Hampton's account of conflict in the state of nature is that even longsighted individuals will not cooperate in ordinary iterated PD's because they will fear they might cooperate with a shortsighted individual who will defect. In Hampton's view, they reason that because the majority of people in the state of nature are shortsighted, the probability of interacting with a shortsighted individual is much greater than that of interacting with a longsighted individual. But if they could reliably tell the difference between shortsighted and longsighted individuals, the risks associated with cooperation in ordinary iterated PD's, and thus the extent of conflict in the state of nature, would be drastically reduced. Thus, if longsighted individuals are in general able reliably to identify other longsighted individuals, the shortsightedness account of conflict in the state of nature is considerably less plausible. This leads us to Hampton's second argument.

Hampton's second argument is based on the premise that there is something special about the relationship between the sovereign-elect and prospective cadre members, and by analogy between SE's and weak warriors. The fundamental problem with this argument is that it merely asserts, without offering any substantive reasons, the uniqueness of these relationships, a uniqueness which must distinguish them from the multitude of other potentially beneficial long-term, cooperative relationships which individuals would encounter in the state of nature. In particular, Hampton must explain why all such relationships in the state of nature – ones which Hampton concedes are rational to enter into and comply with because they have the structure of an iterated PD – are somehow less perceptibly iterated to the average resident of the state of nature. But surely, if individuals could understand the potential benefits of iterated cooperation with a sovereign-elect, or a sovereign-entrepreneur, they could at least as easily appreciate the potential benefits of cooperating with their neighbors in iterated PD's. After all, each individual's daily experience in the state of nature will provide him with ample evidence of the iterated nature of his interaction with his neighbors. Indeed, it is difficult to concede at the outset that the iterated nature of interaction in the state of nature will, in fact, be lost on most people. But we are granting this fundamental assumption for purposes of assessing Hampton's overall contractarian approach. Nonetheless, it strains credulity to give Hampton the benefit of the doubt by granting this quite broad assumption in the first place, and yet later grant a contradictory assumption in the case of agreements with sovereigns-elect or sovereign-entrepreneurs, with whom neither the prospective cadre members nor weak warriors, respectively, need have had any prior iterated experience. The alleged crucial difference between these select relationships and all the other potential and seemingly obviously long-term relationships in the state of nature is simply unexplained. Yet Hampton's theory requires that individuals in the state of nature will appreciate the iterated nature of only the former but not the latter.

To review, Hampton suggests three strategies for supporting her acquisition scenario of the emergence of a sovereign in the state of nature. The first is to model confederacy agreements as single-play agency games. There are, however, two objections to doing so. First, unlike the people in the Ruler-People game, the SE has no incentive to comply in a single-play confederacy game, despite the fact that the SE moves after the weak warrior. No matter what the weak warrior does, the SE's best move is to defect. Second, neither the Ruler-People game, nor confederacy agreements, can be accurately modeled as single-play games. Agency relationships cannot easily be described in terms of discrete, temporally ordered moves and countermoves determined by short-term incentives. Instead, they are essentially long-term relationships whose rationality derives from the long-term benefits of cooperation over time. Rational cooperation in these relationships does depend on responsive moves over time, as in the iterated PD, but it cannot be said to depend on the one-time response to a first move by another party, as Hampton's agency game model suggests. The second strategy is to exploit the fact that there is a minority population of longsighted individuals in the state of nature. This fact would explain compliance in confederacy agreements even if we model them as iterated PD-like games, but only if longsighted individuals could tell the difference between other longsighted individuals and shortsighted individuals. But if longsighted individuals had such an ability, they would be able to cooperate in ordinary iterated PD's, contrary to Hampton's account of conflict in the state of nature. The third strategy is to claim that everyone in the state of nature would be longsighted for purposes of cooperating in a confederacy agreement. But any account of why this would be so is likely to explain why everyone would also be longsighted for purposes of cooperating in ordinary iterated PD's as well.

In the end, Hampton's theory presupposes that individuals in the state of nature will be longsighted for purposes of creating a political association, but shortsighted for purposes of generating a need for political association in the first place. My objection is that she cannot have her cake and eat it too. Either there are enough seriously shortsighted individuals in the state of nature to support her account of conflict and noncooperation in the state of nature, or there are enough longsighted individuals in the state of nature to explain the success of agreements to form punishment cadres or confederacies. Hampton cannot, however, have it both ways.

Summary of the first horn of the dilemma

We have considered, so far, both of Hampton's accounts of the emergence of a political sovereign in the state of nature. The first account holds that individuals will find it individually rational voluntarily to institute a sovereign. The success of this account depends, *inter alia*, on a demonstration of the individual rationality of empowering a sovereign. A sovereign is empowered once she has an effective punishment cadre to enforce her commands. But we rejected both Hampton's mixed coordination game and incentive arguments which purport to demonstrate the individual rationality of joining a punishment cadre. The second account of the emergence of a sovereign in the state of nature holds that from initial two-party agreements between weak warriors and sovereign-entrepreneurs, there will emerge a set of confederacies which ultimately will be reduced to one dominant confederacy. The head of that confederacy will constitute an effective political sovereign. However, none of Hampton's three strategies for explaining why individuals in the state of nature would comply in confederacy agreements can be sustained: The preferences of the sovereign-entrepreneur in a confederacy agreement don't correspond to those of the party moving second in a single-play agency game; confederacy agreements must be modeled as iterated, not single-play games; the existence of a minority of longsighted individuals in the state of nature can't explain cooperation in confederacy agreements; and it is not possible to discern a unique feature of confederacy agreements which would explain why individuals in the state of nature would cooperate in them but not in ordinary iterated PD's. The institution and acquisition scenarios for the rational emergence of a political sovereign in the state of nature are, therefore, unconvincing.

However, neither Hampton's arguments nor my critique of them can be dispositive, for the individual rationality of instituting a sovereign in the state of nature ultimately will depend upon empirical contingencies which do not admit of proof: Precisely how many individuals in the state of nature are predominantly rational? How many would have other-regarding preferences? What would be the exact nature of the risks and utilities associated with joining a punishment cadre? Could a potential sovereign calculate these accurately? How many individuals would be shortsighted? Would some be shortsighted in certain relationships but not others? And so forth. What, then, is the force of the criticisms I have leveled? If my criticisms are correct, then no political institutions would be likely to emerge from the state of nature. I have not, of course, proved that political institutions could not emerge from the state of nature as a result of the voluntary interaction of predominantly rational individuals. But neither has Hampton proved that political institutions would so emerge. Indeed, Hampton has shown, at most, that a sovereign could be voluntarily instituted in the state of nature. But as I argued earlier, the justification of political authority requires a stronger showing than this. Our political institutions are justified, according to Hampton, only if they are individually rational to create and maintain. Hampton's strategy is to demonstrate the individual rationality of creating and maintaining our political institutions by an inference from the individual rationality of creating and maintaining political institutions in the state of nature. But demonstrating the possible individual rationality of instituting a sovereign in the state of nature suffices only to demonstrate the possible individual rationality, and thus the possible legitimacy, of our political institutions. We are thus left with an indeterminate answer to the question of whether or not our political institutions are in fact legitimate.

THE INDIVIDUAL IRRATIONALITY OF DEPOSING A SOVEREIGN: THE SECOND HORN OF THE DILEMMA

Suppose, however, the foregoing criticisms are not compelling, and Hampton has succeeded in demonstrating that a political sovereign would emerge from voluntary interaction in the state of nature. In this section, my claim will be that this would be more disastrous for Hampton's contractarianism than its failure to demonstrate the emergence of a sovereign in the state of nature. As I earlier indicated, I will argue that if Hampton's arguments succeed, they will render rebellion individually irrational even when it would be collectively rational. Given Hampton's reduction of morality to rationality, which identifies the latter with individual rationality alone, her theory must conclude, therefore, that so long as it is individually rational to comply with a regime – even a severely repressive and therefore collectively irrational regime – that regime is morally legitimate. This result, I will contend, constitutes a *reductio ad absurdum* of Hampton's ethical reduction – the normative foundation of her entire contractarian enterprise.[10]

Hampton clearly recognizes the unacceptability of a contractarian theory according to which a collectively irrational regime is morally legitimate. In fact, in her discussion of the justification conferred by agency theory, she claims that contractarianism extends legitimacy to only those regimes which individuals in the state of nature have reason to adopt and comply with, and claims further that individuals in the state of nature will not have reason to adopt or comply with any irrational regimes. Recall that in Chapter 1 the second tenet of Hampton's justificatory strategy of agency theory holds that regimes are legitimate if rational individuals have a self-interested reason to create them:

> [H]uman beings are justified in creating and maintaining the state [because] rational people [in the state of nature] have a certain compelling reason (either self-interested or other-interested or a combination of both) for leaving the state of nature by creating government, where that reason is (or should be) *our* reason either for creating government if one does not exist or for maintaining it in power if it does. (Hampton, p. 272)

As we have seen, for Hampton, the compelling reason for creating government is self-interest. Hampton adds that "The reason given in tenet 2 for creating the state constrains the

10 The issues raised in this section are also raised in the literature discussing the individual rationality of collectively rational rebellion in contemporary analytic Marxist theory. See, for example, Allen Buchanan, *Marx and Justice: The Radical Critique of Liberalism* (Totowa, N.J.: Rowman and Littlefield, 1982), ch. 5; Jon Elster, *Making Sense of Marx* (Cambridge University Press, 1985), pp. 318–97, 428–46, 528–31; and Richard Arneson, "Marxism and Secular Faith," *American Political Science Review* 79 (1985).

kind of state we should create or maintain (i.e., it tells us what kind of state is a justified political regime)" (Hampton, p. 272). Thus, only those regimes which rational individuals in the state of nature have reason to create are supposed to be justified by contractarianism. But if it can be shown that it might be individually irrational to rebel even against a collectively irrational regime, then agency theory cannot sustain its claim to justifying only political institutions which are collectively rational. For if it is individually rational to obey, rather than to rebel against, a collectively irrational regime, then according to the Hobbesian ethical reduction, such obedience is morally required and such a regime is legitimate.

Hampton's main defense against the *reductio* argument is to demonstrate that rebellion is individually rational when a regime's rule becomes collectively irrational. I shall use the term "collective irrationality" very loosely. A regime, we will say, is collectively irrational with respect to the state of nature when a majority of its subjects are worse off in it than they would be in the state of nature. What is Hampton's argument for supposing that when a regime's rule is no longer collectively rational to maintain, it will be individually rational to rebel against it? In general, her claim is that

> the same 'coordination process' that [a sovereign's] subjects had to follow in order to institute her . . . can be used to depose her and to institute another ruler in her place. . . . [I]f people believe that the market presents them with a better potential leader, they will be able (and in certain circumstances rational) to 'fire' the old leader and 'hire' the new one. So when it is in their interest to do so, *people are able to change the convention about who is ruler.* (Hampton, p. 223)

But the convention which supports a ruler can change only under certain conditions. Hampton must show that these conditions will be met whenever a sovereign's rule becomes collectively irrational.

Hampton claims that rebellion will be individually rational

if two conditions are met. For an individual to find it rational to rebel, he must first believe either

1. that life in a state of nature would be better than life in the present commonwealth under his present ruler, or
2. that life in a commonwealth with a *different* ruler would be better than life in the present commonwealth under his present ruler.

Second, he must believe

3. that many other people were dissatisfied and disposed to follow him in rebellion, so that the risk to his life if he should withdraw his authorization (i.e., refuse to obey the ruler's commands) would not be considerable. (Hampton, pp. 221–2)

The first two conditions above specify the circumstances under which a regime's rule can be understood to be, in some sense, collectively irrational. If the first condition is satisfied, then the regime is collectively irrational relative to the state of nature. If the second condition is satisfied, then the regime is collectively irrational relative to alternative regimes. These two conditions provide necessary but not sufficient conditions for the individual rationality of rebellion. Once either is satisfied, then rebellion becomes rational for an individual only when that individual's expected utility from disobeying the sovereign exceeds that of obeying the sovereign. An individual's expected utility of disobeying the sovereign when either of the first two conditions is satisfied will be a function of (1) how great an improvement the state of nature or an alternative regime would constitute over the present regime, (2) the feasibility of instituting a new regime once the old one is dissolved, (3) the expected costs of rebelling against the present regime, and (4) the probability of rebellion succeeding. Hampton claims that these last three variables will depend on the number of individuals who are willing to rebel, whether there is mutual knowledge of this fact among those willing to rebel, and whether some alternative sovereign is salient:

> [I]f there is common knowledge of dissatisfaction among many of the subjects, and if there is general agreement on which person would be a desirable or salient replacement for the ruler, then rebellion becomes a real possibility. . . . [T]he larger the number of rebels, the fewer the number of supporters that the present ruler can use to thwart and punish the rebels, and thus the more likely an expected-utility calculation will tell any other dissatisfied citizenry to risk rebellion. (Hampton, p. 222)

Hampton's claim is that if a regime's rule becomes collectively irrational, enough individuals will find it in their interest to rebel that rebellion will become individually rational and the ruler will be deposed.

There are two serious problems with Hampton's claim that rebellion will eventually become individually rational whenever a regime's rule is collectively irrational. The first is a problem we earlier confronted when considering the individual rationality of joining a punishment cadre. There I argued, against Hampton, that although the formation of a punishment cadre should be modeled as a mixed coordination game, it is still a problem subject to the free rider and assurance problems. Here, the analogous claim can be made with respect to the collective good of rebellion. Even if we suppose that rebellion is a collective good, and thus that at least a majority of subjects would be better off in the state of nature or in some alternative regime, it does not follow that rebellion is individually rational. An individual will find it rational not to contribute to the provision of the collective good of rebellion, reasoning correctly that whether he disobeys the sovereign will not significantly affect the likelihood of rebellion succeeding. This is just to say that the collective good of rebellion seems either to have the structure of a PD or is a mixed coordination game which, like the cadre-formation game, is nonetheless subject to the free rider

178

and assurance problems. Nevertheless, since I have waived this objection against Hampton's arguments for the individual rationality of joining a punishment cadre, I will continue to do so when it reoccurs, as it does here in our discussion of the individual rationality of rebellion.

There is a second objection to Hampton's arguments for the individual rationality of rebellion. Suppose even a large majority of individuals desires to depose a sovereign, either because her rule is worse than the state of nature or the majority prefers a different sovereign. Suppose further that the members of this majority have mutual knowledge of their shared desire to depose the sovereign. Does it follow that these individuals will be able to overthrow the sovereign? No, it does not. Despite the fact that the sovereign, according to Hampton, can be instituted by a convention among individuals in the state of nature, a similar convention may not emerge for individuals suffering under a collectively irrational regime. There is at least one crucial difference between the circumstances of the state of nature in which a convention to institute a sovereign is possible and the circumstances of an oppressive regime in which individuals wish to depose the ruler. In the latter, there exists an effective punishment cadre under the command of the sovereign, while in the former such a cadre does not exist. The existence of the punishment cadre drastically affects the individual rationality of rebellion. For though individuals in the state of nature may have seemed to have nothing to lose in going along with the institution of a sovereign, individuals living under an empowered regime have much to lose by going along with rebellion. So long as the sovereign retains her cadre, she might well be able to make rebellion individually irrational, even for a majority of individuals which desires to depose her. After all, the cadre of a successfully empowered sovereign has deterrent power sufficient to render compliance with her edicts individually rational. So long as that cadre remains in place, it seems that compliance should continue to remain rational. Even in the worst-case scenario, in which individuals are worse off under the present ruler than they would be in the state of nature, the deterrent force of the punishment cadre could well render the expected utility of obedience greater than that of disobedience for each individual. For example, a strong, entrenched cadre might virtually guarantee certain death for rebels, and be so effective as to render the probability of rebels getting caught very high. It seems clear that rebellion, even under a collectively irrational regime, is unlikely to be individually rational unless the members of the cadre find rebellion rational too.

But the members of the punishment cadre will not necessarily find rebellion rational under the same circumstances that non-cadre members will. This is because cadre members, according to Hampton's account of the individual rationality of joining a cadre, are motivated by positive and negative incentives which apply to them uniquely. Recall that the key to Hampton's case for the individual rationality of joining a punishment cadre was the sovereign's ability to introduce the prospect of positive and negative incentives for those individuals she orders to carry out her punishment commands. She promises them, for example, that they will share in her profits once an effective cadre is in place. She also threatens to use the cadre against them if they do not join it and it is created anyway. These incentives, according to Hampton, enable the sovereign to create her punishment cadre in the first place. And Hampton recognizes that once a minimally effective cadre is provided, a sovereign will benefit from increasing its size beyond minimal effectiveness. But because a more-than-minimally effective cadre is, even by Hampton's lights, an incremental step good subject to the free rider and assurance problems, the sovereign will have to rely heavily upon both positive and negative incentives to retain members of a more-than-minimally effective cadre. Thus, so long as the sovereign continues to provide cadre members with these incentives, they will find it individually rational to remain in the cadre. Despite the fact that even a majority of non-cadre members could be worse off under a regime than in the state of nature, cadre members are likely nonetheless to find remaining in the cadre to be individually rational.

Put another way, the sovereign can retain her cadre so long as members in it find it individually rational to carry out her commands. The members in the cadre will find it individually rational to carry out the sovereign's commands so long as the expected utility of doing so is greater than the expected utility of refusing to do so. And it will be so long as the sovereign has at least positive incentives to offer these members so that by carrying out the sovereign's commands, each is better off in the cadre than in the state of nature. Thus, by seeing to it that membership in the cadre is collectively rational, she can insure that membership in it is individually rational. With respect to cadre membership, Hampton's claim seems to be plausible: A sovereign's power will be revoked by a cadre when membership in that cadre is no longer collectively rational. The same convention which creates that cadre will also enable cadre members to dissolve the cadre when it is collectively rational to do so. But from this, it does not follow that an entire political society will be dissolved when it becomes collectively irrational. So long as the cadre remains intact, obedience to even a collectively irrational regime may well remain individually rational. Hampton's fatal mistake is to regard the convention which serves to empower and depose a sovereign as one which arises throughout the citizenry of the sovereign's domain. In fact, though the process may well be conventional, its domain is restricted to the punishment cadre members, and not beyond. It is the punishment cadre that can "giveth and taketh away" the sovereign's power, not "the people at large."

After she models the relationship between ruler and people as the contingent-move agency game we considered in the previous section, we find Hampton again defending the claim that rebellion will be rational whenever a sovereign's rule becomes collectively irrational:

[C]onsider how the ruler will reason as the first player to move. She knows that if she rules against their wishes, they will fire her: Their keeping her in power when she rules badly ranks lowest for them, whereas their firing her when she rules badly ranks second highest for them. . . . [S]he has a choice between working hard and staying in power (ranked second) or being lazy and being deposed (ranked last). . . . Their preferences and power in this situation have put them in the position of being able to force her to make a first move, which will allow them to achieve their favorite outcome. (Hampton, p. 230)

We can now see the fundamental flaw embedded in this characterization of the ruler-people relationship. First, though Hampton characterizes the agency game as one between the ruler and the people, we have seen that "the people" cannot be treated as a single entity. Rather, "the people" consists of many separate individuals sufficiently many of whom must find rebellion rational before rebellion will occur. And if the collective good of rebellion is like the collective good of a punishment cadre, it will not be provided. Second, and more important, the sovereign need not worry whether she rules as "the people" wish her to rule. Rather, she need worry only that she rules so that she can continue to provide the incentives necessary to render cadre membership individually rational. She must keep the cadre happy, not "the people." And it is clear that a sovereign can keep a cadre happy while making "the people" quite unhappy. The structure of Hampton's argument for the individual rationality of instituting a sovereign unfortunately puts her in a position similar to that of Hobbes. Though she is right to deny that a sovereign's power can be as absolute as Hobbes contends, Hampton ends up with a sovereign whose power is contingent upon the welfare of her cadre members, rather than the entirety of her subjects. As a result, subjects might find themselves, as Locke predicts, being devoured by lions, but unable even to return to the life of mere polecats and foxes in the state of nature, much less to life under a new and better sovereign.

Summary

I have argued that Hampton's arguments for the individual rationality of empowering a sovereign lead to the individual rationality of obeying a collectively irrational regime. This result, coupled with Hampton's version of Hobbes's reduction of morality to individual rationality, would force Hampton to conclude that obedience to even a collectively irrational regime is moral, and thus that such regimes can be legitimate. This constitutes a *reductio ad absurdum* of Hampton's contractarianism. Either Hampton's arguments must be replaced with others which rule out the individual rationality of compliance with collectively irrational regimes, or her version of Hobbes's reduction of morality to rationality must be rejected.

Chapter 4

Kavka's hybrid contractarianism

All political contractarian theories bear the burden of explaining the normative significance of hypothetical results because all of them rest their justification of political authority on an analysis of interaction in some hypothetical scenario. The chief attraction of Hobbesian contractarianism, I have argued, is that its hypothetical scenario purports to be normatively minimalistic, and so promises to beg no fundamental normative questions at the outset. The central problem with Hobbesian contractarianism, however, is that the most plausible arguments for the normative significance of hypothetical results appear to rest on idealistic premises, like those provided by Rawls's normatively rich original position, rather than the realistic premises provided by Hobbes's normatively minimalistic state of nature. Thus, the fundamental challenge for a Hobbesian theory is to provide an argument for the normative significance of its hypothetical analysis which "fits" the definition and analysis of its hypothetical scenario and thereby provides an account of the normative significance of hypothetical results in the normatively barren state of nature.[1]

It is worth pausing to appreciate the difficulty confronting normative justifications based on hypothetical actions. The most common objection to such justifications usually takes

---

1 Put in terms of the overall contractarian schema in Chapter 1, Hobbesian theory must provide a stage-three argument which fits its stage-one definition and stage-two analysis of its hypothetical scenario.

the form of a libertarian objection to hypothetical consent as a justificatory strategy. Libertarian justification, in general, proceeds from a foundational commitment to the value of individual autonomy. Because actual, voluntary consent constitutes a manifest expression of an individual's autonomy, it suffices to justify the limiting of an individual's liberty on a libertarian theory. Justifications for limiting an individual's liberty which are based only on that individual's hypothetical consent, however, appear not to respect that individual's autonomy. For the respect of individual autonomy is thought either to entail actual consent as a necessary condition for the justification of limiting an individual's liberty, or to require actual consent because it provides the best evidence that limitations on liberty are consistent with respect for an individual's autonomy.

The libertarian objection is directed at one particular type of hypothetical justification: the justification based on hypothetical consent. As I have presented this justification, it falls far short of a dispositive critique of hypothetical justifications generally. First, it does not establish that hypothetical consent, under certain circumstances, cannot satisfy a libertarian commitment to individual autonomy. In fact, it might be argued that certain forms of hypothetical consent – say, consent under morally ideal conditions – is more expressive of individual autonomy than even actual consent under morally nonideal circumstances. Second, the libertarian objection does not consider hypothetical justifications generally and thus does not address those based on hypothetical actions other than hypothetical consent, some of which might be consistent with a respect for individual autonomy. And third, it presupposes, without argument, a fundamental commitment to individual autonomy. But we needn't defend the libertarian objection to hypothetical consent in order to generate sufficient reason to doubt the force of hypothetical justificatory strategies generally.

One reason for rejecting the normative significance of hypothetical actions is that, in the theory of moral responsibility, it is axiomatic that credit and blame can be ascribed to individuals only in virtue of actual acts they voluntarily commit. For example, suppose we could provide an accurate reconstruction of an individual's actions under any circumstances. Now imagine the hypothetical actions of an individual, currently in circumstances C, were she to be confronted with the opportunity to save an innocent person's life at no substantial risk or cost to herself. This hypothetical scenario takes place in circumstances C', which are identical to C except that the individual is confronted with the opportunity, and moral necessity, of saving a life. Consider two possible hypothetical reconstructions of this individual's actions in C'. First, suppose that the reconstruction conclusively demonstrates that she would in fact save the person's life. Would we ascribe credit to the individual in actual circumstances C for performing a morally praiseworthy act in hypothetical circumstances C'? Second, suppose the reconstruction demonstrates that she would, in C', fail to meet the requirements of morality. Would we, on this basis, ascribe blame to her in C? Perhaps these hypothetical reconstructions might give us insight into her moral character, and we might think more or less of her depending on her hypothetical actions. But we would nonetheless refrain from ascribing moral credit or blame merely on the basis of non-actual decisions she would make.

This intuition is further reinforced by a purely formal consideration. If hypothetical actions in general provided grounds for ascribing credit and blame, the theory of responsibility would lead to absurd results. Suppose, for example, that I would wrongly kill Jones in circumstance C_1, but rightly save Jones in circumstance C_2. Would I therefore deserve both moral blame and moral credit for hypothetically killing and hypothetically saving the same life? The logical structure of morality appears to rule out the possibility that *all* hypothetical actions have normative significance. If hypothetical action is to have moral significance, there must be some principled way of distinguishing some hypothetical actions from others as having moral weight. Not all hypothetical actions can have moral significance.

Contractarian theories, of course, allege the normative significance not of any kind of hypothetical actions under any circumstances, but only of certain sorts of hypothetical actions under special circumstances. Some contractarians, like Rawls, assert the normative significance of hypothetical *consent* to principles of justice under the specialized circumstances of the original position, while others, like Hampton, assert the normative significance of the hypothetical *emergence* of political association, as well as consent, under the particular circumstances of her version of Hobbes's state of nature. These theorists therefore need to explain why hypothetical consent or hypothetical emergence, under the circumstances of their theory's hypothetical scenario, provides a justification for nonhypothetical individuals. Further, contractarians like Rawls and Hampton must explain why hypothetical consent under circumstances which differ from those of their hypothetical scenario will not have the normative significance they claim for the hypothetical actions which take place in their scenario. For if other hypothetical actions – actions which occur in other hypothetical scenarios – provide normative justifications as well, then it is possible that these justifications will produce results which contradict Rawls's and Hampton's normative conclusions. For example, political association might be justified on Hampton's theory, but anarchy might be justified according to some other hypothetical justification. Each theorist, therefore will want to provide an argument for the unique suitability of his or her hypothetical setting for purposes of generating the normative justification he or she seeks.

In Chapters 2 and 3, we considered Hampton's explanation of the normative significance of the outcome of hypothetical interaction in Hobbes's state of nature and her account of the unique normative suitability of Hobbes's state of nature for purposes of justifying the state. Hampton's argument is grounded firmly in realistic constructionism. Stage one of Hampton's theory defines a realistic state of nature which purports to represent the postpolitical anarchy into which we would descend should we abandon our political institutions. Her stage-two analysis holds (1) that life in that state of nature would be full of conflict and practically void of cooperation, (2) that the formation and maintenance of a political association would end this conflict and facilitate cooperation, and (3) that individuals living in that state of nature would find it individually rational to form and maintain a collectively rational political association. Stage three argues that morality is reducible to individual rationality and concludes that the formation and maintenance of political association is, for us, individually rational and therefore moral, because the stage-one definition of the state of nature accurately mirrors our alternative to political association. Hobbes's realistic state of nature is therefore uniquely suitable for the normative purposes of Hampton's theory: namely, demonstrating the individual rationality, and thus morality, of political association for actual human beings. The crux of her stage-three argument – the reduction of morality to individual rationality – explains the normative significance of hypothetical actions (the individually rational emergence of political authority in the state of nature) and thus fits well with her stage-one definition of a realistic state of nature.

In *Hobbesian Political and Moral Theory*, Gregory Kavka parts company with Hampton and defends a contractarian theory which contains both realistic and idealistic elements. Instead of relying on a reduction of morality to individual rationality, Kavka's stage-three arguments, with one exception, rely on idealistic constructionism to account for the normative significance of the outcome in his theory's hypothetical scenario, and so depart from the traditional Hobbesian contractarian justificatory strategies. The task of this chapter is to evaluate the success of these arguments.

OVERVIEW OF KAVKA'S THEORY

Hampton's goal is to defend the closest approximation of Hobbes's original theory as reason permits. In contrast, Kavka defends what he calls "Hobbesian theory," an explicitly revisionistic version of Hobbes's theory. We can best understand Kavka's novel approach by recasting the initial distinction he urges between Hobbes's descriptive and normative theories. According to Kavka,

> [t]here is a *descriptive* theory of human behavior, which identifies the primary motives and patterns of human action and interaction, and there is a *normative* theory of human behavior, which prescribes proper, or morally permissible, modes of action both within civil society and outside it. Departing from tradition, this book separates these two theories and treats them in succession. . . .
>
> The relationships of dependence between Hobbesian descriptive theory and normative theory run primarily, though not entirely, in one direction. While some features of Hobbesian descriptive theory are selected with normative applications in mind, this theory can plausibly stand on its own. But Hobbesian normative theory cannot. It is specifically designed to deal with, and ameliorate, the human situation as set out in the descriptive theory. Its problems, its limits, and its possibilities are constrained by what Hobbesian descriptive theory tells us about human motives and manners. (Kavka, p. 19)

Kavka treats the characterization of the state of nature, the analysis of interaction in the state of nature, and the description and analysis of a hypothetical agreement to form a political association as all part of *descriptive* Hobbesian theory. The arguments purporting to establish the normative significance of hypothetical actions fall within *normative* Hobbesian theory. However, by treating both the description and analysis of a hypothetical agreement to form a political association, as well as the arguments for the normative significance of hypothetical actions, as part of *normative* Hobbesian theory, a deeper understanding of Kavka's theory is possible.[2] So understood, the importance of Kav-

2 Thus, my use of the term "descriptive Hobbesian theory" is opposed to Kavka's when he maintains, at the end of his Chapter 4, that in the following two chapters (the chapters entitled "Founding the State" and "Power and Order in the State," respectively), "we complete the

ka's contention that Hobbes's descriptive and normative theories can and should be treated as theoretically distinct cannot be overestimated. It is at once the liberating premise which allows Kavka to invoke a variety of arguments for the normative significance of hypothetical actions otherwise unavailable to the Hobbesian contractarian, and the theoretical supposition most responsible for the conceptual confusions which obscure and ultimately undermine his theory.

It is natural to suppose that the principal difference between Kavka's and Hampton's versions of Hobbes's theory is captured primarily by their different characterizations of the state of nature. Hampton's characterization of the state of nature is guided by realistic constructionism, while Kavka's is guided by both realistic and idealistic constructionism. But in what follows, I will show that the difference between their theories lies as much in the difference between the theoretical role played by their states of nature as in their different characterizations of their states of nature.

Kavka's partial embrace of realistic constructionism is evident in his explicit endorsement of using the state of nature for the purpose of constructing a realistic hypothetical postpolitical anarchy:

> The state of nature is used, in Hobbesian theory, as a model of what would happen to *us* if central political authority were removed. . . . [W]hat matters for the explanatory and normative uses of Hobbesian state-of-nature theory is what would

descriptive foundation of the Hobbesian case against anarchy by analyzing the (hypothetical) formation and maintenance of commonwealths" (Kavka, p. 178; emphasis added). For purposes of understanding the logical structure of Kavka's theory, the analysis of the hypothetical formation and maintenance of commonwealths, on my view, is best viewed as part of *normative* Hobbesian theory. As the text below explains, this is because Kavka employs distinct descriptions of the state of nature and the hypothetical setting in which a commonwealth is formed. And the latter is best understood as part of normative Hobbesian theory, and as standing in contrast to the (more or less) purely descriptive theory in which the state of nature is described and analyzed as leading to a war of all against all.

happen in the state of nature whose occupants and background conditions resemble those of modern societies. (Kavka, pp. 123–4)

Here we can understand Kavka as endorsing realistic constructionism, in which the state of nature is supposed to represent the postpolitical anarchy in which actual individuals today would find themselves were political institutions suddenly removed from their society. In line with the demands of this brand of realistic constructionism, Kavka's Hobbesian theory characterizes the state of nature as one in which resources are moderately scarce and populations fairly dense. The parties of the Hobbesian state of nature are also supposed to resemble citizens of actual contemporary States as they would be were they living in the Hobbesian state of nature. Thus, they are "death-averse, concerned with their reputations, forwardlooking, in possession of desires which conflict with others, roughly equal in natural endowments" (Kavka, p. 96), and predominantly egoistic. In holding the parties to be predominantly egoistic, Kavka is adopting a modified and qualified version of Hobbes's psychological assumption that individuals in the state of nature are purely self-interested. Although Hampton spells out this assumption in terms of the "healthy deliberation" conception of rationality, Kavka's predominant egoism holds that "self-interested motives tend to take precedence over non-self-interested motives in determining human actions. That is, non-self-interested motives usually give way to self-interested motives when there is a conflict" (Kavka, p. 64). So far, the Hobbesian state of nature seems to conform with the aims of realistic constructionism, as does Hampton's theory.

The similarities between Kavka's and Hampton's characterization of the state of nature, however, appear to end when Kavka explicitly recognizes a role for idealistic constructionism:

Hobbes's theory of life in the state of nature is idealized . . . [T]he individuals whose behavior and interaction patterns are the content of the theory are not real people, but *idealized* persons assumed to possess certain properties – rationality, certain background beliefs and ways of reasoning, and so on. . . .

The idealized individuals of Hobbes's theory are, with exceptions noted later, assumed to be rational. (Kavka, pp. 84–5)

Kavka concedes that this "rationality assumption is not intended to be entirely realistic" (Kavka, p. 97, n.33). But one of Kavka's rationales for incorporating idealistic assumptions into the Hobbesian state of nature is, perhaps surprisingly, based on considerations more properly associated with realistic constructionism. Kavka claims that Hobbes's theory is

essentially a *hypothetical* theory concerning what (counterfactually) would happen if the social and political ties between persons were suddenly dissolved. Such a theory is called for because actually dissolving society to observe the result would likely be disastrous and irreversible, if not impossible. (Kavka, p. 84)

On this view, the state of nature is a conceptual device which serves principally as a surrogate for empirical experimentation which is unfortunately inadvisable or impossible to conduct. Given that empirical testing is unavailable, Hobbesian theory engages in the next best strategy: to try to predict what a postpolitical anarchy would be like without actually looking at one. Hobbesian theory attempts to do this through the use of a hypothetical scenario whose characterization incorporates idealistic assumptions in order to generate empirical generalizations:

In the absence of the capacity for direct experimentation, such idealization is necessary if it is to be possible to derive any general conclusions about what would occur in a state of nature. At the same time, if the individuals of the theory resemble real persons in enough important respects, their interaction patterns in the state of nature might provide considerable insight concerning how real people would be likely to behave in similar circumstances. (Kavka, p. 84)

If the state of nature really reflected reality – and the individuals in it, for example, were rational only to various degrees at various times – then it would be practically impossible to provide any informative analysis of it. Like any theory which purports to provide a predictive model of reality, Hobbesian theory must abstract from the infinitely many variables in real life, and choose to incorporate only those few variables thought to be substantially determinative of outcomes. Thus, the unavailability of empirical methodology, and the intractability of theoretical models with many variables require even realistic constructionists to employ idealistic constructions in their state of nature. In order to generate any useful empirical generalizations for the purpose of providing a realistic analysis, we must, according to Kavka, engage in some idealization. Even so, Kavka argues that such idealization can be compatible with the aims of realistic constructionism so long as the characterization of the state of nature is otherwise realistic "in enough important respects."

However, in addition to this theoretical rationale for idealistic construction which is itself grounded in a concern for realistic prediction, Kavka also offers an idealistic rationale:

[T]o the extent that the idealized individuals of our theory have features that actual individuals *should* strive to approximate (e.g., perfect rationality, possession of full information), their behavior may be relevant to normative issues concerning the proper organization of society, government and so on. (Kavka, p. 84; emphasis added)

Kavka's claim is that by embedding certain ideals in the state of nature, the outcome of interaction in it will have an ideal character as well. This rationale therefore points to a quite different justificatory strategy than the previous realistic rationale. The latter hopes to produce a normative justification by closely aligning the state of nature with a realistic post-political anarchy whose outcomes are relevant to actual people. The outcomes are supposed to be relevant to actual people because, as much as is possible, the state of nature mirrors their important personal features and circumstances. The former attempts to provide a normative justification by aligning the state of nature with certain ideals which are supposed to characterize both the interaction and outcomes in the state of nature. So we can still understand Kavka's theory as fundamentally committed to the goal of realistic constructionism because the rationales he offers which are based on that goal suffice to justify the inclusion of both realistic and idealistic elements in his state of nature. Nevertheless, we might say that Kavka, at this point in his theory, appears to be "flirting" with idealistic constructionism as well, for he offers at least one rationale for these idealistic elements which is based on idealistic constructionism's goal of embedding normative ideals to generate normatively ideal results.[3]

3 It is instructive to note the justification Kavka offers for one of the exceptions to the ideal rationality assumption in the characterization of the state of nature (an exception which Kavka anticipates when first introducing the assumption; see Kavka, p. 85). In his discussion of cooperation in the state of nature, the exception is made in order to explain why it does not follow that if second-party compliance in state-of-nature agreements is rational, then first-party compliance is rational as well. The explanation is required, in Hobbesian theory, in order to defend the claim that the state of nature will consist in a war of all against all. If there is an argument proving the rationality of second-party compliance in cooperative agreements in the state of nature, and it follows from this argument that first-party compliance is rational as well, then cooperation in the state of nature seems likely.

Kavka's response is that first-party compliance will not be rational because potential first-party compliers will properly fear that some second parties will be irrational. Now this response is inconsistent with the assumption that parties in the state of nature are ideally rational. Kavka presents two rather problematic justifications for making the exception in this context – a context in which it appears Hobbes would be in trouble without it. The first is based on a realistic constructionism strategy:

Thus, the divergence between Kavka's and Hampton's theories begins with the divergence between realistic and idealistic constructionism in their descriptions of the state of nature in stage one of their theories. Nonetheless, Kavka's

> [T]he state of nature is supposed to function as a model of societies of real people dissolved by civil disorder or removal of the State. Insofar as specific but highly common irrational tendencies would contribute to problems in such a situation, they *must* be taken into account if we want our state-of-nature theory to explain correctly the dangers of anarchy and the function of the State. (Kavka, p. 148)

This first justification is obviously at odds with the idealistic constructionism goal we have just considered. If there are certain normative purposes (for example, a stage-three argument) that rely on the state of nature embedding the ideal of rationality, the state of nature cannot simultaneously serve this goal of realistic constructionism. Thus, when Kavka makes the ideal rationality assumption, he justifies it on the ground that it serves an overall normative purpose in the theory. But when the assumption is inconvenient, as it is when it threatens to undermine Hobbes's claim that the state of nature consists in a war of all against all, Kavka justifies making an exception on the ground of realistic constructionism. Which strategy – idealistic or realistic constructionism – has priority? It appears to be impossible to satisfy one at no expense to the other.

The second justification Kavka offers for the exception to the ideal rationality assumption is that "there is no general reason why the state-of-nature population must be regarded as perfectly homogeneous, with regard to rationality or anything else" (Kavka, p. 148). But this justification appears to be inconsistent with another of Kavka's initial justifications for the ideal rationality assumption, namely, that such idealizations are necessary in order to use state-of-nature theory to generate empirical generalizations. The ideal rationality assumption is supposed to be necessary in order to facilitate analysis of what otherwise would be a hopelessly intractable problem of determining the nature of interaction within a population of variously rational and irrational persons. It is difficult to see how Kavka can have it both ways. Either the idealization is necessary for purposes of empirical generalizations or it is not necessary. It is too convenient to invoke such a rationale when it serves present purposes, and then ignore it when it presents an obstacle.

Thus, the ideal rationality assumption, and Kavka's exception to it in the context of analyzing cooperation in the state of nature, foreshad-

stage-two account of interaction in the state of nature reaches the same conclusion as Hampton's: that the state of nature will consist in a war of all against all. Unlike Hampton's analysis, however, Kavka's does not rely on the supposition that individuals in the state of nature are shortsighted. Instead, his analysis is based on the structure of interaction among ideally rational actors who have equally rational, but different, strategies for interacting.

Kavka's account of conflict in the state of nature

Kavka's argument for the claim that the Hobbesian state of nature consists in a war of all against all begins by distinguishing among rational strategies for survival in the state of nature. Kavka distinguishes between "dominators" in the state of nature who "desire conquest, dominion, and power over others for its own sake," and "moderates" "who desire power over others, if at all, only as a means to protect and secure themselves and their possessions" (Kavka, p. 97). The central claim of Kavka's argument for the war of all against all is that, in the state of nature, for both dominators and moderates, "anticipation" is the most rational strategy. Anticipation is the state-of-nature strategy of "striking first or gathering power over others so that one will be in a stronger relative position when battle erupts" (Kavka, p. 97). Notice that if nearly everyone in the state of nature anticipates, not only will individuals lack personal security, but they will be unable to cooperate on mutually beneficial endeavors. Anticipation imposes actual losses as well as opportunity costs in the state of nature.

Kavka considers two objections to the claim that the state of nature, as he characterizes it, will consist in a war of all against all. The first holds that for some, if not all, parties in

ows the inevitable tension between a theory which merges realistic and idealistic constructionism. Ultimately, the two approaches are difficult, if not impossible, to marry.

the state of nature, an alternative strategy of "lying low" in the state of nature may be rational. This strategy recommends that individuals not actively attack others and instead keep to themselves in the hope of being left alone. The second claims that cooperation in the state of nature is rational and possible so that the need for anticipation never arises. Kavka notes that at least some moderates may find it rational not to anticipate provided that no others anticipate because they anticipate only as a means to security, not as an end in itself. If sufficiently few individuals in the state of nature anticipate, then anticipation for at least some moderates may be unnecessary. If we accept the premise that there is a threshold of anticipation in the state of nature before which anticipation is irrational for moderates, and after which anticipation is rational for moderates, we can model cooperative agreements in the state of nature as ones in which defection is, at least for some moderates, "quasi-dominant": "[A] move by one party in an n-person game is quasi-dominant if and only if that move yields a higher payoff for that player than any other move for every likely, plausible, or reasonably expectable combination of moves by other players" (Kavka, p. 113). A "quasi-PD" is one in which defection is a quasi-dominant move. The likelihood that sufficiently few individuals in the state of nature will anticipate, given the presence of even a minority of dominators who always anticipate, is extremely low. Nonetheless, should there be very little or no anticipation, moderates would find it rational to comply with cooperative agreements not to anticipate. Thus, they are in a quasi-PD.

What we have seen, then, is that the Hobbesian state of nature is, according to Kavka, subject to mild scarcity of resources and is fairly densely populated by ideally rational, predominantly self-interested, forwardlooking individuals who are in, at the very least, a quasi-PD with respect to cooperative agreements: everyone would prefer to live under cooperative terms, but no one is likely to find it rational to comply with such terms. Thus, the Hobbesian state of nature, like Hampton's state of nature, consists in a war of all against all.

Hypothetical agreement in Kavka's theory

The description and analysis of interaction in the state of nature complete what I have termed, using a slightly modified version of Kavka's definition, "descriptive" Hobbesian theory. The success of descriptive Hobbesian theory can be assessed in terms of how successfully it is thought to provide a model of postpolitical anarchy. But as we have seen, Kavka's state-of-nature analysis anticipates normative Hobbesian theory by rationalizing the inclusion of idealistic assumptions in the state of nature not only on descriptive grounds, but on normative ones as well. In particular, Kavka argued that the assumption of ideal rationality was justified because it might help to insure the normative significance of outcomes in the state of nature. And this rationale is in line with the justificatory strategy which underpins idealistic, not realistic, constructionism. But if Kavka merely "flirts" with idealistic constructionism in the presentation of Hobbesian descriptive theory, he warmly embraces it when he explicates and defends Hobbesian normative theory.

Normative Hobbesian theory begins with the characterization of a hypothetical scenario in which parties face the alternatives of negotiating and agreeing to form a political association or returning to the state of nature.[4] Kavka stipulates that in this setting, the parties are "assured of physical security" but nonetheless face a "generous but definite time limit on negotiation, or a rising economic cost function for time spent in negotiations (and away from normal economic activities)" (Kavka, p. 237, n. 94). It is in this first half of what I am calling Kavka's normative theory – in the characterization of what I shall call "the hypothetical negotiation scenario" – that the goals of idealistic constructionism firmly

---

4 Kavka stipulates that in the hypothetical scenario, "[t]he *no agreement point* is the state of nature" (Kavka, p. 189).

take hold. According to Kavka, the parties to such negotiations are, by definition, not only ideally rational but "appropriately forwardlooking" (Kavka, p. 190) as well. Kavka initially attempts to reconcile this idealistic characterization of the parties in the hypothetical negotiations with the goal of realistic constructionism by arguing that "we could expect most real people to approximate appropriate forwardlookingness in the context of negotiating a binding social contract" (Kavka, p. 191). But even if they could not be expected to be appropriately forwardlooking, Kavka stipulates that the parties in the hypothetical negotiation scenario nonetheless must be characterized as appropriately forwardlooking because,

> for purposes of *justifying* the permanent and lasting authority of (certain) States, we should be interested in the political arrangements that rational farsighted (i.e., appropriately forwardlooking) people would agree on. (To take a parallel example, we would not consider current environmental policies justified by the observation that they are the policies that rational shortsighted people would agree to, but we might well consider such policies justified if convinced that rational farsighted people would agree to them.) (Kavka, p. 191)

The negotiating parties must be characterized as ideally rational for similar reasons:

> Their rationality is a necessary assumption for any hypothetical contract theory that seeks to display the rationale for, and thereby provide a justification of, the State, for hypothetical agreements, unlike actual ones, can provide reasons for action only if they are rational agreements. The parties' rationality is therefore required if we are to make normative use of Hobbesian social contract theory. (Kavka, p. 190)

The ideal rationality and appropriate farsightedness assumptions are clearly not in the spirit of realistic constructionism, for actual individuals in actual societies are of course neither ideally rational nor appropriately farsighted. In-

stead, the rationale for characterizing the hypothetical negotiation scenario in idealistic terms stems from the justificatory strategy of idealistic constructionism. According to
that strategy, the normative significance of outcomes of hypothetical scenarios is a direct function of the normative
ideals embedded within the scenarios which generate them.
The aim behind the ideal rationality and farsightedness assumptions is to construct the state of nature so it embeds at
least some of our fundamental normative ideals. In this case,
it is intended to embed the fundamental ideals of rationality
and appropriate farsightedness.[5]

The effects of idealistic constructionism in Kavka's normative theory pervade his characterization of the hypothetical negotiation scenario. Not only are the parties ideally
rational and appropriately farsighted, but their negotiations
are subject to additional, highly artificial conditions. The
first I shall call "the coalition prohibition":

> The formation of coalitions, and agreements among individu-
> als and subgroups, are not allowed during the negotiations.
> The purpose of this restriction is to prevent arbitrary and
> contingent features of coalition formation patterns from influ-
> encing the ultimate content of the social contract; and in par-
> ticular to prevent the formation of blocking coalitions that
> could effectively use the threat to veto any agreement as a
> way of winning special advantages. (Kavka, p. 189)

The rationale for the coalition prohibition is the prevention
of parties "winning special advantages" and of the forma-

5 Kavka elsewhere justifies other idealistic elements (e.g., the restrictions on the parties' knowledge of their social position) in the Hobbesian hypothetical negotiation scenario, at least in part, on the ground
that they are necessary, or at least helpful, for purposes of assuring
that parties will be able to reach agreement. Though he does not
specifically offer this justification for the rationality and farsightedness
assumptions, one could plausibly argue that these assumptions serve
this "agreement facilitation" purpose as well. See Kavka, p. 193, for
his discussion of the "agreement facilitation" desideratum in characterizing the Hobbesian hypothetical negotiation scenario.

tion of coalitions with "arbitrary and contingent features." These rationales are not of course consistent with realistic constructionism. For agreements in the real world, among actual individuals, are often characterized by special advantages won by coalitions with arbitrary and contingent features. Instead, these rationales are supported by the justificatory strategy of idealistic constructionism: If the results are to be normatively significant, then the hypothetical scenario must embed certain normative ideals. Special advantages and the arbitrary and contingent are enemies of the normatively ideal.

Hobbesian normative theory further departs from realistic constructionism when, in the characterization of the Hobbesian hypothetical negotiation scenario, Kavka introduces assumptions about the negotiating parties' knowledge. First, he stipulates that the parties will have perfect "general social knowledge," on the ground that such knowledge "will be essential to their intelligently carrying out their task" (Kavka, p. 192). Thus the parties are assumed to know "general facts about human psychology and social behavior – the available findings of the social sciences of psychology, economics, sociology, political science, and so on" (Kavka, p. 192). Second, he introduces knowledge constraints on the negotiating parties which might fairly be called a version of Rawls's famous "veil of ignorance" (albeit a more translucent or "thinner" version than Rawls's "thick" veil). Although Kavka's veil permits parties in the hypothetical negotiation scenario to know certain of their personal characteristics like intelligence and gender, it prevents them from knowing their social positions and a certain category of personal goals:

> [O]ur basic assumption shall be that the parties know their personal characteristics but not their social positions. . . . [W]e must rule out knowledge of personal goals, or other characteristics, that presuppose for their existence or fulfillment the existence of a certain specific governmental system or set of institutions. Not doing so would doom us either to begging

the question in favor of existing institutions (if all parties had goals presupposing them) or likely ending up with irreconcilable differences among various parties whose goals presupposed incompatible institutional arrangements. (Kavka, p. 194)

In addition, the veil prevents the parties from knowing their society's particular characteristics. Thus, parties will not know their society's "history, language, culture, geography, economic system, and so on" (Kavka, p. 192). The reason for this restriction is that "we are seeking general criteria of political legitimacy for institutions, and a general justification for the State, that can extend across societies possessing a wide range of particular characteristics" (Kavka, p. 192).

Thus, while a concern to insure that parties will be able "intelligently" to carry out their deliberations motivates Kavka's assumption of perfect general social knowledge, there are two distinct rationales for Kavka's veil of ignorance. The first is to avoid begging the question against those who object to certain (or any) governmental arrangements. By preventing the negotiations in the hypothetical scenario from reflecting any preferences which would not have existed but for the existence of some political association or other, Kavka hopes to eliminate the objection that the outcome of the negotiations itself presupposes the legitimacy of the political institutions partly responsible for generating it. The second rationale is to facilitate agreement in the hypothetical scenario. Kavka's fear is that if parties have knowledge of their social positions, then the negotiations will deadlock because of the vested interests each party will have in a particular set of institutions.

It should be obvious, then, that neither the rationales for the assumption of perfect social knowledge nor for the veil of ignorance in Kavka's theory can be derived from the goal of realistic constructionism. If the hypothetical negotiations in Hobbesian theory are supposed to reconstruct those of actual individuals in realistic circumstances, there would be no explanation for increasing or limiting the parties' knowledge in any way. The avoidance of begging the question and the facilitation of agreement are purely theoretical considerations wholly unrelated to the goal of constructing a hypothetical situation which actual individuals might face. Instead, they are rationales designed to insure that a hypothetical scenario embeds certain normative ideals and produces outcomes which therefore will have the normative force of those ideals.

Likewise, in yet another departure from the familiar structure of Hobbes's theory, Kavka imposes a set of regulations on the negotiations which reflect a commitment to idealistic constructionism. In particular, Kavka stipulates that "[t]o be adopted, a proposal must receive *nearly unanimous* support, that is, a positive cutoff point above 95 percent" (Kavka, p. 190). The rationale for this stipulation is that

> it prevents a reasonable agreement by the vast majority from being scuttled by the intransigent demands of a relative few with extremely atypical personal characteristics, attitudes toward risk, or aversions to peace and compromise. At the same time, it prevents such 'extremists,' or other clever bargainers, from tailoring agreements to their own personal advantage, by threatening to veto it if it is not formulated as they demand. (Kavka, p. 199)

The less-than-unanimity requirement serves both "to facilitate" agreement – by lowering the standards for what counts as agreement – and to prevent the possible "tailoring" of agreements to personal advantage. The underlying rationale seems to be that such tailoring would be somehow improper or inconsistent with the purposes to which such agreements are to be put. This is consistent with the goal of idealistic constructionism.

In sum, Kavka's hypothetical negotiation scenario – the crux of normative Hobbesian theory – cannot be understood as advancing the goal of realistic constructionism. The ideal rationality and farsightedness assumptions, the coalition prohibition, the perfect general social knowledge assumption, and the less-than-unanimity requirement can be justified only as advancing the goal of idealistic constructionism. And the veil of ignorance, while not exactly designed to embed any normative values, is nonetheless incompatible with the goal of realistic constructionism. It is perhaps best understood as a requirement to insure that the normatively ideal hypothetical scenario produces results that do not beg the question. Thus, one clear difference between Hampton's and Kavka's theories is that the former is based solely on realistic constructionism, while the latter blends elements of realistic and idealistic constructionism. But a close analysis of Kavka's hypothetical negotiation scenario reveals an even more profound difference in Kavka's theory: a difference in the conceptual framework of Hobbesian contractarianism.

RECONCEIVING THE HOBBESIAN CONTRACTARIAN PROJECT

The second half of normative Hobbesian theory is provided by Kavka's arguments for the normative significance of hypothetical actions.[6] But before we can evaluate these arguments, we have to solve a puzzle which emerges from the first half of normative Hobbesian theory just considered. The puzzle is generated by comparing Kavka's description of the hypothetical negotiation scenario in what I have called Hobbesian normative theory with his characterization of the state of nature in Hobbesian descriptive theory. As Kavka notes, traditional treatments of Hobbes's theory do not consider his descriptive and normative theories separately.[7] In-

6 In addition to the hypothetical negotiation scenario and the arguments for the normative significance of hypothetical actions, normative Hobbesian (and Hobbes's) theory also provides an analysis of morality, some of the issues of which we examined in Chapter 2. Kavka discusses these meta-ethical and ethical issues in his chapters seven through twelve.
7 Bear in mind, of course, that when Kavka notes his departure from tradition in treating Hobbes's descriptive and normative theories separately, he does not include, as I do, the hypothetical negotiation

stead, the descriptive theory is integrated into the entire Hobbesian normative argument, much in the way I have suggested in presenting the three stages of contractarian arguments in Chapter 1. Thus, like most contractarians, Hobbes can be understood as offering a three-stage theory. In the first, the state of nature is described. In the second, interaction in the state of nature is analyzed. And in the third, an argument is offered to explain the normative significance of the results of the analysis in stage two. This schema captures not only Hobbes's original theory, but Hampton's reconstruction of it as well. But Kavka's theory cannot be understood quite so easily. A careful reading of Kavka's theory suggests that he provides *two* distinct stage-one characterizations and stage-two analyses: one for the state of nature and one for the hypothetical negotiation scenario. But comparison between the two reveals that they cannot be reconciled in the traditional Hobbesian manner because it is impossible to comprehend the hypothetical negotiation scenario within the state-of-nature scenario. Thus, the traditional Hobbesian framework cannot accommodate Kavka's dualistic theory. This, then, is the initial puzzle: If the hypothetical negotiations constitute a distinct hypothetical scenario from the state-of-nature scenario, how are both constructs related to form a coherent overall Hobbesian contractarian argument? Before we attempt to solve this puzzle, let's see why Kavka's theory can be understood only as a dualistic, nontraditional Hobbesian theory.

We can approach the interpretation of Kavka's theory by first comparing the two different contractarian frameworks represented by Hobbes's original theory and Rawls's theory. In Hobbes's theory, the contractarian project is to describe a state of nature, analyze the interaction in that state of nature, and then, on the basis of some stage-three argument,

---

scenario as part of normative theory. But as I hope to make clear below, this reconceptualization accommodates the most coherent interpretation of his theory.

draw normative conclusions from that analysis. In Rawls's theory, the contractarian project is to describe an original position, define a choice problem in that original position, determine the solution to the choice problem and thus determine the content of the choice that would be made in that original position. The stage-three argument in Rawls's theory consists in his particular arguments for characterizing the original position as he does, using idealistic constructionism, and his general argument for reflective equilibrium.

At first blush, it appears that Kavka's theory fits the paradigm for Hobbes's theory. He does, after all, characterize a state of nature in stage one of his theory and analyze interaction in it in stage two. But both of these stages, as regards the state of nature, take place within his descriptive theory only. The final result of his stage-two analysis of descriptive Hobbesian theory is that the state of nature consists in a war of all against all. It does not address the nature or outcome of agreements or conventions in the state of nature. This task falls within the domain of what I am calling normative Hobbesian theory. When Kavka completes his discussion of descriptive Hobbesian theory, he begins another stage-one characterization project and another stage-two analysis project. But in normative Hobbesian theory, however, these projects concern not the state of nature, but a conceptually distinct hypothetical scenario – what I have already termed a hypothetical negotiation scenario. In other words, Kavka's descriptive theory is less complete than Hobbes's original descriptive theory. For Hobbes follows his demonstration of the war of all against all in his stage-two analysis with an explanation of how and why political association would emerge from the state of nature, but Kavka does not. Kavka follows his stage-two demonstration of the war of all against all in the state of nature with a description and analysis of agreement in a hypothetical negotiation scenario only indirectly related to the state of nature. In Kavka's theory, the formation of political association is best understood as part of the normative, not descriptive, Hobbesian project. Kavka never provides an account of how individuals in the state of

nature would come to agree on forming a political association, or how a political association would emerge from it.[8]
Instead, he offers a conceptually distinct hypothetical negotiation scenario in which idealized parties negotiate under
highly specialized circumstances of negotiation. These circumstances differ dramatically from those of the state of
nature Kavka describes in his stage-two demonstration of
the war of all against all.

There is, unfortunately, considerable confusion surrounding the relationship of the state-of-nature discussion (descriptive Hobbesian theory) and the hypothetical negotiation scenario discussion (part one of normative Hobbesian
theory). Although Kavka occasionally, and quite mislead-
ingly, speaks as if we are to imagine the negotiations he
describes as taking place within the Hobbesian state of nature, his discussion also resists the simple identification of
the hypothetical negotiation scenario with the Hobbesian
state of nature.[9] But whether or not Kavka's rhetoric sup-

---

8 Kavka does, however, review the basics of Hobbes's account of the
institution of a sovereign in the state of nature, but the hypothetical
negotiations from which Kavka's normative conclusions are drawn are
conceptually distinct from that account. See Kavka, pp. 182–8. For a
much more detailed analysis of Hobbes's account of the rational institution of a sovereign in the state of nature, see Chapter 3's discussion
of Hampton's argument for the rationality of instituting a sovereign in
the state of nature.

9 There is considerable textual support for the view that Kavka conceives of the hypothetical negotiations as taking place in the state of
nature. Kavka's outline of the overall Hobbesian argument against
anarchy concludes that "rational parties *in a state of nature* would form
a civil society of an appropriate kind in order to leave that state of
nature" (Kavka, p. 109; emphasis added). Later, he refers to the "various reasonable bargains that might emerge among *state-of-nature negotiators*" (Kavka, p. 201; emphasis added). Similarly, Kavka introduces the task of chapter five, in which the hypothetical negotiation
scenario is introduced and analyzed, as one in which the Hobbesian
argument "demonstrate[s] that, and how, a sufficient concentration of
power [to install a government] could come about and be sustained,
without imposing on its citizens worse costs and harms than they
would suffer *in the state of nature*" (Kavka, p. 180). He then distin-

ports the view that the hypothetical negotiation scenario and the state of nature are conceptually distinct in Hobbesian theory, an analysis of his characterization of the hypothetical negotiation scenario compels this conclusion.

guishes between Hobbes's institution and acquisition accounts of the emergence of political association in the state of nature, and explains that for normative purposes, Hobbesian theory (i.e., Kavka's theory) will "rely on sovereignty by institution, Hobbes's version of social contract theory" (Kavka, p. 181) in which the sovereign is instituted *in the state of nature*. Continuing in this vein, just before he begins his characterization of the hypothetical negotiation scenario, he again directly suggests that the task he is engaged in is to describe the "sort of solution rational parties *in the state of nature* would find for their impure coordination problems" (Kavka, p. 188; emphasis added). And in characterizing the hypothetical negotiation scenario, Kavka stipulates that the *"no agreement point* is the state of nature; if no social contract is made, the parties all *remain* in that undesirable condition" (Kavka, p. 189; second emphasis added). In addition, Kavka concludes his discussion of the hypothetical negotiation scenario on page 236 by asking "[h]ow is it possible . . . for state-of-nature parties to come together to negotiate a social contract when they distrust and fear one another?" Finally, in discussing the normative significance of the outcome of the negotiations in the hypothetical negotiation scenario, Kavka claims that "[t]he Hobbesian argument against anarchy demonstrates that some form of State-establishing procedure or interaction would be required by reason *for parties situated in a state of nature*" (Kavka, p. 401; emphasis added). All of these passages suggest that Kavka imagines the hypothetical negotiations to be taking place in the Hobbesian state of nature.

In spite of this evidence, there is also strong textual support for the view that Kavka recognizes that the hypothetical negotiations do not take place in the state of nature. In presenting the logical form of hypothetical contract theories, Kavka's first premise is that "If people were rational and *in such-and-such circumstances,* they would choose or agree to social arrangements of a certain kind" (Kavka, p. 22; emphasis added). Although Kavka is here arguably trying to subsume all contractarian theories within a general framework, this general formulation allows that the choice or agreement to form a political association might take place in something other than the Hobbesian state of nature. More telling is a nearby passage in which Kavka describes Hobbes's original project and contrasts it to his own Hobbesian project:

[Hobbes] imagines rational and predominantly self-interested persons *living in a situation of anarchy choosing among remaining in that*

Consider, for example, Kavka's veil of ignorance. First, recall the veil's restriction on social knowledge which precludes parties from knowing their particular society's "history, language, culture, geography, economic system, and so on" (Kavka, p. 192). This would appear to be a strange

> *situation*, living under a government with limited or divided powers, or living under a government with unlimited and undivided powers. . . . But suppose we replace these premises with more plausible ones that are in accord with other principles of Hobbes's philosophy. Then we emerge with a Hobbesian hypothetical contract theory that justifies obedience to limited governments of certain sorts . . . [and] *uses circumstances of choice that are appropriate to the problem of political obligation* . . . (Kavka, p. 23; emphasis added)

Here Kavka suggests that the circumstances of choice in Hobbes's theory (namely, the state of nature), are inadequate and need to be replaced with "circumstances of choice that are appropriate to the problem of political obligation." Before beginning his discussion of the formation of a political association, Kavka notes that

> [o]ur presentation . . . will diverge much further from Hobbes's text than our presentation of the earlier parts of the argument against anarchy did. This divergence is necessitated by the rejection of certain of Hobbes's main substantive assumptions about political sociology, and by the desire to develop Hobbesian social contract theory in a methodologically explicit and defensible manner. (Kavka, p. 180)

And in describing Hobbesian theory as a hypothetical contract theory, Kavka explains that "it seeks to justify certain social arrangements by claims about what rational people would select or agree on *under appropriately specified conditions*" (Kavka, p. 182; emphasis added). Again, the language Kavka employs resists the simple equating of the hypothetical negotiation scenario with the state of nature. Finally, in response to the concern that parties negotiating to form a political association might fear for their own safety during negotiations (presumably because they are in the state of nature during these negotiations), Kavka reminds us that

> the social contract is, within Hobbesian theory, a hypothetical one. Its content is what such-and-such parties so situated would agree to, *where the characteristics of the parties and situation are not all intended to be realistic*. In particular, we can simply *stipulate* that the contractors have nothing to fear from one another during negotiations . . . [W]e may unobjectionably stipulate the security problem out of existence. (Kavka, p. 237; first emphasis added)

restriction for parties living in a state of nature. Are there, strictly speaking, economic systems in a state of nature, as this restriction would imply if the hypothetical negotiations are imagined to take place in the state of nature? Next, consider the veil's requirement that parties in the hypothetical negotiation scenario cannot know "their *actual* personal social position[s]" (Kavka, p. 194; emphasis added), and thus that their "*present* individual social positions remain a mystery to them" (Kavka, p. 195; emphasis added). If the parties negotiating are in the state of nature, how could they have social positions to know about? Kavka lists "occupation" and "power of public and private offices and positions that one occupies" (Kavka, p. 192) as examples of social positions which parties would not be allowed to know during their negotiations. He illustrates the prohibition against knowledge of social position by noting that "a party may know, for example, that she is an intelligent, success-oriented woman, but not that she is an upper-middle-class attorney earning a high income and having substantial status and political influence in her community" (Kavka, p. 194). But in the Hobbesian state of nature, there are no "occupations" per se, or public offices which individuals could occupy. There can be no political influence because there is no politics. There are no public offices because there is no government. There are no attorneys because there are no courts, no law schools, no professions, etc. And although some groups of individuals may fare better than others, there is nothing like the class system we associate with the term upper-middle-class. There is only a war of all against all. The individuals who might enter into negotiations in the Hobbesian state of nature are individuals living without political association, and as such have no present social positions.[10]

10 We might try to reconcile Kavka's veil of ignorance with the view that the hypothetical negotiations take place in the Hobbesian state of nature by imagining that the parties to the negotiation are in a post-political anarchy, having just lived in a political association. But this strategy fails to explain why Kavka finds it necessary, for example, to stipulate that during negotiations the parties' "*present* individual social

The most natural way to comprehend Kavka's hypothetical negotiation scenario, with all its artificial and idealized
constraints, is to conceive of it as a version of Rawls's original position, rather than a version of Hobbes's state of nature. And Kavka's rhetoric to the contrary notwithstanding,
his discussion of the hypothetical negotiation scenario invites this interpretation. In fact, Kavka directly acknowl-
edges the analogy between the hypothetical negotiation scenario and Rawls's original position in discussing the rationale
of his veil of ignorance:

> To explain how our limited restrictions on the parties' knowl-
> edge are intended to operate, it will be useful to contrast them
> with Rawls's restrictions on knowledge. . . .
> There are useful elements in both early and later Rawlsian
> contractarian theory that can be incorporated into Hobbesian
> theory. (Kavka, pp. 195–6)

positions remain a mystery to them" (Kavka, p. 195). If the parties
were in a postpolitical anarchy, they would have only *former* social
positions. Moreover, one of Kavka's rationales for prohibiting knowledge of one's particular social position is that such knowledge will
likely lead to irreconcilable conflict, for example, among "the rich who
prefer strong property rights and the poor who favor redistribution"
(Kavka, p. 193). But again, the parties in the state of nature could
know, at most, that they *were* rich, not that they *are* rich. For in the
state of nature possessions are not secure, and whether they will retain
their riches in the state of nature or a future political association is an
open question. Of course, so long as they are able to maintain their
previous economic position in the state of nature, they will want to
preserve or improve their position in a future political association,
depending on whether they are rich or poor, respectively (though
even the rich still want to improve, not merely maintain, their position). This might lead to an increased likelihood of disagreement. For
a discussion of the role of knowledge of social position in agreement
facilitation, see the previous section in this chapter entitled "Hypothetical Agreement in Kavka's Theory." Nonetheless, this view still
reduces to the view that the parties are in what amounts to an original
position. For it would be postpolitical in name only. A real postpolitical anarchy would, like Kavka's state of nature, not be subject to all of
the artificial conditions present in the hypothetical negotiation scenario.

Once we interpret the hypothetical negotiation scenario as Kavka's version of a Rawlsian original position, it begins to make more sense. The parties in the hypothetical negotiation scenario are actual people who are to imagine themselves in a particular hypothetical setting. Kavka stipulates that, in the hypothetical negotiation scenario, "[t]he *no agreement point* is the state of nature" (Kavka, p. 189). But while their point of no agreement is the Hobbesian state of nature, they are nonetheless not *in* the Hobbesian state of nature. Instead, they are in an original position and their task is to choose a form of political association as an alternative to the state of nature. So conceived, we can understand how it is possible that individuals, in the absence of Kavka's veil of ignorance, would have knowledge of their present social positions and their current (political) society's characteristics. It makes perfect sense to say that a party "may know . . . that she is an intelligent, success-oriented woman, but not that she is an upper-middle-class attorney earning a high income and having substantial status and political influence in her community" (Kavka, p. 194). And there is no question but that without the veil, the parties are likely to have preferences that derive from their particular political association's structure, and thus that the outcome of the negotiations will in some sense be tainted by these preferences.

This reconceptualization of Kavka's project also helps to explain why knowledge of one's current social position is relevant to whether agreement will be reached in the negotiations. A party's knowledge of her riches, for example, would enable her to target various proposals as more or less favorable to her because she would know that her fortunes will turn on the fortunes of the rich in a future political association. Similarly, others' knowledge of their poverty would enable them to target opposing alternative arrangements which would be to their advantage. When parties in Kavka's hypothetical negotiation scenario are able to target opposing alternatives, we have reason to believe they will have more difficulty reaching agreement than if their ability to forecast their fortunes under various proposals were decreased. For while their ability to target opposing proposals increases the potential grounds for disagreement among the parties, the parties' ability to target alternatives is unfortunately not accompanied by any increase in their ability to persuade others to agree to their alternative. This is because a party would be able to use his knowledge of the status he had before entering the hypothetical negotiations as leverage in negotiations only if the no agreement point for the negotiations were the status quo before negotiations. Thus, if the point of no agreement were the status quo before negotiations, the rich, for example, might be more able to hold out for concessions than the poor, who arguably stand to lose more from returning to the status quo ante, and to gain more from reaching agreement on a mutually advantageous political association. But the no agreement point for the negotiations is the state of nature, *not* the current society of the actual individuals imagining themselves in the hypothetical negotiations. Thus, while knowledge of one's present social position will enable parties to identify those proposals which best advance their interests (assuming they can maintain, for example, their economic position during negotiations), and will therefore lead to disagreement between the parties, such knowledge offers no concomitant increase in any party's bargaining leverage which might increase the likelihood of agreement being reached.[11] The result of allowing parties' knowledge of their present social positions therefore would likely be a decrease in the probability of the parties' reaching agreement.

Thus, Kavka's characterization of the hypothetical negotiation scenario seems naturally to fall into place once we abandon the traditional assumption that the formation of political association in Hobbes's theory takes place within the same state of nature which, for Hobbes, Hampton, and

---

11 The assumption would appear to follow from Kavka's stipulation that "the contractors have nothing to fear from one another during negotiations" (Kavka, p. 237).

Kavka alike, consists in an inevitable war of all against all. Instead, we should understand Kavka's theory as having two stage-one definitions and two stage-two analyses. He defines both a state of nature and a distinct hypothetical negotiation scenario, analyzes the former as leading inevitably to a war of all against all, and analyzes the latter as leading to the formation of a political association. Kavka's description and analysis of the state of nature constitute what I have called "descriptive" Hobbesian theory, while his description and analysis of the hypothetical negotiation scenario constitute what I have called the first part of "normative" Hobbesian theory.

We can now solve part of our initial puzzle by putting Hobbesian descriptive theory and the first part of Hobbesian normative theory together. Both theories are joined directly only at one point: where Kavka defines the hypothetical negotiation scenario's point of no agreement as the Hobbesian state of nature. In Rawls's theory, the failure of individuals in the original position to reach agreement simply means Rawls's theory fails to produce a result. In Kavka's theory, failure of individuals to reach agreement in the hypothetical negotiation scenario would mean those individuals must live in the state of nature. Thus, the parties in Kavka's and Rawls's versions of the original position all seek to maximize their prospects in a future political association they might form by agreement. But the penalty of not reaching any agreement in Kavka's original position is life in the Hobbesian state of nature, while the parties suffer no penalties for failing to reach agreement in Rawls's original position.

In the final analysis, then, Kavka's theory never provides what we have previously called an internal solution to the state of nature problem.[12] He purports to prove that the state of nature would be collectively irrational relative to a political association, and he purports to demonstrate that individuals in a hypothetical negotiation scenario would agree to form a political association. But he never shows that individ-

12 See n. 8.

uals in the Hobbesian state of nature gripped by the war of all against all would themselves form a political association.

With this understanding of Kavka's contractarianism, we are now in a position to consider the second part of normative Hobbesian theory, the stage-three arguments for the normative significance of the hypothetical actions in Kavka's theory. To complete the solution to our puzzle, this second half of Hobbesian normative theory must be successfully integrated with Kavka's unique dualistic presentation of a distinct state of nature and hypothetical negotiation scenario.

KAVKA'S JUSTIFICATORY STRATEGIES

I have not presented the details of Kavka's second stage-two analysis: the analysis of the outcome of the hypothetical negotiation scenario.[13] Kavka does have a substantial discussion of why parties in that situation would come to agreement, and what the nature of the terms of that agreement would be. Kavka argues that individuals in his state of nature would agree to terms of political association which specify certain "economic measures, government powers, and individual liberties" (Kavka, p. 210). Our present concern, however, is not to evaluate the content of the agreement which would be reached in Kavka's state of nature, but rather to determine whether Kavka has given us reason to believe that agreements reached by hypothetical individuals in the hypothetical negotiation scenario provide actual people like us with what Kavka calls a "good moral reason" for abiding by such agreements. Kavka offers three arguments which purport to account for the normative significance of agreements reached in the hypothetical negotiation scenario. The first of these seems to accord with the goals of realistic constructionism.

13 Kavka's analysis of the outcome of bargaining in the hypothetical negotiation scenario is discussed in the section entitled "Evaluating the Application of the Inheritance Principle to Hobbesian Contractarianism."

Kavka's hybrid contractarianism

The realistic reconstruction account

Kavka presents the first argument for the normative significance of hypothetical outcomes when he claims that "according to [hypothetical consent theory], people have good
moral reasons for obeying [certain sorts of] political authorities because *they* would in certain counterfactual (i.e., non-
actual) circumstances consent to do so" (Kavka, p. 399; emphasis added). Kavka ultimately invokes other principles to
explain why such hypothetical consent provides a justification for actual individuals. But even if these principles suffice to explain the normative significance of such hypothetical consent, this strategy for justification would nonetheless
be ill-suited for Kavka's theory because it does not fit with
his hypothetical negotiation scenario. For the parties to Kavka's negotiations are ideally rational and appropriately farsighted, hardly suitable surrogates for actual individuals. If
Kavka had maintained the traditional Hobbesian strategy of
analyzing agreement in the state of nature instead of his
hypothetical negotiation scenario, his theory might have
provided a more appropriate context for generating an
agreement designed to reconstruct the choices of actual individuals. Although the individuals in the Hobbesian state
of nature are for the most part idealistically rational, Kavka
allows that some individuals are sometimes irrational when,
as noted earlier, he assesses Hobbes's argument for the
rationality of second-party compliance in the state of nature.[14] And although individuals in Kavka's state of nature
are farsighted, they are not necessarily appropriately farsighted, as are the individuals in the hypothetical negotiation scenario.[15] Thus, there are relatively few theoretical

14 See n. 3, this chapter, for a discussion of the exception to the ideal
    rationality assumption and its relation to the question of second-party
    compliance.
15 Kavka's describes individuals in the state of nature as forwardlooking
    or farsighted, but never says they are *appropriately* farsighted. That
    adjective is reserved for his characterization of the individuals in the
    hypothetical negotiation scenario. Compare, for example, Kavka's de-
    scription of state-of-nature individuals as "forwardlooking creatures"

barriers to employing Kavka's state of nature as a conceptual device for reconstructing actual individuals' actions under hypothetical circumstances.

But given that Kavka's theory provides a distinct account of hypothetical agreement in an original position populated by ideally rational and appropriately farsighted parties, and not the state of nature populated by some irrational individuals who are not necessarily appropriately farsighted, his theory cannot hope to provide a justification for political authority by reconstructing actual individuals' actions. Kavka's Hobbesian theory proves at most that hypothetical and ideal, not actual and realistic, individuals would agree to political association in the hypothetical negotiation scenario. Any argument which purports to explain the normative force for actual individuals of the hypothetical agreements reached in Kavka's negotiation scenario cannot plausibly rely on the

(Kavka, p. 97) with his description of parties to the hypothetical negotiations:

> The parties to these negotiations are assumed to be . . . appropriately forwardlooking. . . . *Appropriately* forwardlooking parties consider their long-run as well as short-run desires and interests and give their desires and interests at different times equal weights in decision-making. . . . *We noted earlier that forwardlookingness, in the sense of concern for future well-being, is a general characteristic of human beings. But this feature is compatible with shortsightedness, that is, discounting more temporally distant goals or outcomes because of their distance.* . . . [F]or purposes of *justifying* the permanent and lasting authority of (certain) States, we should be interested in the political arrangements that rational farsighted (i.e., appropriately forwardlooking) people would agree on. (Kavka, p. 191; emphasis added)

> Although Kavka does maintain that "most real people . . . approximate appropriate forwardlookingness in the context of negotiating a binding social contract" (Kavka, p. 191), he stipulates that individuals in the hypothetical scenario are appropriately farsighted *by definition*, whereas no such stipulation is made in the context of his state-of-nature discussion. Thus, his state of nature, unlike his hypothetical negotiation scenario, does not idealize the forwardlookingness of individuals and would therefore be a more plausible venue for employing a realistic justificatory strategy which seeks to reconstruct actual persons' ctions.

claim that the individuals in that scenario are accurate surrogates for actual individuals. The fact is that no actual individuals are ideally rational and appropriately farsighted. Thus, there is considerable reason to doubt that the behavior of Kavka's idealized parties accurately predicts the behavior of actual individuals negotiating under those same circumstances.

Moreover, because agreement in Kavka's theory takes place in the hypothetical negotiation scenario and not the state of nature, the circumstances of agreement are not themselves realistic. But realism often underlies the purported significance of the hypothetical consent of actual individuals. Indeed, Kavka sometimes writes as if this is the strategy of Hobbesian justification. The idea seems to be that Hobbesian theory recognizes the normative force of actual consent, but "because dissolving society to observe the result would be likely disastrous and irreversible, if not impossible" (Kavka, p. 84), Hobbesian theory is forced into the realm of hypothetical consent. If Hobbesian theory cannot get the actual consent of actual individuals, then it will settle for the hypothetical consent of actual individuals.

But under what conditions are we to imagine individuals giving their consent? Presumably, we are to imagine them giving such consent when faced with the alternative of entering a postpolitical anarchy like the state of nature. But even if they did realistically represent actual individuals, Kavka's negotiating parties give their consent under the idealized circumstances of the hypothetical negotiation scenario, complete with its coalition prohibition and veil of ignorance. Kavka's theory at most tells us what we would do under idealized circumstances of choice, not what we would do if really confronted with the alternative to political association. Any argument for the normative significance of the hypothetical consent which is based on realistic constructionism therefore seems bound to fail if applied to Kavka's theory. His theory neither reconstructs realistic individuals nor realistic circumstances of choice. Whatever its explanation, the normative force of Kavka's hypothetical

analysis cannot be based on considerations of realistic constructionism.

More generally, realistic reconstruction strategies for providing justification are, in and of themselves, normatively
incomplete. For example, Hampton's theory purports to
demonstrate that realistic people would agree to form a
political association if they were in the realistic circumstances of her state of nature. But the mere fact that she has
accurately reconstructed choices actual individuals would
make under realistic circumstances, by itself fails to explain
why individuals are in any sense morally bound by such
choices. After all, as the libertarian insists, it is one thing
actually to agree, and quite another to agree merely in some
nonactual possible world. Explanations of the normative force
of hypothetical consent which rely on realistic constructionism therefore bear the burden of not only providing the
reconstructions they claim to provide, but explaining why
realistic reconstructions provide justification. In Hampton's
theory, that explanation is provided by the reduction of
morality to individual rationality. In Kavka's theory, no such
explanation can be found. Instead, the ultimate case for the
normative significance of hypothetical consent in his theory
must be found in distinct justificatory principles which rely
on idealistic, not realistic, constructionism.

The "no reasonable objection" account

According to Kavka, "[an] alternative defense of the claim
that hypothetical consent theories produce moral justifications is based on the idea that there can be no reasonable
objections to arrangements that would be agreed to under
appropriate conditions" (Kavka, p. 401). The idea is supposed to be that the circumstances under which the parties
in the hypothetical scenario make their choice are ones which
guarantee that all and only those "reasonable" objections to
various forms of political association will be made. In particular, Kavka claims that the hypothetical negotiation scenario
embeds our ideals of rationality and morality. Thus, if we

agree that the perfect general social knowledge assumption,
the less-than-unanimity requirement, the veil of ignorance,
the coalition prohibition, and the ideal rationality and appropriate farsightedness assumptions successfully and adequately embed the fundamental ideals of rationality and
morality (or freedom and equality, as Kavka later argues)[16]
in the hypothetical negotiation scenario, then, Kavka argues, we have good reason to suppose that disagreement
with the terms of outcomes emerging under such circumstances could not possibly be principled or justified. If an
actual individual were to judge the imposition of those terms
on her to be objectionable and instead insist that some alternative set of arrangements is justified, her judgment would
be necessarily unreasonable: "[a]fter all, if one's grounds for
these judgments were good ones, they would have been
acknowledged by the rational bargainers, who would therefore have chosen (the) alternative arrangements" (Kavka, p.
401). According to Kavka, once the hypothetical negotiation
scenario is conceded to be normatively ideal, all reasonable
objections to any political association must be ones which
the parties in that scenario would voice themselves. For if
an objection would not be raised in an ideally rational and
moral hypothetical scenario, it must be contrary either to
rationality or morality and is therefore unreasonable. According to this view, a fundamentally rational and moral
hypothetical scenario will produce all and only those objections which are reasonable. The only reasonable way to
criticize a political association which would be consented to
in Kavka's negotiation scenario is to question whether that
scenario sufficiently embeds our fundamental conceptions

16 Kavka claims that the "circumstances of agreement and the characteristics of the parties – rationality, reasoned agreement, freedom, and
equality – represent fundamental moral values concerning the conditions and nature of human interactions" (Kavka, p. 400). See the
section in this chapter entitled "The 'No Reasonable Objection' Account" for a discussion of the nature of the values Kavka claims are
embedded in the hypothetical negotiation scenario.

of rationality and morality.[17] Once we grant its morality and rationality, however, we must grant the legitimacy of its outcomes.

The novelty of this account of the normative significance of hypothetical consent lies in its understanding of hypothetical consent as a device for operationalizing the definition of "a reasonable objection."[18] It purports to provide us with a relatively simple test for determining whether an objection is reasonable: An objection is reasonable if and only if the parties in the ideally rational and moral hypothetical scenario would make it. The idea is that an objection is rational and moral only if ideally rational-moral persons in ideally rational-moral circumstances would raise it. Unfortunately, even if we concede that a hypothetical scenario adequately embeds the fundamental ideals of rationality and morality, it does not follow that only those objections which the individuals in that scenario would raise are reasonable. This is because the operational definition of reasonableness, to which the "no legitimate objection" account is wedded, incorrectly presumes that a hypothetical rational-moral person in ideally rational-moral circumstances could voice any objection an equally rational-moral *actual* individual could make in equally idealized circumstances. But there is at least one objection – perhaps the deepest and most frequently raised objection – to the use of hypothetical consent as a justificatory device which rational-moral actual individuals in idealized circumstances could raise, but which ideal, but nonetheless hypothetical, individuals in a hypothetical setting could not. This is the quintessentially libertarian objection, considered earlier, that the principle of hypothetical consent is incompatible with the more basic principle of

17 See Kavka, pp. 402–7, for a discussion of the nature of this objection and Kavka's responses.
18 In some respects, this strategy for understanding hypothetical justification recalls T. M. Scanlon's approach in his "Contractualism and Utilitarianism," reprinted in A. Sen and B. Williams, eds., *Utilitarianism and Beyond* (Cambridge University Press, 1982).

actual consent, a principle entailed by a fundamental commitment to respect for individual autonomy. The chief libertarian objection to the principle of hypothetical consent is that hypothetical consent bears no relevant relationship to actual consent, the only act which libertarians recognize as justifying the imposition of constraints on an individual's liberty.

The point here is not of course that the libertarian's commitment to the principle of actual consent is necessarily reasonable. It would beg the question against the principle of hypothetical consent to presuppose, as this libertarian argument would have it, that the only satisfactory account of the justificatory force of hypothetical consent would be one which somehow reduces hypothetical consent to actual consent. The hypothetical consent advocate will naturally deny that actual consent constitutes the only source of justification for limiting individual liberty. Rather, the point is that the "no reasonable objection" account of the normative force of hypothetical consent is wedded to an operational definition of "a reasonable objection" in which it is logically impossible for the libertarian objection to be raised. The libertarian objection is eliminated not because it is somehow inconsistent with rationality or morality, but merely because it is an objection which cannot be made by hypothetical individuals who, by definition, do give their consent to the hypothetical bargain in question. The hypothetical individuals who are parties to the hypothetical negotiations cannot object to an outcome on the ground that they were not party to it. They are, of course, the only parties to it! Thus, whereas actual rational and moral individuals do not give their actual consent to the terms of hypothetical bargain, the hypothetical individuals in the hypothetical negotiations do give their actual consent. Only the former therefore can object to the imposition of the terms of the hypothetical bargain on the ground that they have not consented to such terms.

We might wonder, however, whether hypothetical individuals in the hypothetical negotiation scenario could object, as a matter of principle only, to the imposition of the terms of their agreement on others who are not party to the hypothetical agreement, even if they could not object to the imposition of those terms on themselves. We might ask, in other words, whether the libertarian objection could be raised by the hypothetical individuals in the hypothetical negotiations, not as an objection on their own behalf, but as a principled objection on behalf of others who are not party to their agreement. Unfortunately, the answer is "no." These individuals will voice objections only to those outcomes which are inconsistent with pursuit of their predominantly self-regarding interests, and they need have no self-interested reason to object to an outcome as violating an actual consent requirement because the imposition of the terms of their agreement does not violate the requirement that they give their consent. Nor, *ex hypothesi,* do they have concern for whether the outcome might be legitimately imposed on others without those others' actual consent. These agents are not moral agents with a moral incentive to agree only on moral outcomes, but rather are predominantly self-interested agents doing their best for themselves under morally constrained circumstances. The hypothetical individuals attending Kavka's hypothetical negotiations cannot be relied upon to possess the motivational capacity to consider the interests of those not party to their agreement.[19] The hypo-

19 The parties can, and according to Kavka do, consider the well-being of family members, future family members, and some friends. But they are in all other respects, predominantly egoistic. Moreover, in another context, Kavka argues that:
   Predominant Egoism places no limits on the scope and strength of motives such as fair play for people in an established position of well-being and security. . . . [And] even for those not in such a position, Predominant Egoism allows that many of them might be somewhat motivated by considerations of justice or fair play and some of them might be highly motivated. . . . [F]inally . . . adopting or developing a sense of fair play or justice can be entirely consistent with promotion of one's long-term interests. To the extent that this is so, the Predominant Egoism hypothesis does

thetical negotiation scenario in Kavka's theory is not designed to reveal the nature of hypothetical deliberations over
principles of political legitimacy, for such deliberations need
never take place in his state of nature. Rather, it is designed
to help us calculate the consequences of rational, predominantly self-interested decision making under morally constrained circumstances. The hypothetical individuals in Kavka's hypothetical negotiation scenario are simply not designed
to generate "in principle" objections to political authority.

Thus, by insisting that "if one's grounds for [one's op-
posed] judgments were good ones, they would have been
acknowledged by the rational bargainers" (Kavka, p. 401),
the "no reasonable objection" account illicitly predetermines
that the libertarian objection cannot be made, not because of
its incompatibility with the norms of rationality and morality, but because of the hypothetical character of its operational test for the reasonableness of an objection. The "no
reasonable objection" account of hypothetical consent therefore begs the question against libertarianism.

Still, if the "no reasonable objection" defense begs the
question against the libertarian commitment to the actual
consent principle, the actual consent principle appears equally
to beg the question against the hypothetical consent principle. The "no reasonable objection" defense unjustifiably rules
out a libertarian objection to the justificatory force of hypothetical consent. But in the absence of an independent argument supporting the libertarian commitment to actual consent as a necessary condition for the justification of political
coercion, the libertarian's objection to the normative force of

not undermine the potential efficacy of appeals to the motive of
fair play. (Kavka, p. 405)
But if rational self-interest and the requirements of morality conflict,
most parties, because they have predominantly self-regarding interests, will not have the motive to conform. Moreover, while it may be
possible that some parties will be morally motivated, and so will raise
an objection to the imposition of their bargain on others who are not
party to the bargain, there is no guarantee that the objection will be
raised.

hypothetical consent is no more compelling than the hypothetical consent advocate's insistence that hypothetical consent can have justificatory force. Neither position appears to have the upper hand. Kavka cannot therefore rely on the "no reasonable objection" argument to discharge his burden of demonstrating the normative significance of hypothetical actions.

The inheritance principle account

The "no reasonable objection" account we have just considered conceives of the hypothetical negotiation scenario as a tool to be used for fleshing out the moral and political implications of our basic normative values. Although this idealistic account of the normative significance of hypothetical action does not succeed, Kavka's central normative argument rests on a similarly idealistic account. Kavka argues that the hypothetical negotiation scenario embeds the normative values of rationality, reasoned agreement, freedom, and equality, much in the same way Rawls's original position is supposed to embed certain Kantian ideals. According to Kavka, the results of human interaction under the circumstances of the hypothetical negotiation scenario are supposed to "inherit" the normative values which characterize or constrain that scenario. Thus, the claim is that the principles of political association to which individuals in the hypothetical negotiation scenario might agree have the same normative status as the circumstances, individuals, and procedures in that scenario. And that normative status is supposed to suffice to justify the imposition of the outcome of the hypothetical negotiation on actual people who have not participated in such negotiations. This argument rests, according to Kavka, on the general principle that

> rational-moral relations among rational-moral beings are preserved by rational-moral interactions among those beings (i.e., the outcomes inherit the rationality-morality of the parties,

their initial relationship, and the interaction process in question). (Kavka, p. 400)

Let us call the operative general principle "the inheritance principle." It is the cornerstone of Kavka's normative theory and constitutes one of his most important and novel contributions to political contractarianism. But while analysis of the inheritance principle generates a number of insights into the normative force of hypothetical actions, it unfortunately cannot account for the normative force of the outcomes of the hypothetical negotiations in Kavka's theory.

Our principal interest in the inheritance principle derives from its role in Kavka's theory: to explain why the fact that the parties in Kavka's hypothetical negotiations would agree to terms of political association suffices to justify the imposition of those terms on us. The inheritance principle is, in other words, a "bridge principle": a principle which connects the results of his stage-one state-of-nature definition and stage-two hypothetical analysis with his stage-three justification of political association. But, as Kavka has formulated it, the precise content of the inheritance principle is subject to a number of possible interpretations. Before considering whether it provides an adequate basis for Kavka's normative conclusion, my task in this section will be to explicate the most convincing version of the principle which Kavka might defend.

The task of interpreting the inheritance principle is complicated because the inheritance principle purports to be a perfectly general principle whose application therefore extends beyond Hobbesian contractarianism. Thus, whether the inheritance principle is a defensible bridge principle for Kavka's theory would appear to depend, at least in part, on whether it can be defended as a general principle, and only then on whether it can be successfully applied to Kavka's theory. It is possible, however, that a general version of the inheritance principle has strengths or weaknesses not shared by a narrower version of the principle tailored to its application in Kavka's theory. Any ambiguities in the formulation of the general principle thus will be resolved in favor of that meaning which most coheres with its application to Kavka's theory, and not necessarily with the most defensible version of the general principle. Once the meaning of the inheritance principle is fixed, I will turn to its direct application in Kavka's theory.

Evaluating the inheritance principle as an independent principle. The inheritance principle invokes the notions of "rational-moral relations," "rational-moral persons," and "rational-moral interactions," but does not specify their content. What makes a person a rational-moral person? What makes an interaction a rational-moral one? What does the claim that a relation is a rational-moral one mean? And what does it mean to say that a rational-moral relation is "preserved"?

Let's begin with the question of what it means to say that a rational-moral relation is "preserved." Temporarily setting aside the question of what it means for a relation to be rational or moral, we can ask simply what it means to "preserve" any relation. Kavka gives us some help when he parenthetically restates the inheritance principle as holding that "*the outcomes* inherit the rationality-morality of the parties, their initial relationship, and the interaction process in question" (Kavka, p. 400; emphasis added). According to Kavka, the relation between parties which results from their interaction is one type of outcome of their interactions. Although the parties' interactions might also produce other types of outcomes (e.g., pollution, pain, happiness, money, knowledge, etc.), the only type of outcomes of interaction which the inheritance principle specifically addresses are relations between parties. Thus, when it states that "rational-moral relations . . . are preserved," the inheritance principle can be understood as claiming that whatever rational-moral relations exist between the parties before their interaction will also exist between the parties after they interact, so long as their interaction is rational-moral.

Now that we have some idea of what it means for a relation to be preserved, we need to define the notions of rational-moral relations, persons, and interactions. In order to refine the meaning of these terms, it will be useful to separate our analysis of the inheritance principle into two distinct prongs. We can begin by considering the rationality prong of the inheritance principle. That prong states that "rational relations among rational persons are preserved by rational interactions." Let's consider each of the key phrases in this principle.

What does the phrase "rational interaction" mean? Presumably, we can define this phrase in terms of the actions of "rational persons": "rational interaction" is interaction between "rational persons." There is little question that, for Kavka, a rational person is someone who follows individually rational strategies (e.g., a utility maximizer). "Rational interaction" is therefore nothing but "interaction between rational parties." But is individually rational interaction the result of individual actions which are merely consistent with individual rationality or actions which are compelled by rationality? Kavka addresses this issue when he notes that

> one might doubt that the rational-moral status of inputs is transmitted to outputs, when the rational-moral interactions which (hypothetically) produce the latter are optional, as opposed to necessary, for the parties in question. (Kavka, p. 401)

As a solution, Kavka substitutes for his original version of the inheritance principle a somewhat weaker version according to which

> rational-moral relations among rational-moral beings are preserved by rational-moral interactions among them, *if these interactions (or interactions of their kind) are required by reason.* . . . (Kavka, p. 401)

Thus, we should understand "rational interaction," on the weaker version of the inheritance principle that Kavka ultimately endorses, to mean "interaction which results from individual actions compelled by individually rational strategies."

228

Finally, consider the meaning of the phrase "rational relation." How should we interpret the inheritance principle's claim that the relation between two parties, either before or after their interaction, is rational? There are two possible interpretations. First, the claim that the parties have a rational relation to one another might mean that each has behaved rationally in his past interactions with the other. On this interpretation, the parties' relationship before interacting is rational only if each has been individually rational when interacting with the other. Then the inheritance principle's claim is that so long as they continue to interact according to individually rational strategies, their relationship will continue to be rational in this sense. But this claim is true by definition. For, according to this interpretation, the very meaning of the claim that a relation is rational is that it resulted from individually rational interaction. In claiming that a rational relation will result from individually rational interactions between persons who have previously had nothing but individually rational interaction, the inheritance principle is making a circular claim. Substituting the phrase "a relation resulting from individually rational interaction" for the phrase "a rational relation," the inheritance principle's claim would be that "a relation resulting from individually rational interaction will result from individually rational interactions between persons who have previously had nothing but individually rational interaction."

A second interpretation of "a rational relation" is a relation which is, in some sense, collectively rational. One definition of a collectively rational relationship would be one which is Pareto optimal.[20] On this view, two parties have a rational relation if and only if there is no way they could interact to make one better off without making the other worse off. The resulting version of the inheritance principle would claim that rational interaction among rational parties

---

20 A state of affairs is Pareto optimal if and only if no one could be made better off in another state of affairs without making someone else worse off.

in a Pareto optimal state of affairs will result in a Pareto optimal state of affairs. Obviously, if two parties are rationally related, on this interpretation, there are no Pareto superior[21] actions to take. Any interaction necessarily will make at least one party worse off. Nonetheless, if each acts to maximize his own welfare in an individually rational fashion, the resulting state of affairs might be one which is Pareto optimal as well.

Another definition of a collectively rational relationship is one which is at least Pareto superior relative to a previous state of affairs. This definition is problematic, however, because it is unclear what the relevant point of comparison is when assessing the collective rationality, so understood, of a relation between two parties before they interact. They have a rational relation, on this view, only if the current state of affairs in which they find themselves is one which is Pareto superior relative to some other state of affairs. But if we understand this to mean merely that there is some state of affairs relative to which theirs is Pareto superior, then virtually all persons will enjoy rational relations before they interact. Yet it is difficult to discern in the inheritance principle any criterion for choosing some relevant state of affairs for purposes of assessing the Pareto superiority of an initial relation between parties. It is much easier, however, to determine the relevant point of comparison in assessing the Pareto superiority of the state of affairs which results from interaction between parties. For we would presumably determine whether the resulting state of affairs is Pareto superior by comparing it to the previous state of affairs characterizing the parties' prior relationship. To make the most sense of this interpretation, we might simply reduce the claim that the parties' initial relationship is rational to the claim that both parties are individually rational. Then we might take the inheritance principle to claim that the state of affairs

21 A state of affairs, S_1, is Pareto superior to a state of affairs, S_2, if and only if at least one person is better off in S_1 than in S_2 and no one is worse off in S_1 than in S_2.

which will result from rational interactions between individually rational actors will be Pareto superior to the state of
affairs which obtained before their interactions.

Unfortunately, both of these collective rationality interpretations of the claim that a relation is rational appear to be
false. The first claims that individually rational interaction
between persons in a Pareto optimal state of affairs necessarily will lead to a Pareto optimal state of affairs. But the
Pareto optimality of an initial state of affairs only insures
that any other state of affairs will be Pareto inferior to it. It
does not insure that another state of affairs – even ones
which result from individually rational interaction – will be
Pareto optimal. For the single-play prisoner's dilemma proves
that individually rational actors are capable of interacting to
produce Pareto suboptimal results, irrespective of whether
their starting point is Pareto optimal. Similarly, the interpretation of a rational relation as a Pareto superior state of
affairs is demonstrably false as well. Again, the single-play
prisoner's dilemma proves that voluntary and individually
rational actions can lead not only to Pareto suboptimal results, but Pareto inferior results as well.

Thus, the only defensible interpretation of "a rational relation" is as "a relation that results from individually rational interaction." This is an interpretation which threatens
to make the rationality prong of the inheritance principle
trivially true. The triviality of this principle is, however, a
consequence of my previous interpretation of the meaning
of the claim that a rational relation is "preserved," an interpretation there is some reason to question. That interpretation held that the claim that a relation is preserved is equivalent to the claim that the relation between the parties before
their interaction remains the same after their interaction.
This interpretation takes the literal phrasing of the inheritance principle seriously: "rational-moral relations *among
rational-moral beings* are preserved by rational-moral interactions among them" (Kavka, p. 401; emphasis added). But
Kavka follows this statement of the inheritance principle
with a parenthetical restatement which holds that "the out-

comes inherit the rationality-morality of the parties, their initial relationship, and the interaction process in question" (Kavka, p. 400). This formulation suggests not only that it is the relation between the parties who interact which is preserved for them through rational interaction, but also that we can think of the resulting relationship between the parties as a type of relationship which is rational not just for those parties but for other parties as well. Rational interaction between rational parties insures not only the rationality of their relationship for them, but also the rationality of that relationship per se. But what could it mean to say that a relationship per se is rational, if not that it is rational for the parties whose interaction produced it?

Kavka suggests the answer to this question when he explicates the weak version of the inheritance principle he ultimately endorses. The weak version of the inheritance principle states that "rational-moral relations among rational-moral beings are preserved by rational-moral interactions among them, if these interactions (*or interactions of their kind*) are required by reason . . ." (Kavka, p. 401; emphasis added). This formulation can be understood as suggesting that the relationship between rational parties which results from their rational interaction will be rational for other individuals for whom interactions of the same kind are rational as well. Thus, the fact that a given relationship resulted from rational interaction among rational beings indicates the individual rationality of acting to bring about that relationship between all persons similarly situated.

But even this interpretation verges on the trivial. For once we determine that others are similarly situated to the parties, it follows necessarily that their rational interaction would lead to the same outcome. Otherwise, they would not, by definition, be sufficiently similarly situated for purposes of the application of the inheritance principle.[22] Even so, this

22 I follow Kavka here in interpreting the phrase "similar circumstances" to include certain crucial characteristics of the parties themselves, like

version of the rationality prong of the inheritance principle can be useful. If we take our initial inquiry to be a search for the individually rational action for two less-than-perfectly rational actors, the inheritance principle invites us to approach the answer by imagining two ideally rational parties in the same circumstances. Whatever actions these ideally rational parties would take, and whatever outcome would result from their interaction, would be rational for the two nonideally rational actors as well. Of course, if we are capable of extrapolating about what the ideally rational parties would do, and what outcome would result, one might think there is little point in going through the exercise. For we should just ask directly what is individually rational to do in the nonideally rational actors' situation. If we could determine what the ideally rational parties would do, then by the same token, we could directly determine what the nonideally rational actors rationally should do. But, in the present context, this is the only claim the inheritance principle makes about rationality. It invites us to use a hypothetical scenario merely as a heuristic device for answering questions about the requirements of individual rationality under various circumstances. In essence, when we want to know the individually rational course of action for actual persons in one set of circumstances, the inheritance principle directs us to imagine what ideally rational individuals would do in similar circumstances. Whatever the latter would do is what individual rationality requires the former to do. Thus, whatever relationship would result between the ideally rational parties – i.e., whatever outcome the ideally rational parties

similar preference structures. Of course, if parties with different preferences were in similar circumstances, it does not follow that the same actions which are rational for different, but ideally rational, persons in those circumstances would be rational for them. But given similar preferences, the inference goes through. On this interpretation, then, the inheritance principle necessarily has no counterexamples. Any purported counterexample necessarily constitutes an example of persons not sufficiently similarly situated.

would produce – would be an ideally rational relationship for the nonideally rational actors, i.e., the outcome they rationally should produce. In this sense, the relationship which results when ideally rational parties interact is ideally rational for everyone in similar circumstances. Thus, the outcome of ideally rational interaction is itself rational, not just for those rational individuals who interact rationally, but for anyone in similar circumstances.

We have, then, reasoned through a number of possible interpretations of the rationality prong of the inheritance principle and fixed on its most defensible interpretation. The most plausible version of the rationality prong of the inheritance principle holds that if individually rational actors, who have previously interacted in an individually rational manner, interact by following individually rational strategies, the relationship between them which results will be rational for them and for others in similar circumstances. To say that the resulting relationship between them is rational is merely to say, tautologically, that it resulted from individually rational interaction. To say that the resulting relationship is rational for others in similar circumstances is merely to say, tautologically, that if others, in sufficiently similar circumstances, were to act according to individually rational strategies, the resulting relationship between them would be the same as the resulting relationship for the individually rational parties. We considered but rejected two alternative interpretations of the phrase "rational relations" which invoked different notions of collective rationality. Neither the Pareto optimality nor Pareto superiority versions of collective rationality could yield a defensible version of the inheritance principle.

There is, however, a principle similar to the inheritance principle which would properly license an inference from the collective rationality of an outcome resulting from interactions between ideally rational parties, to the collective rationality of that outcome for nonideally rational, but similarly situated actors. Let us call this the "collective rationality principle." Note, however, that this principle does not purport to establish the collective rationality of the outcome from the fact that ideally rational parties would, for example, agree to it. Instead, it claims that if a given outcome can be demonstrated by independent means to be collectively rational for the ideally rational individuals, then it is collectively rational for every set of individuals facing sufficiently similar circumstances. Thus, suppose two ideally rational parties are faced with the choice between outcomes A, B, and C, and we can prove that C is collectively rational relative to A and B. If two nonideally rational actors are similarly situated, and thus face the same choice between A, B, and C, then we can infer that C will be collectively rational for them as well. But note that the ideal rationality of the parties plays no role in supporting the inference of the collective rationality of the outcome. All the collective rationality principle requires is some method for determining the collective rationality of a state of affairs in a given set of circumstances. Once this is determined, the collective rationality principle simply states that this state of affairs is collectively rational in all similar circumstances. Because we cannot infer the collective rationality of that state of affairs from the fact that rational interaction between ideally rational individuals would produce it, the ideal rationality of the parties in those circumstances becomes irrelevant. Instead, the real work is done by some independent argument establishing an outcome's collective rationality in a given set of circumstances.

Now let's consider the morality prong of the inheritance principle. That prong holds that "moral relations between moral persons are preserved by moral interactions among those beings (i.e., the outcomes inherit the morality of the parties, their initial relationship, and the interaction process in question)." We can begin our interpretation by asking what it means for a moral relation to be "preserved."[23] My

---

23 We might think of the morality prong of the inheritance principle as grounded in what Rawls calls "pure procedural justice":

> [P]ure procedural justice obtains when there is no independent criterion for the right result: instead there is a correct or fair procedure such that the outcome is likewise correct or fair, what-

interpretation here follows the interpretation of the notion of "preserving" rational relations. The claim that a moral relation between moral persons is preserved by moral inter- action among those beings at the very least means that the relationship between the interacting parties which results from their moral interaction has the same moral status as their preinteraction relationship. Thus, if moral parties have, for example, a morally acceptable or morally ideal relation- ship before interacting morally, the result of their moral interaction will be a relationship which is also morally ac- ceptable or morally ideal, respectively. And while this claim is not tautological, it would appear to be almost as uncon- troversial as its counterpart in the rationality prong of the inheritance principle. Indeed, it is hard to imagine how one could deny, for example, the moral acceptability of the rela- tionship between two moral persons whose initial relation- ship is moral and which results from their morally accept- able interaction. But we might try to follow our analysis of the rationality prong further, and interpret the inheritance principle as not only licensing an inference about the moral- ity of a resulting relationship for the parties whose moral interaction produces it, but for other individuals as well. Recall that this interpretation follows Kavka's explication of the inheritance principle in which "outcomes inherit the . . . morality of the parties, their initial relationship, and the interaction process in question" (Kavka, p. 400). The sugges- tion is that the relationship which results from moral inter- action between moral persons who have moral initial rela- tionships are not merely moral *for them,* but are moral for others similarly situated as well. That is, the outcomes of their interactions are per se moral under similar circum- stances. Unfortunately, this interpretation of the morality

ever it is, provided that the procedure has been properly followed. (Rawls, p. 86)

According to the inheritance principle, once we are assured of the morality of the "inputs," so long as the interaction which follows is moral, the outcome must be moral as well.

prong cannot be sustained. To see this, consider the definition of a "moral relation."

What does it mean to say that the relationship between
two parties is moral? At a minimum, it presumably means
that neither party has moral grounds for complaint against
the other. At a maximum, it presumably means that each
party has, without exception, treated the other in a morally
ideal fashion. Given these definitions, we can see why the
morality prong of the inheritance principle cannot generate
per se moral outcomes. Imagine some circumstance in which
individuals who have, for example, a morally acceptable
relationship (e.g., they have no moral grounds for complaint
against one another) interact in a morally acceptable fashion.
The relationship which results, we have said, may be inferred to be morally acceptable for them as well. But what
would it mean to say that the relationship would be morally
acceptable for others similarly situated? If it simply means
that if others in similar circumstances undergo the same
interactions, then that relationship will be morally acceptable for them too, then the claim is uncontroversial. But
what if others do not undergo the same interactions? What
would it mean for that outcome to be morally acceptable for
them? If we use Kavka's intended application of the inheritance principle as our guide, the claim would have to be that
it is morally acceptable to impose that outcome on others
similarly situated. For Kavka ultimately hopes to demonstrate that the outcome of his hypothetical negotiation scenario legitimately may be imposed on nonhypothetical persons.[24] But this claim, unlike its counterpart in the rationality
prong of the inheritance principle, is too strong.

24 Kavka also claims his goal is to prove that nonhypothetical individuals
have a good moral reason in favor of obeying a political authority that
would be agreed to in his hypothetical negotiation scenario. This
formulation of his conclusion can be substituted in the text's discussion, *salva veritate,* for the claim that the outcome can be imposed on
nonhypothetical persons. Thus, the text's arguments will equally apply to an interpretation of the morality prong of the inheritance prin-

Suppose, for example, that the morally acceptable inter-action between two moral persons consists in reaching a voluntary agreement and that this agreement is thereby morally acceptable as well. Clearly, it does not follow that it would thereby be morally justified to impose this outcome on others who have made no such agreement, even if they are in all other respects similarly situated. The morality of an outcome is necessarily relative to the particular actions which generate it, and cannot, like the individual rationality of certain actions, be inferred to hold for others similarly situated who have nonetheless not yet interacted to produce the outcome themselves. Put another way, the individual rationality of an outcome can be inferred for individuals who have not acted to produce the outcome, from the fact that the interaction of ideally rational individuals in their circum-stances would produce the outcome. Thus, that outcome would be the result of action required by individual rational-ity for anyone in similar circumstances. However, the moral justification for imposing an outcome for individuals who have not acted to produce the outcome cannot be inferred from the fact that the moral interaction of persons under similar circumstances would produce the outcome. For the only reason it is morally permissible to impose the outcome on those individuals who, for example, agree to the out-come, is that they have in fact agreed to the outcome. The first defensible version of the morality prong of the inheri-tance principle thus seems to support only the unsurprising claim that an outcome which results from moral interaction between individuals whose initial relationship is moral is itself a moral outcome for them. Such an outcome can be legitimately imposed on them.[25]

ciple which holds that outcomes produced by moral interaction among moral persons provide others with a good moral reason in favor of accepting that outcome for themselves.
25 Even this claim is importantly ambiguous, for it fails to state who can morally impose the outcome on whom. Even if an agreement takes place under morally acceptable circumstances, it may be that the agreement licenses only the parties to the agreement to enforce the

The inheritance principle does, however, say that an outcome's morality can be inferred if it results from the moral interaction of moral persons. And we have not yet defined the terms "moral interaction" and "moral person." Following our analysis of the rationality prong, we can define "moral interaction" as "interaction between moral persons." In turn, we might define a "moral person" as "one who is morally ideal." Such a person must, for example, possess morally ideal virtues like honesty and integrity, and must, for example, act out of, and only out of, a motivation to do what is morally correct. Defining "moral person" this way might help to explain how we could infer the moral legitimacy of imposing on others the terms of an outcome which results not from their interaction but from moral interactions under moral circumstances among moral persons. Thus, if we imagine two morally ideal persons, in the sense I have described, and we determine that their interaction would produce a given outcome, then we might have reason to infer that it would be morally justified to impose that outcome on others similarly situated, who have, because they are less than morally ideal, not interacted as the morally ideal persons would.

The idea behind this strategy is analogous to the idea behind the inference made under the rationality prong of the inheritance principle. We can infer the rational ideal in our circumstances from the behavior of rationally ideal individuals in relevantly similar circumstances. Thus, whatever the rationally ideal individuals would do is what we rationally should do in those same circumstances. Likewise, we can infer the moral ideal in our circumstances from the behavior of morally ideal individuals in relevantly similar

agreement against one another. Thus, the moral legitimacy of an outcome cannot be equated with the moral legitimacy of anybody's imposing the terms of that outcome on those whose interactions have produced it. In short, morality incorporates what we might call a "standing requirement," in which outcomes can be imposed only by those individuals who, in virtue of the substantive basis for the outcome's moral acceptability, have standing to impose that outcome.

circumstances. Thus, whatever the morally ideal individuals would do is what we morally should do in those same circumstances. As far as it goes, this claim seems plausible. But the above argument we are considering holds not merely that the outcomes produced by morally ideal persons are morally ideal for others in those same circumstances. Instead, it also contends that it would be morally legitimate to impose those outcomes on others. But no credible moral theory would hold that individuals are obligated, or legitimately may be compelled, to conform to the morally ideal. Supererogation is, after all, "above and beyond the call of duty." We cannot infer the moral permissibility of imposing an outcome on one set of individuals from the fact that morally ideal individuals would reach that outcome in the same circumstances, even if we concede that the latter fact proves the outcome is morally ideal. The tasks of determining the morally ideal and the morally required are not one and the same. The former cannot be a surrogate for the latter. And while the morally ideal person will commit all those acts which are morally required of her, she will also commit acts which are morally ideal but not morally required. This is just to say that we "should" do whatever morally ideal persons in our circumstances would do only if we want to be morally ideal ourselves. It is not a requirement of morality, however, that we act in a morally ideal manner.

This problem is somewhat analogous to the problem which faced the rationality prong of the inheritance principle. Recall that Kavka had reason to doubt that outcomes inherited the rationality of the interactions which produced them if those interactions were not "required by reason." Thus, Kavka conceded that outcomes resulting from rationally optional actions might not be, in the requisite sense, rationally required. Similarly, I am now arguing that outcomes produced by morally optional actions are not, in the requisite sense, morally required. Perhaps Kavka's solution to the first problem, properly interpreted, suffices to solve this problem as well. Suppose we interpret the caveat in the definition of the inheritance principle which restricts its application to outcomes that are "required by reason" to mean that the outcomes must be required by moral reasoning. Then the inheritance principle would hold that the only outcomes whose morality can be inferred from moral interactions are those which result from interaction which is required by morality.

We might recast this version of the inheritance principle by changing the definition of "moral persons" from "morally ideal persons" to "minimally moral persons" – that is, persons who do only what is morally required of them. Thus, if such individuals interact in a morally permissible fashion as they must and their previous relationship to one another is moral as well, then we might be able to infer that it would be legitimate to impose the outcome of their interactions on persons similarly situated. For the fact that such an outcome resulted from their interactions indicates that if persons in relevantly similar circumstances were to conform to the requirements of morality, they would reach the same outcome. If similarly situated persons have not reached that outcome, then we can infer they have failed to satisfy the requirements of morality. Thus, given this reading of the inheritance principle, we might have reason to think that imposing the terms of such outcomes on others in similar circumstances would be morally justified.

Although it is ultimately convincing, there is one preliminary objection to this version of the morality prong of the inheritance principle. If the requirements of individual rationality sometimes conflict with the requirements of morality, as many would argue they do, then there could never be any person capable of being both an ideally rational and minimally moral person at the same time. To be sure, an individual might be able, whenever it is possible, to satisfy the requirements of individual rationality and morality at the same time. But no one could be a person who always satisfies both requirements. Every individual would have to choose, at least in principle, a primary allegiance to individual rationality or morality. Yet if the inheritance principle applies only to interactions among persons who are both ideally rational *and* minimally moral, it will have no application. The principle will be moot.

The most natural solution to this problem is to bifurcate the inheritance principle into two distinct principles, much as I have done in the present discussion of it. Instead of dividing the inheritance into two prongs, we can simply divide the principle into two principles. The first holds that rational relations among rational individuals are preserved by rational interaction, if those interactions are required by rational reason. The second holds that moral relations among minimally moral individuals are preserved by moral interaction (or alternatively, that moral relations among moral individuals are preserved by moral interaction, if those actions are required by moral reason). Given this interpretation, the inheritance principle avoids the problem generated by the potential conflict between individual rationality and morality.[26] Each principle is evaluated on its own terms, and neither presupposes that any one individual is both ideally rational and minimally moral all the time.

So understood, the morality version of the inheritance principle appears to be persuasive: The hypothetical actions of minimally moral persons can indeed be legitimately imposed on nonhypothetical individuals similarly situated. Kavka's inheritance principle, properly interpreted, provides a compelling account of the normative significance of certain hypothetical actions in particular contexts. However, in the following section, in which the application of the inheritance principle to Kavka's theory is evaluated, I will argue that it is ill-suited for purposes of explaining the normative significance of the hypothetical actions in Kavka's hypothetical negotiation scenario. Although my argument will not call into question the validity of the inheritance principle per se, it does purport to undermine its role in

---

26 Of course, another alternative would be to join Gauthier or Hampton's Hobbes and argue that morality can be reduced to individual rationality. For discussion of this possibility, see Chapter 5.

explaining the justification of political authority in Hobbesian contractarianism.

Summary

In this section, I have attempted to provide the most defensible interpretation of the inheritance principle for Kavka's
purposes. This interpretation yields to distinct principles
which together license (1) the inference of the individual
rationality and morality of an outcome for those rational and
moral persons who interact in a rational and moral fashion
to produce that outcome, (2) the inference of the individual
rationality of that outcome for other individuals in similar
circumstances who, because of their lack of rationality, have
not acted to produce that outcome, and most importantly,
(3) the inference of the moral legitimacy of imposing the
outcome of the interaction among minimally moral persons
in one set of circumstances on other individuals in relevantly
similar circumstances. But these principles do not allow us
to infer the collective rationality for either those who produce the outcome or those in similar circumstances. However, the discussion of the collective rationality prong of the
inheritance principle suggested a distinct principle – the
collective rationality principle – which can be successfully
invoked to license the inference directly from the collective
rationality of an outcome in one set of circumstances to that
outcome's collective rationality in a similar set of circumstances. But the collective rationality principle requires some
independent means of determining the collective rationality
of an outcome in the first set of circumstances. And such a
determination cannot be made by inferring the collective
rationality of an outcome from the fact that it results from
interaction between ideally rational individuals.

*Evaluating the application of the inheritance principle to Hobbes-
ian contractarianism.* How might the inheritance principle account for the normative significance of the outcome of interactions in Kavka's hypothetical negotiation scenario? Those
interactions are, as the inheritance principle requires, under-

taken by ideally rational parties. Therefore, if we are in circumstances substantially similar to those faced by the parties in the hypothetical negotiation scenario, then the inheritance principle allows us to infer that their actions would be individually rational for us to perform, and in this sense, that the outcome of their interactions would be rational for us. But are we in sufficiently similar circumstances as the parties in the hypothetical negotiation scenario for the rationality prong of the inheritance principle to apply to us? Kavka claims that we are, for the hypothetical negotiation scenario is constructed to represent the choice that we in effect face every day. Just as the parties face the exclusive alternatives of anarchy or political association, so do we. And just as the alternative of anarchy for them consists in the Hobbesian state of nature, a war of all against all, so our alternative of anarchy consists in the Hobbesian state of nature as well. But the individual rationality of the parties' interactions in the hypothetical scenario is a function not only of the choice they face, but the circumstances under which they choose. And their circumstances for choosing between the state of nature and various forms of political association are quite different than those that we do or would face in reality. In particular, they are assured of coming to agreement, in part, because they are, for example, blocked from forming voting coalitions and ignorant of their present social positions. These features of their circumstances of choice dramatically affect the individual rationality of their choices. In fact, some of Kavka's own rationales for including these features in the hypothetical scenario state their purpose to be the facilitation of agreement. We will justifiably suspect, then, that under the circumstances we do or would face in choosing between anarchy and various forms of political association, the individually rational actions for us might differ from those of the individuals in the hypothetical negotiation scenario. It is, of course, surely the case that were we in their circumstances, the individually rational actions to take would be those taken by them in those circumstances. But the individual rationality of their interactions is relevant to determining what is individually rational for us only if their circumstances sufficiently mirror ours so that we might infer the latter from the former. However, we have good reason to doubt such an inference can be made. The fact that we can form coalitions, for example, might lead to a deadlock in negotiations due to blocking coalitions. And the fact that we do know our present social positions will enable us to target various forms of political association as ones which best advance our interest at the expense of others' interests. Such targeting, as noted earlier, will increase the probability of disagreement in negotiations and further stymie the prospects for reaching agreement. Thus, the fact that our circumstances of choice will differ dramatically from the circumstances of choice in Kavka's hypothetical negotiations undermines any inference from the individual rationality of their actions to the individual rationality of those actions for us. We have no reason to believe, then, that the outcome which results from their choice between the state of nature and various forms of political association would result from our facing the same choice, even if we concede either that we in effect face such a choice now, or that we will face such a choice in the future.

Although we cannot infer the individual rationality of certain choices for us from the individual rationality of the choices of Kavka's hypothetical parties, perhaps we can infer the *collective rationality* of the outcome of their interaction for us. Despite the fact that, as noted previously, we cannot use the inheritance principle to infer the collective rationality of an outcome from the individual rationality of the actions that produce it, we might try to use the collective rationality principle instead. It might be the case that the hypothetical scenario is so constructed as to insure both the individual and collective rationality of its outcomes. In fact, Kavka's account of the choice that his hypothetical parties would make, if correct, suffices to establish that all the forms of political association they might choose would share in common the property of being collectively rational relative to the state of nature. He purports to prove that the parties in the hypothetical negotiation scenario would agree only to form political associations which are collectively rational.

Kavka argues that the parties to the hypothetical negotiations would be guided by the "disaster avoidance" principle of rational decision making. This principle recommends that when an

> agent faces a choice among potential disasters [for him] under uncertainty . . . [he should choose] the course of action that minimizes the probability of ending up with a disastrous outcome, the act with the lowest disaster potential. The basic intuition underlying the principle is that under uncertainty, with much at risk (as there will be if disastrous outcomes are possible), it is rational to play it safe by doing one's best to avoid unacceptable outcomes. (Kavka, p. 203)[27]

Reasoning in accordance with the disaster avoidance principle, the parties necessarily will agree, according to Kavka, on some form of political association which incorporates an economic minimum and certain fundamental political rights for everyone. Such a State necessarily will be collectively rational relative to the state of nature. Kavka maintains that the parties to the hypothetical negotiations would voluntarily agree to a State only because

> it solves their security problems *without imposing on them harms or risks worse than they could expect to suffer under anarchy*. The terms of the founding agreement insure this by providing the parties with physical security, economic security and opportunity, personal and civil liberties, safeguards against tyranny, and minimal risks of revolution. This [demonstrates that the] . . . State is rationally preferred to the state of nature. (Kavka, p. 236; emphasis added)

27 Note that this principle differs from Rawls's maximin principle which recommends that when making decisions under uncertainty, individuals choose that outcome which maximizes the minimum utility an agent might receive. See Kavka, pp. 205–9, for a comparison between the disaster avoidance and the maximin principles.

If we grant that Kavka's claim is correct, and that the parties to his negotiations would in fact only agree upon those forms of political association which are collectively rational relative to the state of nature, then it follows that those same forms of political association would be collectively rational for us. For by demonstrating the collective rationality of certain forms of political association for the parties in the hypothetical negotiation scenario, Kavka has thereby – by virtue of the collective rationality principle – demonstrated the collective rationality of those forms of political association for everyone whose alternative is the state of nature. In short, Kavka's demonstration, if successful, proves that those forms of political association are collectively rational relative to the state of nature. From this claim, it follows that they are collectively rational for us, granting (as we are) that our alternative to political association is the Hobbesian state of nature Kavka describes. Although the inheritance principle cannot be used in Kavka's theory to explain why it would be individually rational for us to agree to a political association, the collective rationality principle can be used to explain why the political association to which parties in the hypothetical negotiation scenario would agree is also collectively rational for us.

Hobbesian contractarianism purports, however, to establish more than the mere collective rationality of political association. Kavka claims that it demonstrates the moral legitimacy of political association. His claim is that Hobbesian contractarianism proves that those forms of political association to which his hypothetical negotiators would agree legitimately can be imposed on us (or alternatively, that we have good moral reasons for obeying political authorities in states of the sort which his hypothetical parties would agree to form). The collective rationality of a State provides one reason for obeying its commands, but it hardly suffices to establish its moral legitimacy. The inheritance principle, of course, claims that the morality of an outcome might be inferred from the morality of the interactions producing it. Can the inheritance principle justify an inference from the

morality of the outcome of Kavka's hypothetical negotiations to the morality of imposing the terms of that outcome
on us? Can the inheritance principle demonstrate that because the individuals in the hypothetical setting have moral
reason to obey the political authority they create, we would
therefore have a moral reason to obey a similar political
authority as well?

I have argued that there is a defensible version of the
inheritance principle which licenses an inference from the
actions of minimally moral individuals to the moral legitimacy of imposing the outcome of their interactions not only
on them, but on others similarly situated. But Kavka cannot
avail himself of this version of the inheritance principle because the parties to the hypothetical negotiations are not
minimally moral. Although they interact under what Kavka
supposes to be moral circumstances, and their *ex ante* negotiation positions are supposed to be morally unobjectionable
as well, they are motivated not by a concern to conform to
morality, but by a concern to advance their predominantly
self-regarding interests.[28] Moreover, if Kavka were to stipulate that the parties were minimally moral persons, he would
risk begging the question against those who reject his conception of what the minimal requirements of morality are.
The resulting justification of political association would be
no stronger than his independent arguments for the moral
theory presupposed in his hypothetical negotiation scenario. In another context, Kavka argues that even predomi-

---

28 The key to understanding why the parties' *ex ante* positions going into
the hypothetical negotiations are morally unobjectionable is that whatever their current position in society, the point of no agreement for the
negotiations is the state of nature. This fact greatly reduces, if not
eliminates, any bargaining leverage they might have by virtue of previously acquired undeserved, or unfair, advantages. Contrary to Rawls,
however, Kavka maintains that knowledge of their personal characteristics does not constitute an unfair advantage in the negotiations,
largely because he thinks the correlation between personal characteristics and future well-being in a prospective political association is
tenuous, and that individuals will also care for the well-being of family
members and friends who are not advantaged by favorable personal
characteristics. See Kavka, pp. 195–9.

nantly egoistic parties are capable of being motivated by moral considerations, like maintaining rules of "fair play."[29] But even if we concede this, the mere possibility of various parties sometimes having moral motivations of varying strengths hardly suffices to guarantee that all or even most parties are minimally moral parties in the sense I have described. To be sure, Kavka, in any event, presupposes certain moral propositions in constructing his hypothetical negotiation scenario. We have seen, for example, that the coalition prohibition is in part justified on the ground that it prevents unfairness in the voting procedure. But the moral suppositions already embedded within Kavka's hypothetical setting are a far cry from the complete moral theory he would need to presuppose if he were to stipulate that the parties were minimally moral, and thus complied with all moral requirements.

Nor will it help to return to the alternative explication of the more robust version of the inheritance principle. Instead of positing minimally moral persons, that explication simply interpreted the inheritance principle as licensing the inference of an outcome's morality from the fact that interactions "required by moral reasoning" produce it. But to determine what is required by moral reasoning, Kavka will require no less than the same complete moral theory he would need to determine what minimally moral persons would do. These two determinations are one and the same.

Kavka might respond that while the parties to the hypothetical negotiation are not morally motivated, their interactions, and thus the outcomes of their interactions, are guaranteed to meet all moral requirements because they take place under "moral circumstances." This response rejects the notion of embedding a complete moral theory in the hypothetical setting by defining the parties as having moral motivation. Instead, it seeks to embed sufficiently many moral ideals into their circumstances to insure that even outcomes resulting from rational actors "ruthlessly" pursuing predominantly self-regarding interests will be morally

29 See Kavka, p. 405.

acceptable. In effect, the claim is that, try as they might to be ruthless, the circumstances of negotiation will insure that the parties will be able to act only as morality requires.

The fundamental problem with this account is that even if it is correct, it cannot explain why the outcomes of the parties' interaction in the hypothetical negotiation scenario can be morally imposed on us. For unlike the version of the hypothetical negotiations in which the parties are minimally moral, the results of interaction in Kavka's negotiations – even conceding the morality of the circumstances surrounding the negotiations – are not necessarily morally required. Even if the circumstances guarantee that parties will not be able to act contrary to moral requirements, they would not guarantee that the parties will commit only those acts required by morality. For the outcomes of interaction in his scenario might be either merely morally permissible or morally ideal, yet not be morally required. And if the outcomes are not morally required, then we have no moral reason to impose them on others in similar circumstances. For the only intuition supporting the imposition of an outcome among one set of actors on another is that both are similarly situated and the former are doing what is necessary to comply with morality. Under these circumstances, failure to produce this outcome constitutes a *violation* of morality. But if one set of actors is merely acting consistently with morality, by committing either morally permissible or morally supererogatory acts, there is no moral reason why others in a similar situation should be compelled to do the same. The fact that the individuals in the hypothetical negotiations are operating under morally constrained circumstances cannot guarantee that the outcome of their interaction is one which morality requires. And the only device for assuring that the outcomes are morally mandatory requires Kavka to characterize his parties as minimally moral (or equivalently, to restrict the application of the inheritance principle to those outcomes which are required by moral reasoning). But this strategy, as I have argued above, will jeopardize the normative force of the Hobbesian justification of political association by grounding it in a pretheoretic or independently supported commitment to an entire moral theory. Such a strategy risks begging the question against those who would reject that theory, a risk Kavka is at pains to avoid.

Summary

In this chapter, I have explicated Gregory Kavka's Hobbesian theory and provided a critique of its central normative arguments. Kavka's theory constitutes an innovative and unique effort to combine both Hobbesian and Rawlsian insights in a dualistic contractarian framework. In addition to providing a stage-one definition and stage-two analysis of the state of nature, Hobbesian theory also presents a stage-one definition and stage-two analysis of a hypothetical negotiation scenario. Although the former accords, for the most part, with the goals of realistic constructionism, the latter aligns predominantly with the goals of idealistic constructionism. By stipulating the state of nature to be the point of no agreement in the hypothetical scenario, Kavka joins these two otherwise distinct hypothetical settings to form a coherent overall Hobbesian argument.

The foundation for the normative argument to establish the legitimacy of political association is provided by three distinct stage-three "bridge" principles, each of which purports to provide an account of the normative significance of the outcome of Hobbesian theory's hypothetical negotiation scenario. The first seeks to explain the normative force of agreements reached in the hypothetical negotiations by treating them as realistic reconstructions or predictions of the choices actual individuals would make. But this realistic strategy founders on the disparity between the idealistic characterization of the parties and circumstances of the hypothetical negotiations and the realistic character of the actual persons and circumstances that setting would, according to this argument, have to reconstruct. The second bridge principle relies on the idealistic construction of the hypothetical negotiations to argue that any outcome it produces necessarily would be one to which no legitimate objection could be made. For it defines a legitimate objection as one which would have been made by the parties to those negotiations. Apart from whether this claim would otherwise be plausible, this principle illicitly rules out as illegitimate the fundamental libertarian objection which a nonhypothetical individual who was not party to the hypothetical agreement might raise if that outcome were imposed upon him: namely, that imposing that outcome on him violates his autonomy because he did not give his actual consent to the outcome. Although the libertarian objection begs the question against the proponent of hypothetical consent, the "no legitimate objection" account begs the question against the libertarian objection through its operational definition of a legitimate objection. That definition excludes the possibility of the libertarian objection being raised as a consequence of the hypothetical structure of the definition of a legitimate objection, rather than on the ground that it is incompatible with reasoned rational and moral decision making.

The third and final bridge principle I considered is the inheritance principle. Once bifurcated into two prongs, this principle can be given an interpretation which provides a defensible general account of the normative significance of hypothetical actions. But the resulting principle is revealed to have a rationality prong of primarily heuristic value, its substantive content being tautological, and a morality prong of limited, albeit nontautological, scope. The former merely suggests that in order to determine what is ideally rational for nonideally rational actors in one set of circumstances, we simply imagine what ideally rational actors would do in similar circumstances. The latter demonstrates that what minimally moral persons would do in one set of circumstances would be morally required for others to do in similar circumstances. But when applied to Hobbesian contractarianism, this principle fails to provide an adequate account of the normative significance of the outcome of the hypothetical negotiations. Although as a distinct principle, the collective rationality principle demonstrates at most that such outcomes would be collectively rational for us, the inheritance principle cannot explain why these outcomes would be morally legitimate to impose on nonhypothetical persons.

The failure of the inheritance principle to account for the normative significance of these outcomes is due to the failure of the hypothetical negotiation scenario to insure that outcomes it generates are morally required. It can be designed to produce morally ideal outcomes, but these unavoidably will include morally supererogatory outcomes which cannot legitimately be imposed on others. Alternatively, it could be designed to produce morally required outcomes which only minimally moral persons would produce. But while this design would insure the applicability of the inheritance principle, and successfully provide an account of the normative significance of hypothetical agreement in Hobbesian contractarianism, it would also require an independent or pretheoretic commitment to a robust moral theory. Such a commitment would seriously undermine the normative minimalism to which Hobbesian contractarianism aspires and instead would invite the charge that the theory begs fundamental normative questions at its foundation. In the final analysis, Kavka's creative attempt to merge realistic and idealistic constructionism is undermined by the inevitable tensions these contradictory strategies create. For the normative principles upon which the ultimate conclusion of contractarianism is built can at most support one strategy or the other, but not both.

Chapter 5

Gauthier's moral contractarianism

Hobbesian contractarianism is traditionally thought to be a political theory, one which purports to refute the anarchist and establish the conditions for the legitimate exercise of political coercion. But the province of political theory is not entirely independent from other normative inquiries. Indeed, it might be argued that much of political philosophy, properly conceived, falls within the larger rubric of moral theory, insofar as its defining inquiry concerns the nature of the justification or legitimacy of political authority. For the question of whether a political authority is legitimate is the same question as whether that authority is *morally* justified.[1] It should be unsurprising, then, that the contractarian framework might serve not only as a theoretical approach to understanding the question of political legitimacy, but also as a perspicuous methodology for exploring the nature of moral justification in general. In fact, it would be surprising if in the course of any theoretical exploration of the nature of political legitimacy, the question of moral justification did not also arise in its own right. This prediction is borne out in Hampton's work, where Hobbes's justification of the state is seen to depend on a meta-ethical reduction of morality to individual rationality. Similarly, in Kavka's enterprise, the normative force of agreement in his hypothetical negotiation

---

1 Indeed, these issues seem to merge in Rawls's work, where rational choice in a contractarian setting is used to derive moral principles (i.e., the principles of justice) which set forth the conditions for political legitimacy.

scenario is seen ultimately to depend upon whether that scenario adequately embeds certain fundamental moral ideals.[2]

While the search for political justification will inevitably lead to some meta-ethical inquiry, the latter is an important and arguably more foundational topic in its own right. Contractarian theory therefore can be conceived as raising meta-ethical issues only indirectly, attendant to a principal effort to derive conditions for political legitimacy, or directly, as a primary object in itself. David Gauthier's theory exemplifies this latter conception and is therefore a moral Hobbesian contractarian theory designed to answer a distinct set of questions in moral theory. His theory undertakes to answer the age-old question of the relationship between morality and rationality, and bears on the question of political authority only incidentally, as a consequence of the position it advances in meta-ethics. Yet the implications of Gauthier's theory for political Hobbesian contractarianism are quite direct.

FROM POLITICAL TO MORAL HOBBESIAN CONTRACTARIANISM

The success of any political Hobbesian contractarian theory will require some defense of the claim that political association is, or is quite likely to be, collectively rational relative to the anarchistic state of nature. The most compelling case for this claim would be one which convincingly demonstrates that most interaction in the state of nature has the structure of the single-play PD. For to the extent that the individuals

---

2 A complete assessment of these political contractarians' work, thus, would require not only the internal critique I have provided, but an evaluation of the plausibility of the meta-ethical views their theories presuppose. I have not endeavored to provide such an evaluation other than by arguing that, *pace* Hampton, Hobbes's metaphysical and meta-ethical views do not logically compel him to embrace a reduction of morality to individual rationality; and by arguing Kavka's theory can succeed only by begging fundamental questions in moral theory.

populating the state of nature are rational – as every Hobbesian contractarian in large measure supposes them to be – they would be unable to cooperate in the single-play PD. Or so the game-theoretic definition of the single-play PD would seem to entail.

In *Morals by Agreement*, however, David Gauthier questions the apparently unquestionable claim that cooperation in the single-play PD is irrational. By rejecting the received definition of individual rationality in game theory, Gauthier hopes to prove that rational cooperation in the single-play PD is possible. If his argument succeeds, he has at the very least seriously jeopardized the conventional bases for the claim that cooperation is unlikely in the state of nature. For if individually rational cooperation is possible in the single-play PD, it is all the more likely in the quasi- and iterated PD's which characterize interaction in Kavka's and Hampton's states of nature. In undermining the strongest case for the irrationality of cooperation in the state of nature, Gauthier's argument threatens a crucial plank in the foundation of political Hobbesian contractarianism. The stage-two analysis of the state of nature, to which political Hobbesian contractarians like Hampton and Kavka are committed, would demonstrate neither the individual nor collective rationality of forming a political association. If the state of nature is not a state of conflict, as Hobbes's "war of all against all" scenario claims, then political association cannot be viewed as a solution to a problem of noncooperation in the state of nature. The Hobbesian argument that individuals living in the state of nature would find it rational to create a political association in order to solve their collective action problem would fail. For they would have no collective action problem to solve. Thus, in effect, Gauthier purports to demonstrate the possibility of a collectively rational anarchy, not by defending a different game-theoretic model of the state of nature, but by challenging the conception of rationality according to which defection is thought to be the dominant strategy in a single-play PD.

A theory explaining the rationality of cooperation in the

single-play PD would indeed have profound implications for political Hobbesian contractarianism, as well as the field of rational choice in general. But even if successful, we might still wonder whether such a demonstration serves only the critical purpose of undermining the political Hobbesian contractarian's argument, or serves as well to establish the morality of anarchy. In order to defend the anarchist, it may not be enough merely to refute the contractarian. The failure of a justification of political coercion, we might argue, does not by itself constitute a defense of anarchy. Although individuals living in anarchy have no state to hold accountable for its exercise of force, they nonetheless may have legitimate moral complaints against their fellows. For if morality applies equally in anarchy and polity, the harm one suffers at the hands of others in anarchy provides no less a ground for moral complaint than the harm one suffers at the hands of the state.[3] The moral comparison between polity and anarchy cannot simply prefer the latter in the absence of an independent justification for the former. Instead, it must balance whatever unchecked and morally unjustified state coercion exists under polity against whatever unbridled and morally objectionable behavior takes place in anarchy. Thus, Gauthier's demonstration of the rationality of cooperation in the state of nature, even if correct, leaves room to question the moral legitimacy of anarchy unless he can show that such cooperation is morally acceptable as well. And in order to prove that cooperation in an anarchistic state of nature would be morally acceptable, Gauthier must supplement his account of the rationality of cooperation with a proof of its *fairness* as well. For cooperation can be moral only if its terms are fair.

Gauthier does in fact claim that rational cooperation in the state of nature would be fair, and the central concern of this chapter is to evaluate this claim. But, as I have noted, Gauthier advances the claim that cooperation in the state of

---

3 Of course, Hobbes himself argued that in the state of nature, morality was binding *in foro interno* only.

nature would be rational and fair in the course of building a moral Hobbesian contractarian theory, and not in order to refute the political Hobbesian contractarian. His theory is designed, first and foremost, to uncover the fundamental relationship between morality and rationality, not to address the political Hobbesian contractarian's question of the legitimacy of political association. His central concern is to advance the thesis that the demands of morality can be reconciled, indeed reduced to, the demands of individual rationality, once the latter is properly understood. As a moral theorist, Gauthier hopes to refute the moral skeptic by deriving both the content of moral principles and the motivation to behave morally from the concept of individual rationality. I have just argued that Gauthier's moral enterprise has implications for the political Hobbesian enterprise as well. His refutation of the moral skeptic would serve to refute the Hobbesian contractarian as well, for a demonstration of the morality of anarchy would appear to undermine the Hobbesian case for polity. But while the consequences of Gauthier's theory for political Hobbesian contractarianism are important, his theory deserves to be considered in its own right, as a unique and powerful contribution to moral Hobbesian contractarian thought. In this chapter, my primary objective is to explicate and evaluate Gauthier's moral contractarian theory.

GAUTHIER'S MORAL CONTRACTARIANISM

Gauthier's moral contractarianism is, in its broadest terms, an effort to uncover the relationship between morality and rationality. Gauthier begins by isolating what he takes to be relatively simple and uncontroversial core definitions for these concepts. He defines rationality as it is defined in contemporary microeconomics: rationality is utility maximization.[4] The rational actor seeks to maximize his net ex-

---

4 The notion of utility maximization employed here is the mathematical notion employed by economists whereby the maximization of utility is

pected utility. Defining rationality in this way enables him to contrast rationality with morality by defining the latter as requiring, at least on some occasions, that individuals constrain their rational action. On this view, morality is defined in part as constrained utility maximization.[5] The moral actor sometimes acts so as to constrain his utility-maximizing behavior. Given these definitions, rationality and morality are incompatible. The purely rational individual, at least sometimes, must act immorally; the purely moral individual, at least sometimes, must act irrationally. So conceived, the project of reconciling morality and rationality would appear futile. But Gauthier claims that the rational requirement of utility maximization which generates the apparent contradiction between morality and rationality has been fundamentally misunderstood. Gauthier's argument proceeds from his conception of the role of morality within a rational choice framework.

The rational choice framework

One way of framing the question of whether morality is derivable from rationality is in contractarian terms: Under what conditions, if any, would rational agents agree to constrain their utility-maximizing behavior? Gauthier begins to

represented by the maximization of a utility function, itself generated from an ordinal preference calculus. Talk of utility here does not imply interpersonal comparisons of utility, standard utilitarian moral theory, or any dubious metaphysical commitments. All reference to utility maximization can in fact be replaced with preference satisfaction.

5 This definition provides, at best, a necessary condition for a principle to be a moral principle. Of course, there is surely more to the concept of morality than constraint on utility maximization. And as I explain below, Gauthier recognizes that not all principles of constraint will qualify as moral principles; only those that require fair constraint are plausible candidates. However, even a fair principle of constraint might not qualify as a moral principle. But Gauthier is content to show that moral principles, so understood, can be derived from rationality. He does not reach the question of whether a more robust conception of morality would be similarly reducible.

answer this question by answering another question: Can circumstances be specified in which it would be irrational to impose constraints on one's self-interested, utility-maximizing behavior? In this light, he considers the economist's concept of perfect competition. Under conditions of perfect competition, the individually rational, self-interested behavior of all agents induces a Pareto efficient outcome.[6] Pareto efficient states have no states Pareto superior to them. In optimal equilibria therefore each actor does as well as he can – that is, his utility is maximized subject to the utility maximization of others. If, by acting purely self-interestedly, each agent does as well as he or she can, then it would be irrational for any agent to impose restrictions on the pursuit of his self-interest. If, given the utility of others, I do the best I can by pursuing my self-interest, then I will necessarily do less well by constraining my self-interested behavior. Under conditions of perfect competition, then, the rational actor has no incentive to adopt constraints, moral or other, on his utility-maximizing behavior. Compliance with moral principles would be irrational.

However, when markets fail (which, in the real world, they will do almost without exception) and conditions of perfect competition do not obtain, the self-interested, utility-

---

6 The conditions of perfect competition can be summarized, roughly, as: (1) All individuals in the market behave as price takers (i.e., they choose consumption and production bundles subject to fixed positive prices). (2) All producers sell commodities that are identical with respect to physical characteristics, location, and time of availability. (3) There is no cost involved in exchanging commodities, and there is free entry into and exit from the market. (4) Producers and consumers possess perfect information concerning the price, physical characteristics, and availability of each commodity.

Pareto efficiency is usually defined in terms of preferences: A state, S_1, is Pareto optimal if and only if there is no feasible alternative state, S_2, such that at least one person prefers S_2 to S_1 and such that no one prefers S_1 to S_2. A state, S_1, is Pareto superior to a state, S_2, if and only if at least one person prefers S_1 to S_2 and no one prefers S_2 to S_1. Pareto efficiency can also be defined in terms of utility (roughly) by substituting "is better off in" for "prefers" in the above definitions.

maximizing behavior of each individual leads to a Pareto inefficient outcome – that is, one in which at least some individuals could be made better off without worsening the condition of others. The possibility then arises that, by constraining her utility-maximizing behavior, an individual may be made better off than if she continues, unconstrained, to pursue her self-interest. By introducing constraints on the utility-maximizing behavior of individuals, it may be possible to secure Pareto efficient outcomes in which an individual fares better than she would were she to act as an unconstrained utility maximizer. There would then be a rational motivation for compliance with normative principles – principles which Gauthier argues are moral principles – which require constraint. Though the perfectly competitive market might well be likened to what Gauthier calls a "morally free zone" of "moral anarchy," in which moral constraints are irrational, the imperfectly competitive market represents a "normatively constrained zone," in which moral constraints might well be rational.[7]

Morality, according to Gauthier, is a potential solution to the problem of market failure. Because morality is introduced to govern social interactions only under conditions of market failure, it is rendered fundamentally instrumental. The rationality of morality depends on its being a particular kind of solution to the problem of market failure: one that secures a Pareto efficient outcome by making each individual better off. To be a viable solution to the problem of market failure, morality must be both individually and collectively rational. Moreover, the case for morality generated by the market model is entirely contingent. But the contingency on which it rests is one virtually certain to obtain: markets are never perfectly competitive.

The view that compliance with morality would solve the problem of market failure can, for our purposes, be recast as the view that compliance with morality would solve the single-play PD. To see this, consider the two fundamental

---

7 See Gauthier, p. 84.

problems which underlie the irrationality of cooperation in the single-play PD. First, given that the parties' rational strategies are defined as those which maximize their utility, neither will comply with an arrangement which requires him to forgo his utility-maximizing strategy. Moreover, reaching agreement often presents difficulties in its own right, insofar as each individual will have a stake in striking a deal which disproportionately serves his interests. We might call this "the compliance problem." Second, given the compliance problem, it would be irrational for the parties even to agree on pursuing the non-utility-maximizing strategy. For each would know that the other will be rationally compelled to defect from such an agreement. It would therefore be irrational to waste resources in reaching an agreement to which compliance is irrational and thus inevitably not forthcoming from rational persons. We might call this "the agreement problem." Of course, the costs associated with coming to agreement in the actual example of the single-play PD are trivial, for the cooperative strategy is predefined by the game as mutual non-confession. And the payoffs accruing to each party as a result of joint compliance with that strategy (i.e., the division of the gains from an agreement not to confess) are fixed in the definition of the game (e.g., one year in jail instead of ten). However, other games with the structure of the single-play PD do not come with a predefined apportionment of the gains available to each party as a result of successful cooperation. Thus, the costs of reaching agreement on a cooperative joint strategy, quite apart from the problem of securing compliance with such an agreement, can be quite significant. Individuals must bargain over the division of the cooperative surplus which mutual compliance with a joint cooperative strategy will create. This cost is not worth incurring if joint compliance cannot be expected.

If compliance with moral principles – principles which require the constraint of direct utility maximization – were rational, then both problems underlying the single-play PD could be overcome. For if such constraint is rational, it might be rational for individuals to forgo their directly utility-maximizing strategy and to comply with a nondirectly utility-maximizing strategy. Given that compliance with such a strategy is possible, making the effort to reach agreement on that strategy might be rational as well, provided the problem of agreeing on a division of the cooperative gains can be solved. And the outcome of pursuing this strategy of course would be Pareto efficient. By purporting to demonstrate that compliance with moral principles can be rational, Gauthier thereby hopes to demonstrate how nondirectly utility-maximizing behavior, and thus cooperation in the single-play PD, can be rational.

The problem of deriving morality from rationality, then, can be understood as the problem of demonstrating that in the state of nature, there is a joint cooperative strategy with which most ideally rational individuals would comply, and therefore to which most ideally rational individuals would agree. Gauthier's derivation of morality from rationality, thus, requires him to provide an account of how ideally rational persons could come to agree on a joint cooperative strategy (assuming that compliance with such an agreement would be rational), and then an account of the rationality of compliance with that strategy. The account of how ideally rational persons in the state of nature could come to agree on the division of the cooperative surplus generated by mutual compliance with a joint cooperative strategy constitutes Gauthier's substantive theory of morality. It provides the derivation of the content of the principles of morality from individual rationality. The account of why ideally rational persons would comply with this agreement constitutes Gauthier's motivational theory of morality. It provides the derivation of the motivation to comply with moral principles from individual rationality. Once his motivational theory of morality is in place, then, the overall structure of Gauthier's problem becomes clear. He must demonstrate that ideally rational individuals in the state of nature would be able to solve what amounts to a mixed coordination game like the Battle-of-the-Sexes game we considered in Chapter 3. If these individuals are unable to agree on a division of the gains from cooperation, they will be unable to realize any gains at all. Each individual has an incentive to cooperate in order to generate mutual gains, but to insist on the largest share of the gains as a condition precedent to his cooperation. In Gauthier's project, the derivation of the substantive and motivational theories of morality is provided by a theory of the solution to this rational bargaining problem so conceived.[8]

Thus, compliance and agreement are inexorably linked in Gauthier's rational choice framework. There is no sense in pursuing agreement on a cooperative joint strategy if rationality precludes compliance. And there is no point in demonstrating the rationality of such compliance, if rationality precludes securing agreement on a cooperative joint strategy. In this chapter, I will grant Gauthier's two central claims, but only in their weakest form. First, I will grant that there exists some solution to the agreement problem: There is a correct theory of the bargaining process which demonstrates how and why rational agents will agree on some joint cooperative strategy. Thus, I will concede, for present purposes, that there is some solution to the problem of securing agreement on a joint cooperative strategy among ideally rational agents. Second, I will grant that there exists some solution to the compliance problem: It is, under certain circumstances, individually rational to cooperate in the single-play PD. In particular, I will assume, for present purposes, that Gauthier's theory of constrained maximization, explained

---

8 There are any number of constraints, various subsets of which would enable individuals to capture the surplus. We might say, then, that various sets of constraints all possess the efficiency property, that is, each set will be capable of bridging the gap between the suboptimal equilibrium of the PD and the optimal equilibria of perfect competition. Alternatives differ, however, in the manner in which they distribute the gains from cooperation. In pursuing agreement on a set of moral constraints, each actor is exploring alternative ways of distributing the gains from cooperation. Moral maxims, therefore, have an intrinsic distributional component.

later, is correct. By granting these claims, I have already given more ground to Gauthier than many of his critics are prepared to concede.[9] But these concessions fall far short of conceding Gauthier's ultimate claim to have derived morality from rationality. For as we have seen, if Gauthier's model is to derive morality from rationality, he must demonstrate not only that rational individuals in the state of nature will agree to constrain their directly utility-maximizing behavior and will comply with that agreement, but that their agreement will be fair. The principles of constraint to which rational individuals agree must be fair and impartial if they are to qualify as moral principles. Thus, I will take issue with the relatively stronger claims Gauthier advances in order to defend his claim that morality can be derived from rationality. I will reject his contention that the only constraining principles with which rational persons in the state of nature would comply are fair ones, and that therefore the only constraining principles to which such parties would bargain are fair as well.

The claim that ideally rational individuals in the state of nature would agree to and comply with only fair principles appears, on its face, to be obviously false. In a bargaining situation, failure to secure agreement returns parties to their prebargain positions – the status quo ante. The way in which the parties evaluate their prebargain position will naturally influence their bargaining behavior in ways that are likely to affect outcomes. If inequity or unfairness exists in the initial position, it is likely to be influential in the bargaining process. Even if it is not influential there, however, it will be transmitted by the bargaining process to the outcomes, thereby raising doubts about the fairness of the resulting principles.[10] The initial problem with the claim that rational bargains are fair ones, then, is the problem of the unfair status quo ante: The principles chosen in bargaining from

9 See, for example, Peter Vallentyne, ed., *Contractarianism and Rational Choice* (Cambridge University Press, 1991).
10 See n. 15.

unfair initial positions will almost certainly be unfair; yet the unfairness of the outcome of bargaining would not appear to preclude its rationality. Rational bargains, we would normally believe, need not be fair ones. So why does Gauthier think that morality would be the outcome of a rational bargain?

One solution to the problem of the unfair status quo ante is to follow Kavka (and Rawls) and simply define the bargaining scenario as one in which all parties begin bargaining from a fair status quo ante. Instead of advancing the counterintuitive claim that every rational bargain is fair, Gauthier can maintain that only certain rational bargains – those struck under certain conditions – need be fair. In particular, he can argue that only rational bargains struck from fair initial conditions in the state of nature necessarily produce constraints that are fair and impartial in the sense necessary for them to constitute a morality. The point of Gauthier's enterprise, after all, is to hit upon moral principles, and bargaining from unfair initial positions is unlikely to serve that purpose well.

This simple solution is, unfortunately, too simple. All contractarians, of course, must define their hypothetical scenario in stage one of their argument. But to the extent they presuppose normative values in this definition, they beg the question against those who reject those values. The only normative presupposition Gauthier intends to make in his hypothetical scenario is that of rationality. Were he "artificially" to stipulate that the status quo ante of the parties in his hypothetical scenario is fair, he would have shown only that morality can be derived from rationality and fairness, not rationality alone. Gauthier wants to avoid presupposing any controversial normative value other than his narrow conception of individual rationality. Thus, precluding unfair initial bargaining positions *a priori* would undermine the enterprise of deriving morality from rationality alone. Instead, it derives morality from rationality and fairness.

Instead of defining away the problem of the status quo ante, Gauthier's strategy is to avoid presupposing fairness in his hypothetical bargaining scenario by arguing that, in the state of nature, bargaining from an unfair status quo ante is irrational. Indeed, it is Gauthier's claim that, in the state of nature, the only kind of bargains which are rational to make and keep are ones which not only proceed from a fair status quo ante, but which are fair in all other respects as well. His argument can be put quite simply:

1. Bargaining is rational only if compliance is rational.
2. Compliance is rational only if the bargain outcome is fair.
3. Therefore, bargaining is rational only if it is fair.
4. Therefore, rational bargains must be fair bargains.
5. Therefore, bargaining from whatever unfair advantages one may have *ex ante* is not rational.

Support for the conclusion of the argument is straightforward: Bargaining from unfair positions yields unfair outcomes with which it is not rational to comply. But if it is not rational to comply, then it is not rational to bargain. The upshot of this argument is that demonstrating the rationality of complying with bargains suffices to prove the irrationality of entering into unfair bargains. This, then, is the argument one needs to make in order to derive morality from a bargain-theoretic conception of rationality.

Fairness and constrained maximization

I noted earlier that Gauthier's approach to morality requires a solution to the compliance problem. As a general solution to the compliance problem, Gauthier advances his "theory of constrained maximization." I do not take issue with the theory of constrained maximization as such, but several of the arguments that follow require at least a rudimentary understanding of it and of several distinctions upon which it relies.

Game theorists have long recognized the possible rationality of compliance in the iterated PD, but Gauthier focuses instead on the possibility of rational compliance in the single-play PD. He begins by noting that people are likely to face interaction with the structure of the single-play PD repeatedly over the course of their lives. That is, people can anticipate that they will interact repeatedly in the single-play PD not with the same party but with different parties at different times. If one could acquire a disposition which prevented one from abiding by the maxims of straightforward utility maximization and instead demanded compliance when engaged in a PD-structured bargain, then one could benefit repeatedly from collective action with others similarly disposed. The idea is that such a disposition could serve to precommit a rational actor to compliance in the single-play PD when such compliance is likely to be beneficial. Just as Ulysses's being bound to the mast enables him to hear the Sirens yet resist their call, a disposition to comply in the single-play PD with others similarly disposed would enable an individual over the long run to benefit from cooperation otherwise not possible for rational actors.

In order to bring about compliance in a single-play PD, the disposition Gauthier envisions would have to amount to a self-imposed psychological guarantee of compliance, one which cannot be resisted. If it could be resisted, then it would appear that straightforward maximizers would resist it in PD-structured bargains in order to maximize utility, and so adoption of it would not result in successful collective action. But because Gauthier wants to claim that rational actors so disposed are still making a choice, and thus bargaining, when they cooperate in the PD, he wants the disposition to fall short of psychological compulsion. Nonetheless, because he wants this disposition to influence their choice to cooperate, it must be strong enough to override consideration of direct utility maximization. It is difficult to conceptualize what such a disposition could be and even more troublesome to contemplate its psychological plausibility. But for present purposes, I will grant that such a disposition is plausible to achieve.

The question then is not simply whether it is sometimes rational for strategic reasons to comply with the bargains one strikes, but whether it is rational so to dispose oneself.

Gauthier argues that under certain conditions, it is in fact rational to dispose oneself to compliance. The conditions are, roughly, that a threshold number of compliance-disposed persons exists and that individuals are neither "opaque" nor "transparent" but are instead "translucent" with respect to their dispositions for compliance. In other words, if there is a reasonably good chance that you are negotiating with a compliance-disposed person and the chances are pretty good that you will be identified for what you truly are (a complier or a defector), then it is rational to dispose yourself to compliance. To say it is rational to dispose yourself to compliance is to say that you will maximize your utility over time by doing so. Once you are rationally disposed, it will be rational for you to do what you are disposed to do – that is, to comply even if you may be taken advantage of from time to time by defectors or even if you might do better on occasion by defecting and, thereby, taking advantage of others. The idea is that the benefits from the collective action such a disposition will make possible will outweigh these costs.

In what follows, I grant that constrained maximization is a correct solution to the compliance problem. The crucial issue, I will argue, is whether *narrow compliance* – roughly the disposition to comply only with fair bargains – is uniquely rational.

Fairness and bargaining

Moral principles are constraints. Not every constraint is, however, a moral one. Moral principles are constraints that are "fair and impartial." The outcome of a bargain is moral only if it is fair. In order to argue that the outcome of rational bargaining will be fair, Gauthier must first offer an independent substantive theory of fairness with which to assess the fairness of the outcomes of rational bargains. Gauthier's substantive theory of fairness is not derived from within his contractarian theory. Instead, it is introduced as a pretheoretic and exogenous theory, one which supplies a necessary condition to be satisfied by any principles which purport to be moral principles. Like any moral theorist, Gauthier must accept some criteria of adequacy or correctness against which the results of his theory can be tested. Because Gauthier claims that the normative principles to which rational parties would agree are fair and therefore moral principles, it is incumbent upon him to prove that those normative principles satisfy some plausible theory of fairness. He endorses the view, with respect to distributive fairness, that the distributions are fair if and only if they accord each person gains proportionate to his or her contribution.[11] With respect to initial allocations, he endorses a modified version of the Lockean proviso.[12] Both these views of fairness, in distribution and acquisition, are of course controversial. The former Gauthier assumes but does not defend. The latter, Gauthier claims, is both favored by pretheoretic intuition and would be adopted by ideally rational agents. I do not take issue with Gauthier's substantive claims concerning fairness. Although it is surely possible to question the adequacy of Gauthier's theory of fairness, my intention is to demonstrate the failure of *Morals by Agreement* to generate an adequate moral theory on its own terms and thus its own standards.

Considerations of fairness enter Gauthier's account at three distinct places. The first is within the theory of rational bargaining in which rational persons, it is argued, agree to a set of fair constraining principles as the result of following a uniquely rational bargaining principle.[13] The second is within the theory of constrained maximization in which, it is ar-

---

11 See Gauthier, p. 154: "[I]f a fair or impartial distribution of the cooperative surplus relates the benefit each receives to the contribution he makes, each person's fair share of the surplus is determined by making shares proportional to claims."

12 See Gauthier, pp. 200–32.

13 Gauthier argues that the correct principle of ideal rational bargaining is the principle of "minimax relative concession." This principle and the important condition under which it is thought to obtain are discussed in the section of this chapter entitled "Equal Rationality and Equal Compliance."

gued, rational individuals dispose themselves to comply only with fair constraining principles. The third is within Gauthier's theory of fair initial bargaining positions in which, it is argued, rational bargaining in the state of nature necessarily proceeds from a fair status quo ante.[14] It follows that there are two ways in which constraining principles might be unfair or biased and, therefore, not moral. First, the bargaining procedure itself might be unfair. If it is, the principles specifying the distribution of the cooperative surplus might allow some to gain in greater proportion to their contribution than others. Second, the initial bargaining position might be unfair, in which case even a fair bargaining procedure (i.e., one in which each individual gains in proportion to his contribution) will embed and transmit this unfairness to the constraining principles to which persons bargain.

Unfairness in the initial bargaining position may be transmitted to the outcome of bargaining in one of three ways. First, if as a result of an unfair initial position some parties are able to contribute more to a cooperative venture than others, those advantaged individuals will be accorded greater shares of the cooperative surplus. Then, even if the bargaining process itself is fair in that it accords each a share of the surplus proportionate to his or her contribution, the resulting distribution is unfair because it transmits and amplifies the distortions created by unfairly acquired entitlements. Second, even if advantaged parties in the initial position do not contribute more to the bargain and contribute only that portion of their entitlements which would have been acquired in a fair initial position, the outcome may yet be unfair for either of two reasons. Those unfairly advantaged in the initial bargaining position retain their unfairly acquired entitlements after the bargain. This is just to say that even a fair bargaining procedure need not rectify unjust

---

14 Gauthier suggests a positive theory of just entitlement for the initial position. He holds that rational individuals will bargain only with those individuals whose possessions have been acquired in accordance with his version of the Lockean proviso.

prior distributions. Fair bargaining does not embed a principle of corrective or rectificatory justice.[15] And, it is also possible that those individuals whose entitlements were fairly acquired might have had more to bargain with in the initial position had no one else acquired entitlements unfairly.[16] Third, advantaged parties in the initial position might use their advantage to "coerce," "railroad," or "extort" a bargain from the disadvantaged which fails even to accord the disadvantaged a share of the cooperative surplus proportionate to their contributions. Here the unfair initial bargaining position induces an unfair bargaining procedure. In the first two kinds of cases the distortions existing in unfair starting points are transmitted to outcomes, thus polluting them either because a fair bargaining procedure is unable to rectify or correct prior unfair advantage or because fair bargaining may actually exacerbate prior distortions. In the third case, unfairly acquired initial entitlements are employed to distort the bargaining process itself by "extortion" or "coercion."

In order to derive morality from rational bargaining, the resulting principles must be fair and impartial. To demonstrate their fairness, Gauthier must argue that rational persons in the state of nature will bargain only from fair initial bargaining positions, engage only in bargains whose procedures are fair, and dispose themselves to comply only with constraining principles that result from a fair bargain origi-

15 I argue, in connection with Gauthier's argument from predation, for narrow compliance, that even this sort of unfairness must be sufficient for a bargain and its outcome to be unfair. Despite the fact that individuals who have prior, unfairly acquired entitlements may enter into new bargains, these new bargains must still be treated as unfair from the point of view of narrow compliance. That is, narrow compliers will not have the disposition to comply with these bargains in virtue of the unrectified unfair entitlements of some parties to the bargain. Otherwise, narrow compliance cannot induce individuals to refrain from predation; see the section "Narrow Compliance and Predation."

16 For example, if all players prior to the bargain were playing a zero-sum game, then those who unfairly acquire more entitlements necessarily diminish the entitlements available to others.

nating from a fair initial bargaining position. And of course, Gauthier must argue that such bargaining will take place without the benefit of external means of enforcement adequate to induce compliance. If bargaining is to succeed in the state of nature, it must be because the outcome commands rational compliance on its own merits.

So Gauthier's overall strategy is clear. He is nowhere committed to the view that all rational bargains, under any conditions, are fair. He is committed only to the claim that rational bargaining in the state of nature yields fair and impartial outcomes. He intends to argue that the only kind of bargains in the state of nature that can command rational compliance are fair ones and that bargaining from the unfair entitlements in the state of nature will yield unstable results because the terms of the bargain will be unfair. In the following section, I consider Gauthier's first argument for the unique rationality of complying with fair bargains. According to this argument, unfair bargains will be unstable, and since instability adversely affects the rationality of bargaining, only fair bargaining is rational.

FAIRNESS AND STABILITY

Gauthier begins his discussion of the initial bargaining position by considering a society of rational slaves and masters. In this society, the masters engage in costly coercion in order to force the slaves to do their bidding, while the slaves suffer the effects of coercion. Gauthier observes that this society is suboptimal: Alternative forms of interaction can enhance the well-being of some without making others worse off. In fact, there is a mutually advantageous bargain into which the slaves and masters might well enter. It would be rational, for example, for all to agree to continue their society as is, preserving the advantages and disadvantages of the caste system, while eliminating its coercive component. In such an agreement, masters are committed to eliminating coercion, and slaves are bound to serve their masters voluntarily. The bargain is Pareto improving since masters could then enjoy life free of the costs of coercing, and the slaves would be free of the costs of being coerced. Gauthier notes, however, that once coercion has been banned by agreement, and slaves and masters alike have improved their situation, the slaves will no longer find it rational to comply with their part of the bargain. They will simply walk away from the bargain since, in the absence of coercion, they have no incentive to do the bidding of their masters. The bargain, though Pareto improving, is fundamentally unstable. By demanding pay for services the slaves merely move the bargain along the Pareto frontier, giving them a greater share of the cooperative gains. Were the masters to reintroduce slavery both sides would return to the prebargain state which would fall within the frontier and, which, therefore, would be inefficient. The slaves' walking away and demanding pay is rational; the masters' threat to reintroduce slavery is not credible, since carrying it out would be inefficient. The slaves and masters end up with a situation in which the former slaves sell their labor to former slave owners. This is the stable outcome. The conclusions Gauthier wants to draw from this example are (1) that a bargain originating in an unfair initial position is unstable, (2) that it is unstable because it is unfair, (3) that it is unfair because it involves "unproductive transfers," and (4) that the stable outcome coincides with what would have been the outcome had the bargain originated in fair initial positions.

It is evident that the slaves would eventually find it irrational to continue to comply voluntarily with their agreement. The reason, as Gauthier puts it, is that they are being asked to make unproductive transfers: "An unproductive transfer brings no new goods into being and involves no exchange of existing goods; it simply redistributes some existing good from one person to another. Thus, it involves a utility cost for which no benefit is received, a utility gain for which no service is provided" (Gauthier, p. 197). The slaves have no incentive in the absence of coercion to continue making unproductive transfers. The masters are unable to reintroduce the former coercive arrangement in which slaves were slaves and masters were masters, since doing so would render everyone, including the masters, worse off than they would be under the implicit terms of the postbargain, post-defection arrangement. The masters are stuck with a freer, more egalitarian society – the one, moreover, that all would have agreed to had the initial bargaining position been fair.

Perhaps Gauthier has isolated an example in which a bargain from an unfair initial position will first result in an unstable outcome and eventually in a stable one identical to that which would have resulted had bargaining originated in a fair initial position. It may also be true that the instability in the initial outcome is due to the irrationality, in the absence of coercion, of making unproductive transfers. Gauthier's argument for the rationality of morality requires, however, that the specific case be generalizable: that, in other words, *all* unfair but rational bargains will prove unstable because they will induce rational defection.

One reason for thinking that unfair bargains will occasion rational defection is that unfair bargains involve unproductive transfers, and making an unproductive transfer voluntarily is irrational. The general argument can be put more rigorously:

1. Unfair bargains always require unproductive transfers.

Therefore,

2. Absent coercion, compliance with unfair bargains will always require voluntary unproductive transfers.
3. An act is rational only if it is directly utility maximizing.
4. An unproductive transfer is directly utility maximizing only if it is coerced.
5. Absent coercion, compliance with unfair bargains must be irrational.

Therefore,

6. Unfair and uncoerced bargains between rational individuals are necessarily unstable.
7. Only stable bargains are rational.

Therefore,

8. Only fair bargains are rational.

Consider first the claim, in premise 1, that unfair bargains always involve unproductive transfers. We earlier considered two ways in which an outcome of a bargain might be unfair. It might be the result of an unfair bargaining procedure or it might be the outcome of a bargain from an unfair initial bargaining position. Recall that a fair bargaining procedure is one which distributes the cooperative surplus in proportion to the contributions of individuals. If we consider only those outcomes of bargains which are unfair because they are the result of unfair bargaining procedures, we might suppose that the first premise in Gauthier's argument is correct. After all, if the outcome of a bargain is unfair because it is the result of an unfair bargaining procedure, then some individuals are not gaining in proportion to their contribution and are instead transferring a portion of their fair share to others.

However, if we consider those outcomes of bargains which are unfair in virtue of the unfair initial positions from which they originate, we see that these unfair outcomes need not involve unproductive transfers. Outcomes which are unfair because of the unfairness of the initial bargaining position can be unfair for several reasons, only one of which requires unproductive transfers. This is the case in which, as a result of an unfair bargaining advantage, one individual or group of individuals is able to use his (its) advantage to negotiate in an unfair bargaining process. These are bargains in which unfair initial positions induce an unfair bargaining procedure.

But unfair outcomes can result from unfair starting points for reasons other than the reason that the unfairness of the starting point induces extortion and thus affects the bargaining process, ultimately resulting in an outcome which requires unproductive transfers. An unfair outcome can result instead from a fair bargaining procedure that either distributes the cooperative surplus according to contributions themselves made possible only because of unfairly acquired entitlements, or fails to rectify the unfairness of the initial position so that, though others have not gained in the bargain as a result of their unfair advantage in the initial position, they still retain their relative advantage in the postbargain state of affairs.[17] Neither of these unfair outcomes requires individuals to make unproductive transfers. If it is not rational for individuals to comply with these outcomes, it cannot be because it is irrational for individuals to make voluntary unproductive transfers, since no such transfers need to be made. It is not true, then, that unfair bargains always require unproductive transfers. Premise 1 is therefore false. Thus, it does not follow that, absent coercion, compliance with unfair bargains will always require voluntary unproductive transfers. In fact, they need not require any unproductive transfers, much less voluntary ones. Therefore, premise 2 is false.

Is it true, as is claimed in premise 4, that an unproductive transfer is directly utility maximizing only if it is coerced? No. Whether an unproductive transfer can be directly utility maximizing in the absence of coercion depends on other available options, that is, on the opportunity costs of failing to make the unproductive transfer. We can, in fact, imagine cases in which unproductive transfers may be directly utility maximizing not because they are coerced but because the only alternative is a return to the initial bargaining position, an alternative which is mutually disadvantageous and thus irrational.[18] Return to the initial bargaining position need

17 These bargains, according to Gauthier's arguments, must be treated as unfair; see n. 15.
18 For example, suppose that the community of masters and slaves were to strike a somewhat different mutually advantageous bargain. According to it, the masters would no longer coerce the slaves so long as the slaves would fill undesirable jobs in the masters' manufacturing plants. It so happens, in virtue of contingent features of the relevant labor markets, that no manufacturing is possible without the slaves' filling these positions at the plants. Once manufacturing begins, there

not be the result of coercion; rather, it may be the result of contingent features of the nature of the joint strategy on which all parties agree. Nevertheless, it is a result rational parties must seek to avoid, even at the cost of making an unproductive transfer.

Gauthier believes that unfair bargains are inherently unstable because they involve unproductive transfers. Making an unproductive transfer is irrational because it is not directly utility maximizing. I have shown so far that bargains can be unfair without involving unproductive transfers.

is a huge cooperative surplus which is put to use in a mutually advantageous way. In this arrangement, the slaves are better off because they are no longer being coerced and they are getting paid for their work. The masters are better off because they no longer bear the costs of coercing and they enjoy the benefits of production without having to participate in the undesirable tasks involved in manufacturing. Because the masters handle all financial matters, we might suppose that they retain control over the distribution of the surplus. The masters pay themselves more for their jobs than they pay the slaves for working their jobs. Here, the cooperative surplus, *ex hypothesi*, is not being distributed in proportion to relative contribution. Though the slaves might threaten to strike, such threats would be irrational to carry out. A strike would return the entire community to the mutually disadvantageous initial bargaining position. And, as Gauthier recognizes, bringing about mutually disadvantageous states of affairs is paradigmatically irrational. In this revised slave-master bargain, part of the portion of the cooperative surplus to which the slaves directly contribute is "redistributed" to the masters. Gauthier claims that, in the original slave-master example, the voluntary provision of unremunerated services to the masters by the slaves constitutes an "unproductive transfer." In this example, unlike the original slave-master example, the slaves do not directly "transfer" part of their share of the surplus to the masters. Rather, they voluntarily contribute to the creation of the cooperative surplus knowing that they will not be given their fair share of it. In this case, the unfair distribution of the surplus constitutes an unproductive transfer. Thus, it is not true that an unproductive transfer is directly utility maximizing only if it is coerced. Premise 4 is, therefore, false. We then can say of the "slaves" in our example that they voluntarily comply with an arrangement involving unproductive transfers and that their doing so is rational. Therefore, contrary to 5, compliance with unfair bargains in the absence of coercion can be rational.

Moreover, I have suggested that unproductive transfers, given the opportunity costs of noncompliance, can be directly utility maximizing and therefore can be rational in the absence of coercion.[19] But even if I am mistaken in claiming that unproductive transfers sometimes can be directly utility maximizing, it does not follow that unproductive transfers are irrational on those grounds alone.

An act can be rational even if it is not directly utility maximizing and for the very same reasons that Gauthier thinks that the disposition to comply with certain cooperative strategies, and thus compliance itself, can be rational.[20] Simply recall Gauthier's solution to the compliance problem: the principle of constrained maximization. In the single-play PD, defection is ordinarily understood to be the dominant strategy. But by introducing the distinction between directly and indirectly utility-maximizing conduct, Gauthier purports to demonstrate that defection in the single-play PD is *not* dominant. Compliance with PD-structured agreements, he argues, can be rational even when it is not directly maximizing. Why? Because compliance in particular cases is the result of choosing to have a certain disposition on the basis of directly utility-maximizing considerations. The rationality of compliance is completely a function of the rationality of the choice to dispose oneself to comply.[21] According to Gauthier, compliance with PD-structured bargains is rational,

19 See n. 18.
20 Gauthier argues that if it is rational to choose the disposition to comply with certain agreements, then the actual compliance with those agreements is itself rational, even if it is not straightforwardly, or directly, utility maximizing. I will grant this point. Gauthier's argument for the claim is too extensive to be reconstructed here. He makes and defends the claim in chap. 6, sec. 3.2, pp. 184–7: "An objector might grant that it may be rational to dispose oneself to constrained maximization, but deny that the choices one is then disposed to make are rational. . . . [But] our argument identifies practical rationality with utility-maximization at the level of dispositions to choose, and carries through the implications of that identification in assessing the rationality of particular choices."
21 See n. 20.

then, in virtue of the prior, directly utility-maximizing choice to be disposed to compliance in PD-structured bargains. The disposition to comply is utility maximizing even if on occasion compliance is not directly utility maximizing. In Gauthier's view, the rationality of a course of conduct, the choice of a disposition, or anything for that matter, cannot be determined entirely by inquiring whether or not it is directly utility maximizing.

Similar reasoning can be used to defend the rationality of other nondirectly utility-maximizing acts such as unproductive transfers. Even if compliance with certain mutually advantageous joint strategies that require voluntary unproductive transfers is not directly utility-maximizing, it may be rational to make such transfers in virtue of the rationality of the choice to dispose oneself to make such transfers. At the very least, Gauthier's own argument for the rationality of compliance shows that we cannot infer that certain actions or choices are irrational from the fact that they are not directly utility maximizing. If unproductive transfers are irrational, their irrationality does not follow from their not being directly utility maximizing, at least not if Gauthier's own argument for the rationality of constrained maximization is compelling. So on pain of inconsistency, Gauthier must concede that premise 3 is false.

The argument from the instability of unfair bargains is unsound. Were Gauthier seriously to defend the claim that only directly utility-maximizing behavior can be rational, he would be forced to abandon the argument for rational compliance. Were Gauthier to give up the argument for rational compliance, his entire enterprise would quickly unravel for the obvious reason stated earlier: If it is not rational to comply, it cannot be rational to bargain. It would appear that Gauthier would do better to hold onto the possibility that some nondirectly utility-maximizing behavior can be rational and to give up instead the argument from the instability of unfair bargains.

But there is another, more attractive, line of argument for Gauthier which may allow him to have both constrained maximization and the argument from the instability of unfair bargains. This argument depends on a distinction he draws between two kinds of constrained maximization. In the end, Gauthier does not want to argue that constrained maximization in just any form is rational. Rather, he wants to argue that it is rational to dispose oneself to comply with bargains only if they are fair (Gauthier, p. 178). This is a particular form of constrained maximization, what Gauthier calls "narrow compliance." Because narrow compliance is a form of constrained maximization, its rationality does not depend on its being directly maximizing. So Gauthier's commitment to the rationality of narrow compliance means that he is committed to the principle that nondirectly maximizing behavior can be rational. But, in order to save the argument from the instability of unfair bargains, Gauthier has to give up reliance upon the claim that because unproductive transfers are not directly utility maximizing they are irrational. He can do this by claiming instead that nondirectly utility-maximizing behavior can be rational only when it is required by narrow compliance. Thus, unproductive transfers, which are involved in unfair bargains only, cannot be rational. They are not directly utility maximizing and are never required by narrow compliance. Moreover, given the unique rationality of narrow compliance, unfair bargains necessarily will be unstable because it will be rational for all parties in unfair bargains to defect. They will not have the disposition to comply necessary to secure the success of PD-structured bargains.

However, if narrow compliance is uniquely rational, then Gauthier's argument for the instability of unfair bargains is entirely unnecessary. All of its central premises can be abandoned. Because narrow compliance compels compliance only with fair bargains, unfair bargains, whether the result of unproductive transfers or not, are unstable. The entire discussion of the irrationality of unproductive transfers is beside the point. In short, given that Gauthier ultimately argues for the unique rationality of narrow compliance, it serves no purpose to show that unfair bargains unravel for the reason he gives. The unique rationality of narrow compliance demonstrates a more fundamental flaw in unfair bargains. It would not be rational to negotiate an unfair bargain because it is not rational to bargain in the absence of expected compliance, and narrow compliance precludes abiding by the terms of anything other than fair bargains.

It seems clear, then, that the most important arguments in Gauthier's book are those presented on behalf of the unique rationality of narrow compliance.[22] These arguments are the subject of the following section.[23]

22 Even if one is persuaded of this point by the instability argument, note that by undermining the arguments for narrow compliance that follow, the instability argument will be undermined, for without an argument for the unique rationality of narrow compliance there is no argument for the irrationality of unproductive transfers.

23 In a recent commentary, Gauthier seems to view his argument in *Morals by Agreement* in a different light. He suggests that the case for fair principles is based on establishing the unique rationality of acting in accordance with his version of the principle of ideal rational bargaining, minimax relative concession: "I claim then that it is rational to dispose oneself to narrow compliance, rather than to either broad or less-than-narrow compliance. The argument requires (i) a defense of the rationality of the principle of minimax relative concession; (ii) a defense of the rationality of the proviso constraining interaction to ensure a no-advantage basepoint; (iii) a defense of the rationality of narrow compliance given (i) and (ii)" (David Gauthier, "Reply to Kraus/ Coleman" [paper read at the meeting of the American Philosophical Association Central Division, St. Louis, Mo., May 2, 1986], p. 14.) Though this may have been Gauthier's intention in *Morals by Agreement*, the arguments he presents for the rationality of the proviso, in my view, themselves depend on independent arguments he presents in defense of narrow compliance. First, Gauthier claims he will show the proviso to be rational: "It may seem that reason and the proviso part company, and so, since the proviso ensures impartiality, do reason and morals . . . we deny this" (*Morals by Agreement*, p. 224). But the case for the rationality of the proviso rests entirely on the arguments from displaced costs (*Morals by Agreement*, p. 225) and from equal rationality (*Morals by Agreement*, p. 226), both of which are arguments for the unique rationality of narrow compliance. Thus, Gauthier seems to misunderstand the order of his own analysis. The arguments for the rationality of the proviso *presuppose* the soundness of his argu-

BROAD AND NARROW COMPLIANCE

There is an important distinction between a person "who is disposed to cooperate in ways that, followed by all, merely yield her some benefit in relation to universal noncooperation" and a person "who is disposed to cooperate in ways that, followed by all, yield nearly optimal and fair outcomes" (Gauthier, p. 178). The former are *broad compliers*, the latter *narrow compliers*. As they stand, the definitions of broad and narrow compliance are importantly ambiguous.

Cooperation consists in both agreement and compliance. From what Gauthier says we cannot be certain if narrow compliers have the disposition to agree to and comply with fair bargains only, or the disposition to comply with whatever fair bargains they strike, though they have no particular disposition with respect to the striking of bargains, fair or otherwise. On both accounts, narrow compliers are disposed to comply with any fair bargains they make. On the first account, however, the disposition they have is compound: it includes not only a disposition to comply with fair bargains but a disposition to accept any and all fair bargains and to reject all unfair ones as well. Thus, for them the question of whether to comply with an unfair bargain into which they have entered never arises. Narrowly compliant persons of this sort simply do not make unfair bargains. The disposition to be narrowly compliant in the second sense, however, insures only that, if a fair bargain is struck, a

ments for narrow compliance, not vice versa. Moreover, the strategy I suggest in the text provides a more powerful case for narrow compliance, which does not rest on the rationality of the proviso or on the correctness of minimax relative concession. Additionally, Gauthier's arguments for minimax relative concession rest on assumptions that do not obtain in the state of nature, where Gauthier holds rational individuals would employ that principle (see n. 37 and the section "The Arguments from Rational and Costless Bargaining" in this chapter). Thus, if the only argument for narrow compliance presupposes the successful defense of the rationality of the proviso and of minimax relative concession, the argument would be circular and unsuccessful.

narrowly compliant person will abide by its terms. Narrow compliers, however, would be free to refrain from striking fair bargains and free to make unfair ones.

For the narrowly compliant person of the second sort the decision whether or not to strike a particular bargain will be made on straightforward utility-maximizing grounds. Among the factors relevant to assessing the rationality of entering negotiations with others is the likelihood of their compliance with the outcome. A narrowly compliant person in the second sense will strike either fair or unfair bargains only if she believes that compliance of others is likely. If compliance is likely and the bargain struck is a fair one, the narrowly compliant person is compelled to cooperate. If the compliance of others is likely and the bargain struck is an unfair one, the narrowly compliant person is not compelled to comply. This does not mean she is compelled to defect. She is compelled in no way at all; she is free either to comply or defect. If the bargain is embedded in a single-play PD, she will defect. But her decision to defect follows from the single-play PD structure of the bargain and the dominant rationality of defection in the absence of a disposition to do otherwise. If the bargain is not a single-play PD, however, she can comply or defect depending on the counsel of straightforward maximization. If we restrict discussion to a state of nature in which most bargains have the structure of the single-play PD, then she will usually defect from the unfair bargains she makes – but not because she is disposed to defect and not because she is disposed not to make unfair bargains.

Now consider the narrowly compliant person of the first sort. Because she is compelled to enter into and comply with only fair bargains, no decision she makes requires that she take into account straightforward maximizing considerations. Those factors enter only when she chooses to adopt the disposition to enter into fair bargains only. From then on, she is compelled to turn her back on bargains that are unfair, even if the compliance of others is likely and the terms offered benefit her in disproportion to the gains accorded others.

In this chapter, I will adopt the second formulation of narrow compliance and thus define broad compliance accordingly.[24]

Narrow compliers have the disposition to comply with fair bargains, though, as a matter of their disposition, they need not accept them in the first place. Because their disposition is confined only to fair bargains, they are dispositionally free with respect to their compliance decisions regarding unfair bargains.[25]

24 There are two theoretical considerations which are relevant to the choice between the two alternative formulations of narrow compliance. The first consideration is psychological. Because it is difficult enough to suppose (1) that individuals can voluntarily choose to adopt a disposition to comply with bargains, and moreover that (2) this disposition is conditional upon the fairness of the bargain, it would seem theoretically prudent to avoid adopting an even less plausible definition which requires the same voluntarily adopted disposition in addition to another disposition for accepting and rejecting bargains on the basis of their fairness. Perhaps the bounds of our imaginations can stretch to accommodate the first account, but they positively explode when contemplating the second. The second theoretical consideration is epistemic. Gauthier's argument for constrained maximization depends on individuals being translucent with respect to their dispositions for compliance. Translucence in turn requires some practical explanation of how individuals might be able to tell whether others are constrained or straightforward maximizers. Yet if both narrow compliers and straightforward maximizers can be observed defecting from agreements, "defection records" would not be reliable indicators of individuals' dispositions. Ideally, only straightforward maximizers would ever defect from their agreements. Once an individual defects from an agreement, then it might be plausible to suppose that society has a good chance of marking him as a straightforward maximizer. Epistemic considerations, therefore, favor the first alternative definition which precludes, analytically, the possibility of a narrowly compliant person's defecting from his or her agreements. Thus, psychological factors favor the second characterization of narrow compliance; epistemic ones favor the first.

25 This point bears amplification. In the state of nature, a narrowly compliant person will always comply with fair bargains and always defect from unfair ones. The reason is as follows. The state of nature is a PD in which defection is rational unless one is disposed always to do otherwise and so will never defect. A narrowly compliant person will

Broad compliers have the disposition to comply with any mutually advantageous bargains they enter, though they may choose not to enter certain bargains, fair or not.

I have adopted these formulations for three reasons. First, and foremost, the theoretical motivation for constrained maximization is the single-play PD. The adoption of a disposition to comply with bargains is motivated for rational agents as a strategy for avoiding the suboptimality of the single-play PD. Rational agents can avoid the single-play PD by the adoption of a disposition for compliance. A more complex disposition which disposes agents both to comply and to accept bargains is unmotivated for rational agents.[26] Second, the relevant disposition for compliance must be psychologically plausible. The disposition to comply only with certain bargains is psychologically more plausible, I believe, than the disposition to enter into and to comply with certain bargains only.[27] Finally, Gauthier's own discussions of narrow and broad compliance in *Morals by Agreement* strongly suggest this interpretation.[28] However, as con-

defect in a PD except when he is disposed to do otherwise; and he is disposed to do otherwise only if the bargain is fair. If an unfair bargain is not a PD, a narrowly compliant person need not defect, though he is not compelled to comply either.

26 In addition, Ockham's razor would mitigate against the more complex disposition. It is theoretically unnecessary.

27 See n. 24.

28 In *Morals by Agreement*, Gauthier clearly holds that narrow compliers will not have the disposition to comply with unfair bargains, irrespective of whether they benefit or suffer from the unfairness: "The narrowly compliant person is always prepared . . . to be co-operative whenever co-operation can be mutually beneficial on terms equally rational and fair to all. In refusing other terms . . . she ensures that those not disposed to fair co-operation do not enjoy the benefits of any co-operation, thus making their unfairness costly to themselves, and so irrational" (*Morals by Agreement*, pp. 178–9). If a narrow complier has the disposition to comply with certain fair bargains (i.e., ones according her the greater, unfair share), then she would be defeating herself by trying to ensure "that those not disposed to fair co-operation do not enjoy the benefits of any co-operation." But in his

cerns the arguments of *Morals by Agreement* and my criticism
of them, the two definitions can be shown to be *extensionally*

commentary, Gauthier changes the definition of narrow compliance:
"A narrowly compliant person, as I define her . . . does not refuse to
enter, or to comply with, agreements if her share is more than fair; she
refuses only if she would get less" (Gauthier, Reply to Kraus/Coleman,
p. 13). His strategy is to strengthen his argument against the rationality of broad compliance (i.e., the disposition to comply with mutually
advantageous bargains which accord one the smaller portion of the
cooperative surplus). As it stands, even this redefinition does not help
Gauthier's case, for the definition of narrow compliance I adopt enables narrow compliers to enter into and comply with unfair bargains
as a matter of disposition (i.e., their disposition does not prevent them
from doing so). But narrow compliers, being utility maximizers, will
not comply with unfair, PD-structured bargains, even when the unfairness is in their favor, because they lack the disposition to comply
necessary to override the straightforward, utility-maximizing strategy
of defection in PD-structured bargains. We might suppose, however,
that Gauthier here allows for narrow compliers to be disposed to
comply with unfair bargains on the condition that the unfairness is in
their favor. This redefinition not only makes the envisioned disposition extremely psychologically unrealistic, but it also fails to increase
sufficiently the profitability of being a narrow complier. For the set of
bargains available to narrow compliers is a proper subset of the larger
set of bargains available to broad compliers. Thus, broad compliance
is more profitable than narrow compliance and hence is the rational
disposition to choose. See the discussion of the equal rationality argument in this chapter.

   Consider two of Gauthier's statements. First, he says "in interacting
with you I should dispose myself to comply with a joint strategy only
if it offers me, not a fair share, but a lion's share of the cooperative
surplus" (Gauthier, *Morals by Agreement*, p. 226). Here Gauthier is
clearly isolating a disposition for compliance, and compliance only. No
mention is made of a disposition to accept or reject bargains. Second,
he says, "A person disposed to broad compliance compares the benefit
she would expect from cooperation on whatever terms are offered
with what she would expect from non-co-operation, and complies if
the former is greater" (Gauthier, *Morals by Agreement*, p. 225). Though
this definition seems to conflate agreement and compliance, he seems
clearly to think that the choice to accept a bargain is a straightforward
maximization consideration, not a matter of disposition. The question
the broad complier faces is whether to accept the bargain knowing
that she will comply with it if she does.

equivalent, so someone unpersuaded by my characterization of narrow compliance can substitute the more complex characterization in most arguments, *salva veritate.*[29]

In order to solve the compliance and status quo ante prob-

---

29 Gauthier presents different arguments in his commentary "Reply to Kraus/Coleman." There Gauthier reformulates the definition of narrow compliance. I respond to this reformulation and the argument which relies upon it in n. 28.

   To say that the two alternative definitions of narrow compliance are extensionally equivalent, in this context, is to say that all and only the bargains that narrow compliers can (or will) make in the state of nature given the first definition are bargains that narrow compliers can (or will) make in the state of nature given the second definition. To see that the definitions are extensionally equivalent, consider first the bargains broad and narrow compliers will make if we use the first definition. Broad compliers will be able to make fair and unfair bargains among themselves, and so long as they do not have unfairly acquired entitlements as a result of unfair bargaining, they will be able to make fair bargains with narrow compliers. Narrow compliers will be able to make fair bargains with other narrow compliers and with broad compliers who have legitimately acquired entitlements (if their entitlements were unfairly acquired, then bargains with them would be necessarily unfair (see the section "Narrow Compliance and Predation" in this chapter). No unfair bargains involving narrow compliers will be possible. Next, consider the bargains made by broad and narrow compliers if we use the second definition. Broad compliers will be able to make fair bargains among themselves and with narrow compliers just as above. However, they are, in principle, also able to engage not only in unfair bargains among themselves, as above, but also in unfair bargains with narrow compliers, for narrow compliers now may make any bargains they wish. However, even though narrow compliers presumably might, under certain conditions, like to make advantageous, unfair bargains among themselves and with broad compliers, rationality prevents any such bargains from taking place. Broad compliers will not make any unfair bargains with narrow compliers because narrow compliers are not credible in unfair bargains. Their disposition to comply with bargains, unlike the broad compliers' disposition, is contingent upon the fairness of the bargain. In the state of nature, most bargains have the structure of the PD, and so narrow compliers will defect from unfair bargains because it is the uniquely rational action, in lieu of a disposition to comply. Broad compliers, who will comply with such bargains, know that narrow compliers cannot comply, as a matter of straightforward utility maximization,

lems simultaneously, Gauthier's rational choice model of morality requires that narrow compliance be uniquely rational. In what follows, I distinguish among four arguments for the irrationality of broad compliance and the rationality of narrow compliance. These are arguments from predation, displaced costs, translucence, and equal rationality. I consider each in turn.

NARROW COMPLIANCE AND PREDATION

Gauthier writes: "Someone disposed to comply with agreements that left untouched the fruits of predation would simply invite others to engage in predatory and coercive activities as a prelude to bargaining. She would permit the successful predators to reap where they had ceased to sow, to continue to profit from the effects of natural predation after entering into agreements freeing them from the need to invest further in predatory effort" (Gauthier, p. 195). According to the argument from predation, it is rational to exclude from bargaining those individuals who have unfair initial entitlements because doing so would discourage them from stealing as a prelude to bargaining. Narrow compliance, as I have defined it, insures the exclusion of individuals with unfair entitlements from bargains with narrow compliers.

and so will not enter into unfair bargains with narrow compliers. Likewise, narrow compliers will not make unfair bargains among themselves because each knows the other is bound by rationality to defect. Thus, irrespective of the definitions of narrow and broad compliance we adopt, the same set of bargains are available to narrow and broad compliers: Unfair bargains can take place only among broad compliers, and fair bargains can take place among both narrow and broad compliers so long as they have not already profited unfairly in previous bargaining, thus rendering all bargains they enter unfair.

When I later have occasion to discuss the rationality of "less-than-narrow" compliance, the difference between the two formulations we have just considered and the two analogous definitions of less-than-narrow compliance will be important. There we will not be able to treat the two as extensionally equivalent.

Before evaluating the argument from predation, we should note at the outset that in order for the argument to get off the ground, it must be the case that anyone who acts as a predator in the state of nature will be excluded from bargains with narrow compliers. But the criterion for exclusion from bargains with narrow compliers exclusively concerns the fairness of the bargains they are considering and is connected to prebargain predation only via the effect such predation will have on the fairness of bargains entered into by formerly predatory individuals. Thus, the argument can work only if bargains with formerly predatory individuals will be necessarily unfair. Prebargain predation must "taint" an individual so that all the bargains he enters necessarily will be unfair.[30] These bargains will be ones with which narrow compliers will not comply (they will defect in single-play PDs unless disposed to comply), and thus ones into which narrow compliers will not even enter. It is a consequence of this argument, then, that an individual who has unfairly acquired entitlements is analytically unable to enter into a fair bargain. Even if he bargains according to a fair bargaining principle, and his unfairly acquired entitlements in no other way adversely affect the other parties' bargaining gains (e.g., the prebargain situation is not a zero-sum game where unfairly acquired entitlements for A necessarily mean unfairly less entitlements for B and C), the fact that he retains his unfairly acquired entitlements in the postbargain outcome renders the distributions necessarily unfair. Thus, necessarily, bargains which fail to rectify prior unjust distributions are unfair. If this were not the case, then individuals would be free to engage in prebargain predation so long as they did not use the fruits of their predation in future unfair bargains, where their unfair advantage enables them to coerce others into complying with bargains resulting from unfair bargaining principles.

It is clearly desirable and rational to attempt to discourage

---

30 Except, perhaps, if they somehow rectify the previous entitlements unfairly acquired through predation.

individuals from attacking in the state of nature. Suppose there were so many narrow compliers in the state of nature who excluded those with unfair initial entitlements from the benefits of cooperation that the benefits from predation did not exceed the costs of exclusion from cooperation. Then, as Gauthier claims, it would be irrational to engage in predatory behavior, and individuals would be discouraged from doing so. But we cannot simply assume that there are, or always would be, a sufficient number of narrowly compliant individuals in the state of nature to make prebargain predation irrational. And even once a threshold population of narrow compliers has been reached, and prebargain predation becomes irrational, it does not follow that it is rational for any particular individual to be narrowly compliant.

Consider two possible scenarios. In one, the population of narrowly compliant individuals falls below the threshold necessary to induce others to refrain from predation. In the other, the population exceeds that necessary to deter predation. Should the threshold population of narrow compliers in the state of nature not obtain, there is no reason to think that the members of the narrow compliance population will be spared from predation by non-narrow compliers. Narrow compliance would be costly since it would require someone to forgo certain mutually advantageous, but unfair, bargains. At the same time, the potential benefit of narrow compliance, that is, deterring predation, would not obtain. Thus, narrow compliance would not be rational, let alone uniquely rational.

Now consider the case in which the threshold of narrowly compliant persons in the overall population is met or exceeded. When this condition is satisfied, it is rational to refrain from engaging in predatory behavior. But is it rational to be narrowly compliant? No. Whether or not an individual is narrowly compliant, others will not prey on him. If they do, they will be excluded from advantageous bargains with the narrow compliers. But being a narrow complier is not a necessary condition for cooperative interaction with narrow compliers. The only precondition is that one not engage in predation. Non-narrow compliers who do not engage in predatory behavior will not be excluded from cooperative bargains with narrow compliers. It is rational not to be excluded. Broadly compliant persons also will be included as long as they are not predatory. Thus, broad compliance is a rational disposition both when the number of narrowly compliant persons in a population falls below or exceeds that necessary to foreclose predation. The only circumstance in which it is uniquely rational to be narrowly compliant occurs when one's decision is decisive in reaching the threshold population size in which predation results in a net loss to the predator and is thus irrational. The probability that any one person's choice of a disposition toward compliance could be decisive is extremely low. And even where one person's choice could affect the expected utility of predation, the probability of any one particular choice being decisive is even lower. So the rationality of narrow compliance is simply not established by the argument from predation.

DISPLACED COSTS AND RATIONAL COMPLIANCE

The argument from displaced costs is really just Gauthier's earlier argument that, because unfair bargains involve unproductive transfers, narrow compliance is uniquely rational. Gauthier writes:

> If interaction is to be fully cooperative, it must proceed from an initial position in which costs are internalized, and so in which no person has the right to impose uncompensated costs on another. For if not, the resulting social arrangements must embody one-sided interactions benefitting some persons at cost to others. Even if each were to receive some portion of the cooperative surplus, yet each could not expect to benefit in the same relation to contribution as his fellows. *Interactions based on displaced costs would be redistributive, and redistribution can not be part of a rational system of co-operation.* (Gauthier, p. 225; emphasis added)

The claim is that unfair bargains always result in displaced costs and that because displaced costs are redistributive, they are irrational. Redistributive outcomes are irrational, according to Gauthier's earlier claim, because they require unproductive transfers. But recall that (in the instability argument) his argument for the irrationality of unproductive transfers, and thus redistribution, depended on the claim that unproductive transfers were not directly utility maximizing. However, as I pointed out earlier, Gauthier cannot claim that any act that is not directly utility maximizing is necessarily irrational, for his central thesis of constrained maximization, if correct, proves the exception: It is rational to dispose oneself *ex ante* to comply with certain nondirectly utility-maximizing bargains; thus compliance with these bargains, even though they are not directly utility maximizing, is rational. In order to prove that unproductive transfers are irrational, Gauthier has to argue that only one brand of constrained maximization is rational: narrow compliance. He could then hold that all nondirectly utility-maximizing behavior is irrational unless it is required by narrow compliance. Because unproductive transfers will never be required by narrow compliance, it follows that unproductive transfers cannot be rational. But this strategy cannot work. On pain of circularity, Gauthier cannot, in the displaced costs argument, argue for the unique rationality of narrow compliance on the ground that the alternative of broad compliance involves unproductive transfers and is thus irrational when his only argument for the necessary irrationality of unproductive transfers (made earlier in connection with the instability argument) relied upon the claim that narrow compliance is uniquely rational.[31] We had best move on.

---

31 In addition, I have already rejected the claim that broad compliance necessarily involves unproductive transfers. See the section "Fairness and Stability."

TRANSLUCENCE AND COMPLIANCE

The rationality of constrained maximization in part depends on the ability of constrained maximizers to recognize straightforward maximizers and other constrained maximizers. The easier it is to recognize what sort of maximizer an individual is, the more probable it will be that (1) constrained maximizers successfully bargain to mutual advantage with other constrained maximizers, (2) constrained maximizers will not be exploited by straightforward maximizers, and (3) straightforward maximizers will be excluded from cooperative interaction. As the probability of (1)–(3) increases, the expected utility of being a constrained maximizer increases and the expected utility of being a straightforward maximizer decreases.

A "transparent" individual is one whose disposition is unmistakable. Transparent individuals are always recognized correctly for the kind of maximizers they are. An "opaque" individual is one whose disposition is very difficult to detect. Opaque individuals are often mistakenly identified as constrained maximizers when they are in fact straightforward maximizers and vice versa. Gauthier claims that in fact individuals are "translucent." They admit of various degrees of translucence so that some individuals, who have finely honed skills of recognition, can do very well at recognizing constrained and straightforward maximizers, and most people stand a pretty good chance of recognizing individuals to be the type of maximizers they are.

We can reformulate Gauthier's claim about the relationship between the rationality of constrained maximization and the recognizability of constrained maximization as follows: the higher the degree of transparency, the less the potential benefit of cooperation must be in order for constrained maximization to be rational; or, the lower the degree of transparency, the greater the potential benefit of cooperation must be in order for constrained maximization to be rational.

Gauthier claims that "as practices and activities fall short of fairness, the expected value of cooperation for those with less than fair shares decreases, and so the degree of translucency required to make cooperation rational for them increases" (Gauthier, p. 178). The point is that it can be rational to be a constrained maximizer who accepts unfair bargains only as individuals approach transparency. The expected utility of constrained maximization is a function of the likelihood of interacting with constrained maximizers, the potential gain from such interaction, and the potential loss from interacting with a straightforward maximizer. In turn, the likelihood of interacting with a constrained maximizer, and not interacting with a straightforward maximizer is, in part, a function of translucency. So if it is going to be rational to dispose oneself to comply with unfair bargains, in which the potential gain need not be considerable, the likelihood of success must be very high. Thus, the rationality of disposing oneself to compliance with unfair, though mutually advantageous, bargains will be in part a function of translucency. In order for the expected utility of compliance with an unfair bargain to be greater than the expected costs for the bargaining partner receiving the smaller share of the gains, the bargaining partner receiving the larger share of the gains will have to be less opaque than otherwise. Thus, a disposition to comply with unfair bargains is unlikely to be rational.

Gauthier's account of the relationship between the rationality of the disposition to comply with unfair bargains and translucency is essentially correct. But the translucency argument fails to take degrees of unfairness into account. Surely not all unfair bargains are equally unfair. And where the stakes are large enough, even unfairly small portions of a surplus may be large enough to make the expected utility of broad compliance high enough to outweigh its expected loss. My principal objection to the translucency argument is that Gauthier cannot assume that all unfair bargains are ones in which the potential gain, the unfair share of the surplus, will be critically low. It may be sufficiently high if either (1) the bargain is not extremely unfair and/or (2) the cooperative surplus is very large. There will surely be some unfair bargains with which no rational person ought to comply. But from this it cannot follow that there are no unfair bargains with which rational persons ought to comply. The latter claim must be true, however, for narrow compliance to be uniquely rational.

NARROW COMPLIANCE AND EQUAL RATIONALITY

Gauthier's entire enterprise rests on his demonstrating the unique rationality of narrow compliance, that is, the disposition to comply only with fair bargains. It is one thing to establish the rationality of constrained maximization; it is another thing to establish that compliance is rational only if the terms of an agreement are fair. Consideration of predation, displaced costs, and the translucence of character do not appear to provide the argument Gauthier needs. The deepest and, in many ways, the most promising argument for narrow compliance relies upon the concept of equal rationality. The argument from equal rationality can be put as follows:

1. Equally rational individuals will comply under the same conditions.

Therefore,

2. If some individuals comply under different conditions than others, these individuals cannot be equally rational.

Therefore,

3. If some people are narrowly compliant, and others are broadly compliant, some individuals are not as rational as others.
4. But all individuals are equally rational, *ex hypothesi.*

Therefore,

5. Either everyone must be broadly compliant or everyone must be narrowly compliant.
6. It is never rational for everyone to be broadly compliant.

Therefore,

7. It is uniquely rational for everyone to be narrowly compliant.

The argument rests on two central premises. The first, premise 6, is that it cannot be rational for everyone to be broadly compliant. The second, premise 1, is that equally rational individuals will comply under the same conditions; thus, broadly and narrowly compliant persons cannot both be equally rational.

The irrationality of broad compliance

Gauthier's argument for the claim that it is not rational for everyone to be broadly compliant is:

A. If you will comply for any benefit whatsoever, i.e., if you are broadly compliant, then in interacting with you I should dispose myself to comply with a bargain we strike only if it offers me, not a fair share, but the lion's share of the surplus.

Therefore,

B. If some persons are broadly compliant, then others, interacting with them, will find it advantageous not to be broadly compliant, or even so much as narrowly compliant. It is rational for them (those demanding the lion's share) to be less-than-narrowly compliant.

Therefore,

C. It is not and cannot be rational for everyone to be . . . broadly compliant. (Gauthier, pp. 226–7)

Consider premise A of the argument. According to Gauthier, constrained maximizers, whether narrowly or broadly compliant, cooperate only with persons they have reason to believe are similarly constrained. They want to make it costly for others to be straightforward maximizers, by excluding them from the benefits of cooperation, and beneficial for others to be constrained maximizers. This will increase the desirability of being a constrained maximizer and thus increase the number of constrained maximizers in the population. And this in turn increases the probability of constrained maximization being rational. Now suppose that you have the disposition to comply with any mutually advantageous bargains into which you enter, and I know this.[32] That is, I know you are broadly compliant. Does it follow that I should dispose myself to comply only with agreements that afford me a lion's share of the cooperative surplus? That is, does it follow that I should be less-than-narrowly compliant? Surely not.

First, from the fact that you are broadly compliant it does not follow that you will enter into any mutually advantageous agreement. All that follows is that you will comply with any mutually advantageous agreement into which you enter. And were you to know that I am not even narrowly compliant (which you would be as likely to know as I am likely to know that you are broadly compliant), you would know that the only successful cooperative agreements between us would be ones which accorded me the lion's share of the surplus. You would enter into a bargain with me only if your squirrel's share of the surplus were sufficiently large to make such a bargain rational for you. Depending on your other opportunities, you might not strike a deal with me at

32 Note that this supposition presupposes my knowledge of whether you are a broad or narrow complier. But even if constrained maximizers are transparent, it does not follow that broad and narrow compliers can be easily distinguished. This is yet another obstacle facing the view that only narrow compliance is rational – it requires a further epistemic ability to distinguish not only constrained from straightforward maximizers, but narrow from broad compliers as well.

all. In general, broad compliers might well enter into few bargains with less-than-narrow compliers – only those affording the broad compliers enough to make the bargain rational. And since less-than-narrow compliers are known not to comply with bargains affording them less than a lion's share of the surplus, broad compliers will find it rational to enter into bargains with them only when the surplus is so large that their small share is still worth pursuing.

Whether it is worth pursuing depends of course on the opportunity costs. The range of unfair bargains worth entering into for those destined to receive the unfair, extremely small reward is nowhere near as large, we might reasonably suppose, as the range of unfair and fair bargains into which broad compliers might enter with one another. Were I a broad complier, the range of bargains in which each of us could count on the other to comply would be maximal, so we would likely strike more bargains and gain more as a result. Broad compliers faced with other broad compliers will know that they can successfully cooperate on a much larger set of joint ventures and so will almost always find some strategy on which to agree. But broad compliers know that less-than-narrow compliers will have the disposition to comply only when they get the lion's share. Thus, it is less likely to be rational for broad compliers to interact with less-than-narrow compliers than it will be for them to interact with other broad compliers. If I am considering demanding the lion's share, then I must realize that one consequence of my doing so is that you might be a broad complier and yet decide not to bargain with me at all. So it may be irrational for me to be less-than-narrowly compliant even if I know you are broadly compliant! Certainly we can draw no inference about what it would be rational for me to demand of you in the absence of my knowledge of your other alternatives.

Second, even if it would be desirable for me to be a less-than-narrow complier when interacting with a broad complier, it does not follow that it is rational for me to become less-than-narrowly compliant. The dispositions of narrow and broad compliance are not conditional upon certain bargains with certain sorts of people. Individuals are either broad or narrow (or less-than-narrow) compliers, period. They cannot be broad compliers when interacting with some people but narrow compliers when interacting with others. Though I might rationally prefer to be a less-than-narrow complier while I am interacting with you, the rationality of my actually being a less-than-narrow complier will depend on the distribution of dispositions throughout the population with whom I interact. If everyone but you were narrowly compliant, then it would still not be rational for me to be a less-than-narrow complier, even if you are broadly compliant.

Nor will it help to employ the alternative definition of broad and narrow compliance discussed earlier. Although the previous argument against the rationality of less-than-narrow compliance relies upon defining the dispositions in question not to include a disposition to accept certain bargains, the claim that broad compliance of some leads to less-than-narrow compliance of others is incorrect, even on the alternative definition. Suppose that broad compliers do in fact have the disposition *both* to accept and comply with *any* mutually advantageous bargain, no matter how unfairly small their share of the cooperative surplus. Then, presumably, a less-than-narrow complier would have the disposition to accept, offer, and comply with only those unfair bargains which accorded him a lion's share of the surplus. Now, does it follow that it is rational to be a less-than-narrow complier if someone else is a broad complier? We have already seen that the presence of one broad complier will be unlikely to affect the rationality of being a less-than-narrow complier for anyone else. The rationality of the latter will at best be a function of the number of broad compliers in a population. But the number of broad compliers required in order to make less-than-narrow compliance rational is very large. For less-than-narrow compliers will never be able to strike cooperative agreements with each other. There must be so many broad compliers, and so few less-than-narrow compliers, that the costs of being a less-than-narrow complier (i.e., of failing to make agreements with other less-than-narrow compliers) is outweighed by the benefits of exploiting broad compliers. But these benefits are possible only when cooperative efforts consist of agreement between few enough narrow compliers, and enough broad compliers, that the less-than-narrow compliers can still receive their lion's share. The more less-than-narrow compliers involved in a cooperative venture along with the broad compliers, the less the lion's share for each less-than-narrow complier. And so the more less-than-narrow compliers in the world, the less there will be opportunities to engage in cooperative bargains according lion's shares to some and squirrel's shares to others. One wolf among a flock of sheep fares well. Ten wolves among two sheep fare poorly. So even if we define broad and narrow compliance to include a disposition to accept and comply with certain agreements, we see that even in a population of many broad compliers, it does not necessarily follow that it is rational to be a less-than-narrow complier.

The central premise in the argument, premise A, is false. It does not follow from the fact that someone is broadly compliant that others ought to be less-than-narrowly compliant. In fact the reverse might be true. Thus, premise B does not follow: If some persons are broadly compliant, then it is not necessarily the case that others interacting with them will find it advantageous not to be broadly compliant, or even so much as narrowly compliant. Premise C is also false: It can be rational for everyone to be broad compliers. For being a broad complier may afford everyone the best opportunity to reach agreement and to benefit from cooperative ventures.

Equal rationality and equal compliance

I have so far argued that premise 6 in the equal rationality argument is false: It can be rational for everyone to be a broad complier. Thus, the truth of premise 7 does not follow from the conjunction of premises 5 and 6, and the argument for the unique rationality of narrow compliance is now incomplete. But the crux of the argument, premise 1, so far remains intact: Equally rational individuals will comply under the same conditions and thus everyone must be either broadly or narrowly compliant. Some people cannot be narrowly compliant and others broadly compliant. The "impossibility" is presumably a conceptual one, following from the definition of "equal rationality."

The equal rationality of the parties in the initial position, however, is largely irrelevant in determining the rationality of broad and narrow compliance. One's reasons for being a broad or narrow complier depend on one's bargaining advantage in the state of nature and the preexisting size of the populations of broad and narrow compliers. Given acceptable populations of broad and narrow compliers, if one is advantaged, then one can afford to hold out for fair bargains. Opportunity costs will often force the disadvantaged to acquiesce in unfair bargains. Though parties in the initial position may be equally rational, they are not necessarily equally advantaged. Thus, they may comply with bargains under very different conditions.

For advantaged individuals, it will never be rational to be narrowly compliant, for the adoption of that disposition would preclude them from ever profiting from their advantage. The only question they must face is whether it is rational to engage in unfair bargains. Because anyone who gains unfairly in a bargain will be excluded from bargaining with a narrow complier even on fair terms, even advantaged individuals must weigh the benefits of using their advantage against the costs of being excluded from whatever population of narrow compliers exists or will exist in the future.[33]

33 The reason that unfairly acquired prior entitlements render individuals ineligible in otherwise fair bargains in the future is that even bargains with fair bargaining principles must be treated as unfair if they transmit prior unfairnesses. This was an assumption necessary to make sense of the argument from predation (see n. 15 and the section "Narrow Compliance and Predation"). If we drop this assumption,

Ultimately, then, the only question which an advantaged individual must confront is whether he ought to engage in unfair bargaining, not whether he ought to be a narrow complier. Under no circumstances will it be rational for an advantaged individual to be a narrow complier, for by becoming narrowly compliant he forfeits the possibility of profiting from his advantage when the benefits of so doing outweigh the costs (i.e., of exclusion from bargaining with the population of narrow compliers). Individuals who are not advantaged will of course desire that there be a large enough population of narrow compliers so that advantaged individuals have incentive only to engage in fair bargaining. But, as I earlier demonstrated, even from this it does not follow that any one particular disadvantaged individual ought to become narrowly compliant.[34] In fact, unless his decision to become narrowly compliant can break the threshold beyond which the costs of unfair bargaining for advantaged individuals outweigh the benefits, it is irrational for any single disadvantaged individual to be narrowly compliant. Broad compliance allows him to benefit from all bargains with narrow compliers and from those unfair bargains with advantaged individuals in which he gains the lesser, unfair, share.

What, then, can we say about the possibility of a population of equally rational individuals being divided between broad and narrow compliers? Simply this: In the absence of a preexisting large population of narrow compliers, it is not and will never be rational for anyone, advantaged or not, to become a narrow complier. For advantaged individuals, narrow compliance is never rational. For disadvantaged individuals, it is rational only when their choice to become narrowly compliant is decisive, which requires at least some

then advantaged individuals could, in principle, profit unfairly in bargains and then bargain on fair terms in the future with narrow compliers. So much the worse for the case against the rationality of exploiting one's advantage: It would be possible to avoid incurring *any* costs for using one's unfair advantage!

34 See the discussion in the section "Narrow Compliance and Predation."

preexisting population of narrow compliers. But if this is so, then there will never be any population of narrow compliers, for it will never be rational for an individual to become narrowly compliant in the first place. Alternatively, if we stipulate the existence of a large population of narrow compliers, without explaining how it was ever rational for any of them to become narrow compliers, then it still would be irrational for any of the remainder of the total population to become narrowly compliant. They might just as well be broad compliers who restrict their bargains to fair ones. In this case, we see that a population of rational individuals could include both broad and narrow compliers, though the evolution of such a population would remain a mystery. In any event, equal rationality, it appears, does not entail equal compliance, and the last argument for the unique rationality of narrow compliance has failed.[35]

THE ARGUMENTS FROM RATIONAL AND COSTLESS BARGAINING

In addition to the arguments I have considered, Gauthier offers two additional and interdependent, though less developed, arguments for the claim that, necessarily, rational agreements in the state of nature will be fair. The first is premised on his theory of rational bargaining; the second is premised on the concept of costless bargaining.

35 I have not discussed Gauthier's argument that the correct principle of ideal rational bargaining *entails* that rational individuals will not bargain from anything less than fair initial positions. I discuss his principle of ideal rational bargaining in the next section. It is my claim that the correctness of this principle depends on the implausible, if not incoherent, characterization of the initial choice problem as being costless. Thus, we need not wonder whether his principle, if correct, would entail the fairness of the initial bargaining position. For there is no proof of its correctness that does not depend on an assumption I reject.

Rationality and fair bargaining

Suppose I am right that the argument from narrow compliance is unsound. It can be rational to dispose oneself to comply with the rational bargains one strikes, even if those bargains are not fair. That is, we cannot derive the fairness of bargained outcomes as a consequence of a theory of rational compliance. This does not mean that we cannot derive it from a theory of rational bargaining. Suppose the correct theory of rational bargaining had as its consequence that a rational bargain was a fair one. Then, if moral principles must be fair ones, they might still be determined by the outcome of a rational bargain.

Gauthier advances a theory of rational bargaining, the principle of minimax relative concession. According to this principle, each individual shares in the surplus proportionate to his relative contribution. Since fairness requires proportionate distribution, rational bargaining turns out to be fair bargaining. The outcome of every rational bargain is fair. Therefore, even if it is rational to be broadly compliant, the bargains with which one complies are fair ones.

The problem with this argument is that it ignores the potential unfairness of the initial positions. As we have already seen, even if the rational bargaining process itself is fair, such a process may nonetheless exacerbate, and will in any event preserve rather than rectify preexisting inequalities. Unless rational bargaining effects corrective justice, the outcome of a rational bargain can be unfair even if the rational bargaining which produces it is procedurally fair.

The possibility remains that this sort of unfairness need not concern the rational choice model of morality. After all, one could argue that the substantive principles of morality can be fair but not rectificatory. Why should we think that correct moral principles ought to address issues of corrective justice? In my view, a theory of morality which ignores corrective justice is unacceptable. But even if it were acceptable, a rational choice theorist of morality would still have to prove that the correct ideal principle of rational bargaining was a fair one. Gauthier claims to have done this, but his proof depends crucially on the characterization of the initial choice problem as taking place within the context of costless bargaining.

Costless bargaining

One of the most common objections leveled against Rawls is that his characterization of the original position is not normatively neutral. Because it is not, the two principles of justice do not derive from the concept of rationality fleshed out as Rawls thinks it should be – namely, as individual rational decision under uncertainty. Instead, the principles are derived from rationality embedded within a Kantian normative framework. As I have explicated Gauthier's theory, it constitutes an effort to derive morality from "pure rationality." This explains Gauthier's efforts to impose minimal constraints on the decision problem. The one important constraint he imposes, but inadequately discusses, is that bargaining in the state of nature is costless in terms of utility and time.[36]

If bargaining is in fact costless in time and utility, it is possible to argue that rational bargaining will invariably lead to fair outcomes. Rational bargaining will give rise to unfair outcomes if initial inequities allow one party to extort shares that exceed his relative contribution or if the inequities are simply transmitted to the outcomes. If bargaining is costless, however, then those disadvantaged in the state of nature have nothing to lose by refusing to join in a cooperative effort unless the terms of the bargain are fair. At the same

36 Gauthier writes that "bargaining is cost-free, both in terms of utility and time, so that no one need come to a decision without full consideration; bargaining is unpressured. Thus, each bargainer can employ only his rationality to appeal to the equal rationality of his fellows. In addition to rationality, there are only each person's preferences and possible actions to consider, and it is about these that everyone bargains" (Gauthier, *Morals by Agreement*, p. 156).

time, they cannot expect to receive terms more favorable to them than fair terms, because other cooperators will object and hold out for fair terms at no cost to them. Thus, everyone can expect fair terms, regardless of the initial distribution of holdings. Provided they are equally rational, they will get fair terms. Cooperation assumes that the contribution of others is necessary; the costlessness assumption guarantees that all bargaining will be on terms that are fair to all contributing parties. The costlessness assumption, which is thought necessary to insure that the outcome in Gauthier's bargaining scenario is explained by rationality alone, turns out to have extraordinary normative consequences. It nullifies all advantages and induces all parties to comply under exactly the same terms. The assumption does what the arguments for narrow compliance could not do: It solves both the compliance and status quo ante problems. It has to be too good to be true, and it is.

The assumption enables Gauthier to derive morality from rationality but at the cost of robbing the argument of its essential state-of-nature character. The motivation for rational individuals to cooperate in the state of nature, after all, is the existence of costs. These are forgone opportunities in the form of a surplus unattainable given the defection problem. If the state of nature were itself costless in Gauthier's sense, no need for a theory of rational bargaining would arise. Truly costless interaction would be efficient, and no need for a mechanism to solve a market failure problem would emerge. In a costless world, no market failures would emerge. The entire state-of-nature enterprise unravels quickly once one introduces the costlessness condition.

A sympathetic reading of Gauthier sees the costlessness assumption as part of his attempt to isolate a concept of "pure rationality." This assumption, we might say, is intended as a constraint in the state of nature only during bargaining, a constraint similar to the constraint Kavka introduces into his hypothetical bargaining scenario according to which the parties are assured of physical security during their negotiations. But even Kavka observes that "if assured of physical security during negotiations [perhaps] the parties would never end them" (Kavka, p. 237). Kavka's solution is to impose a generous but definite time limit on negotiations after which security would no longer be guaranteed. Gauthier, however, has no such limitation on his costlessness assumption. And should he introduce a limit on the time during which negotiations are costless, the costlessness assumption will no longer support the claim that rational parties will bargain only on fair terms. For, in effect, by limiting the costlessness assumption, Gauthier necessarily would introduce costs into the bargaining scenario. Parties would have to anticipate the arrival of the deadline, and their failure to come to an agreement, even on unfair terms, would constitute an opportunity cost. In the end, the costlessness assumption must either be granted entirely or abandoned. There would appear to be no middle ground.

Moreover, once we grant the costlessness assumption, it is unclear how to make sense of it. Rational individuals who incur no costs for failing to reach agreement have, *a fortiori*, nothing to gain in bargaining. For if they did, there would be, necessarily, costs (opportunity costs) of forgoing or delaying agreement. Bargaining is rational therefore only if it takes place within the context of costs, and costless contexts necessarily render bargaining irrational. The costlessness assumption, far from being an innocent attempt to constrain the decision problem in a normatively neutral way, turns out to be too strong. It may even be incoherent.[37]

37 Note that even if we hold the costlessness assumption to be coherent and legitimate within the context of deriving a principle of ideal rational bargaining, this will not help Gauthier's case for the fairness of bargaining in the state of nature. For even though we assume individuals to be perfectly rational in the state of nature, it is doubtful that rationality requires that they employ a principle of bargaining the unique rationality of which has been proved only in a costless setting. The principle of minimax relative concession, even if uniquely rational in costless contexts, need not be, indeed is unlikely to be, uniquely rational in costly contexts. And the state of nature is, by definition, costly. Thus, we see that "ideal rational principles" of this sort have

Arguments from rational and costless bargaining

Summary

There is a significant theme which emerges from the preceding critique of Gauthier's theory: The very problems of collective action which motivate the need for constrained maximization emerge again at the level of choice between the alternative forms of constrained maximization, broad and narrow compliance. The rationality of narrow compliance ultimately depends upon the incentives available for inducing individuals to be narrow compliers. And while we can imagine it sometimes being rational to want a population that is largely, if not exclusively, narrowly compliant, the problems of collective action prevent individuals from forming such a population. Once a threshold of narrow compliers exists, there will be an incentive for others to "free ride" on that population and be broad compliers. The conundrum of collective action, even when solved at one level, reoccurs at another, in this case foiling an ambitious attempt to ground morality in rationality.

no implication even for ideally rational agents when the derivation of such principles depends on artificial conditions considerably different from those in which even ideally rational agents might find themselves (e.g., the state of nature).

Chapter 6

The limits of Hobbesian contractarianism

The contractarian approach to normative questions is distinguished from others in part by its commitment to understanding normative questions as ones amenable to hypothetical analysis, and by its aspiration to derive normative conclusions from uncontroversial premises. If we suppose descriptive propositions to be less controversial or at least in principle more demonstrable than normative ones, then the strongest argument for a normative conclusion will proceed from descriptive premises. As I noted at the outset, however, one of the principal obstacles facing normative theory is the naturalistic gap – the apparent logical gulf between descriptive premises and normative conclusions. If no normative conclusions can be inferred from descriptive premises alone, as Moore's naturalistic fallacy suggests, then the most we can hope for are arguments supporting normative conclusions which proceed from normatively minimalistic premises, premises which though not purely descriptive, are so uncontroversial that they hold force for most people.[1] Such an ambition certainly falls short of the aspiration to build universally compelling normative conclusions from demonstrable premises presupposing no prior normative commitments. But it is no mean feat to support a substantive normative conclusion on grounds to

---

1 For a discussion of the naturalistic gap, and the difficulties in assessing Moore's argument, see Chapter 1, n. 20.

which most people are, or on reflection would be, committed.

Contractarianism does not, then, purport to cross the naturalistic divide. Instead, it offers an array of theories designed to argue from admittedly normative premises to normative conclusions. Within the contractarian tradition, theories range from those which presuppose highly controversial and complex normative premises (i.e., normatively idealistic theories employing idealistic constructionism in the design of their hypothetical setting), to those which presuppose relatively uncontroversial and theoretically simple normative premises (i.e., normatively minimalistic theories employing realistic construction in the design of their hypothetical setting). Pure Hobbesian contractarianism occupies the latter end of this spectrum and thus promises to provide the most powerful form of contractarian political or moral theory possible short of a pure reduction of normative concepts to descriptive ones.

Of the Hobbesian contractarian theories we have examined, Hampton's commitment to realistic constructionism makes hers the most normatively minimalistic. Her realistic construction of the hypothetical scenario resists idealizations. The individuals and circumstances characterizing her state of nature are, for the most part, realistic: They purport to describe the reality we would face in anarchy. On the other hand, Kavka's theory is perhaps the most idealistic, for despite his substantially realistic state of nature, his hypothetical negotiation scenario is intentionally constructed to embed and thus presuppose a number of arguably controversial normative ideals. Finally, Gauthier's theory probably falls between Hampton's and Kavka's, for by its nature, Gauthier's project of deriving morality from individual rationality requires that he exclude any other substantive normative ideals from his hypothetical bargaining scenario. Nevertheless, despite the commitment to normative minimalism inherent in Gauthier's theory, his hypothetical scenario is necessarily populated by ideally rational individuals and to that extent presupposes more than the minimal rationality Hampton's theory requires. Gauthier's theory, then, presupposes the norm of ideal rationality in a way that Hampton's does not.

In contrast to the normative minimalism of Hobbesian contractarianism, idealistic contractarian theories like Rawls's openly endorse a comparatively rich set of normative assumptions as central premises in their argument. As a result, idealistic and realistic contractarian theories have different strengths and weaknesses in providing a complete defense of their conclusions. A complete defense of a contractarian theory's conclusion has two parts. The first part must establish a justification for undertaking a hypothetical inquiry in order to generate normative conclusions. For any given contractarian theory, such an argument must explain the normative significance of hypothetical action, and in so doing, must justify the particular description of the hypothetical setting to which that theory is wedded. The argument must explain why hypothetical action is normatively significant under certain conditions, and then demonstrate that those conditions are satisfied by the particular hypothetical setting defined by the theory. The second part must demonstrate that the individuals in the hypothetical setting defined by the theory would interact as the theory alleges they would. This demonstration consists of an analysis of interaction in the hypothetical setting according to which the hypothetical scenario would unfold as the contractarian claims.

Idealistic and realistic theories face different obstacles in providing the first part of this contractarian defense. On one hand, idealistic theories have available to them arguments for the normative significance of their hypothetical scenarios which are not available to their realistic competitors. For the gap between the set of relatively rich normative premises built into their hypothetical settings and the normative conclusions they purport to derive is relatively small. Although the reason why hypothetical actions ground normative conclusions is never self-evident in either type of theory, *ceteris paribus*, it is easier to reason to robust normative conclusions from the relatively thick normative premises of idealistic theories than from the relatively thin ones of normatively minimal theories. On the other hand, given the relatively strong normative premises presupposed by idealistic theories, they must either explain why they do not beg the question at the outset or restrict the application of their normative results to those who are willing to endorse without argument their normative presuppositions. The challenge for idealistic theories is less to prove that their normative conclusions follow from their premises – if anything, the latter seem to follow too easily from the former – than to explain why their conclusions are informative and not merely circular or question-begging. By comparison, the normative minimalism in the construction of the hypothetical setting of realistic theories to a great extent insulates them from these concerns.

In providing the second part of the contractarian defense, idealistic theories seem to have the upper hand. For realistic theories must have hypothetical settings which reflect some alleged empirical truths in order to support their claim that their setting actually represents a particular state of affairs which would have taken place or would take place under certain conditions (e.g., a hypothetical state of anarchy predating any political association or one which is supposed to ensue upon the termination of a political association). It is difficult to design such a hypothetical setting in order to guarantee that interaction in it would generate a result desired in advance. The constraints on its design are exogenously given by the goal of realistic construction, and it is thus less amenable to "tailoring" in order to insure a particular outcome. Idealistic theories, however, are less concerned to provide an accurate reconstruction of some scenario and instead seek primarily to embed certain normative values in their hypothetical setting. In the course of doing so, there are arguably fewer constraints preventing them from designing the hypothetical setting to generate a particular result. In the extreme case, an idealistic theory could simply stipulate, for example, that the parties in the hypothetical scenario must choose among possible political associations, and by so stipulating eliminate the necessity of proving that they would not choose anarchy. A realistic theory could not help itself to this assumption.

Perhaps because of their vulnerability to charges of circularity, idealistic theories reflect a preoccupation with the first part of the contractarian defense. In particular, idealistic theories like Rawls's devote enormous effort to justifying the normatively rich description of their hypothetical settings and explaining the sense in which their conclusions are informative. The technical analysis of interaction of their hypothetical settings typically receives less extended treatment and occasions less controversy. Realistic theories are less susceptible to charges of circularity and thus devote comparatively little attention to justifying the description of their hypothetical setting. Far from accusing Hobbes of begging the question, Hobbes's critics have seized upon the paucity of normative assumptions in the state of nature, and challenged his claim that the amoral, rational, self-interested residents of his state of nature are capable of forming a government. As a result, the central focus in realistic contractarian theory has been on the analysis of interaction in the hypothetical setting. Contemporary Hobbesian scholars have sought, above all else, to evaluate and in most cases to vindicate Hobbes's assertion that political association would emerge from rational interaction in the state of nature. Thus, although proponents of idealistic theories have devoted considerable attention to justifying the construction of their hypothetical setting, they have paid comparatively less attention to proving that interaction in that setting would generate the results they claim. And although advocates of realistic theories have focused intensely on the task of analyzing interaction in hypothetical scenarios, they have spent comparatively less time justifying the construction of their hypothetical setting.

It is clear, however, that theoretical priority must be given to the first part of the contractarian defense. For in any contractarian theory, idealistic or realistic, there is little point in demonstrating that a given outcome would result from interaction in a hypothetical setting if there is no reason to suppose that the outcome would be normatively significant. And as between idealistic and realistic theories, the latter face a far more serious challenge in explaining the normative significance of their hypothetical outcomes. Unlike the idealistic theories, Hobbesian theories must traverse the considerable gap between their normatively sparse hypothetical settings and their normatively rich conclusions. But Hobbesian contractarians have instead focused their attention on the analysis of their hypothetical settings, and have done comparatively little to discharge their burden of establishing the normative significance of their results. Yet it is this burden more than any other which has so far defined, at its foundation, the philosophical limits of Hobbesian contractarianism.

In previous chapters, we have seen that Hobbesian contractarians devote the bulk of their efforts to deepening their analysis of their hypothetical settings, but pay comparatively little attention to the normative foundation on which such analyses must rest. Hampton's consideration of the normative foundation of Hobbes's argument comes principally at the end of her book, in a brief chapter presenting the inferential argument. But the connection or "fit" between this normative argument and the prior stages of her theory is far from clear. And upon analysis, as I have argued, it is difficult to align her definition and analysis of the state of nature with the inferential argument (e.g., her state of nature models a prepolitical anarchy but the inferential argument relies on predictions about a postpolitical anarchy). Even more striking, however, is the absence of any defense of the Hobbesian reduction of morality to individual rationality, the linchpin of Hampton's reconstruction of Hobbes's theory. Instead of assessing the viability of such a reduction, Hampton merely argues that Hobbes's philosophical commitments in metaphysics and the philosophy of mind logically compel him to endorse it, commitments which I argued in Chapter 2 neither compel nor undermine a reduction of morality to rationality. Similarly, although Kavka sketches several accounts of the normative force of hypothetical actions, these accounts are left almost entirely undeveloped.

Notwithstanding Hobbesian contractarians' lack of attention to the normative foundations of their theories, their detailed and sustained analysis of interaction in Hobbesian hypothetical settings is indeed impressive. There can be no question that our understanding of such settings has been deepened considerably as a result. Hampton's analysis of the state of nature helps to clarify the relationship between individual rationality, shortsightedness, the content and source of desires, and conflict in anarchy. In so doing, her argument reveals the fallacy in supposing that the iterated nature of interaction in the state of nature undermines Hobbes's claim that the latter consists in a war of all against all. For even the iterated PD will not obviate conflict and facilitate cooperation in a population with even a significant minority of shortsighted individuals. And her analysis of the emergence of a sovereign in the state of nature not only illuminates the relationship between the prisoner's dilemma, bargaining problems, coordination problems, and their solutions, but puts to rest the claim that all contractarian theories must, at some point, argue that the state would receive the hypothetical *consent* of individuals in the state of nature. For contractarian theories can argue that the state might simply emerge from a process of rational interaction in something like a free market of competing confederacies, and thus need not result directly from an agreement to form a government. Similarly, Kavka's analysis of the state of nature introduces the important distinction between the two different, equally rational, strategies of anticipation and lying low, and provides an alternative game-theoretic account of conflict based on the quasi-PD.

But for all their game-theoretic sophistication, neither Hampton, Kavka, nor Gauthier manages to overcome the traditional difficulty confronting this second part of their

316

contractarian defense: the problem of collective action. I have argued that Hampton's demonstration of the rational emergence of a sovereign from the state of nature fails because the individuals in the state of nature would be unable to empower a sovereign. Moreover, if a sovereign were empowered according to the scenario Hampton suggests, individuals living under that sovereign would be potentially unable to disempower the sovereign, even if the sovereign's rule makes life worse than life in the state of nature. In both instances, the failure of Hampton's argument can be traced to a failure to surmount a collective action problem. In both cases, Hampton's efforts to overcome the rational incentive to free ride, and the concomitant assurance problem, are unsuccessful. A sovereign therefore might well be unable to form an effective punishment cadre, and a rebellion might well fail to gain sufficient momentum for individuals to find it rational to join.

Kavka's argument of course does not even purport to demonstrate that a sovereign would emerge from the state of nature. His game-theoretic efforts are confined to establishing the proposition that the state of nature would likely consist in a war of all against all. But his stage-two analysis takes place in a conceptually distinct hypothetical negotiation scenario, one in which agreement on sovereign-rule is facilitated by definition, not game-theoretic argument. Finally, Gauthier's argument for the reduction of morality to individual rationality founders on the free rider problem as well. Even if we concede the validity of his principal game-theoretic innovation – the principle of constrained maximization according to which it is rational to dispose oneself to comply in the single-play PD – Gauthier is unable to demonstrate the unique rationality of narrow compliance, the disposition to comply only with fair bargains. Broad compliers, those with the disposition to comply in unfair as well as fair bargains, will be able to free ride on the collective benefits produced by narrow compliers. The free rider problem thus undercuts Gauthier's defense of narrow compliance, the crucial link between his argument for constrained maximization and the reduction of morality to individual rationality.

So although Hampton, Kavka, and Gauthier have exploited game theory to facilitate a deeper and more systematic analysis of interaction in hypothetical settings, I have argued that in the end, the standard problems of collective action have once again proven intransigent. The present forms of their arguments fall short of establishing their conclusions, but it is possible that some new formulation might surmount these problems. And it is this allure which I suspect is in large measure responsible for the attention contemporary theorists have paid to the second part of the Hobbesian contractarian defense. Collective action problems are technical puzzles, and as such hold considerable fascination for philosophers, game theorists, and economists, whose instincts and training compel them to search for a solution. There is a sense, perhaps not unfounded, that success is possible, if just one innovation can be found or one definition slightly changed. Just as Hampton hoped that redefining the empowerment problem as one creating a minimally effective punishment cadre might solve the free rider problem attending the empowerment of the sovereign in the state of nature, so another will hope to restructure or reconceive the hypothetical analyses Hampton, Kavka, and Gauthier have presented to avoid the collective action problems which remain. Indeed, the application of decision and game theory to contractarian thought accounts for much of the progress Rawls made in rediscovering the utility of contractarian analysis in *A Theory of Justice*. One of the most influential innovations in Rawls's work is the central role it provides for rational choice theory in political and moral philosophy, a role which has been fully imported into contemporary Hobbesian contractarianism.

Yet, after careful examination of the Hobbesian alternatives to Rawls's theory, game-theoretic analysis seems to have taken on a life of its own, its relevance for the ultimate normative purpose of the Hobbesian project left unclear. For in the absence of some argument which connects such an analysis to a normative conclusion, there would appear to be little point to undertaking the analysis in the first place. The quintessentially philosophical task of Hobbesian contractarianism, no less than any other approach to political or moral philosophy, is to establish a moral conclusion. No matter how extensive or clever, an analysis of hypothetical interaction cannot bring us any closer to a moral conclusion without some argument explaining why hypothetical interaction of any kind has bearing on the question of political legitimacy or morality. Of the theories we have considered, only Gauthier's devotes as much attention to defending the position that his conclusion turns on his game-theoretic analysis of his hypothetical setting as he devotes to engaging in that analysis itself. Neither Hampton nor Kavka adequately explores the arguments necessary to defend in order to establish the relevance of the extensive game-theoretic analysis of interaction in their hypothetical settings.

The philosophical limits of Hobbesian contractarianism, in the final analysis, are the philosophical limits of normative theory. Although the secondary game-theoretic questions appear more readily amenable to analysis, the challenge of Hobbesian contractarianism must first be to answer the primary normative questions which explain why anyone in political or moral philosophy should care about answering these secondary questions at all. Hobbesian contractarianism promises to provide both a stronger justification for political association and a stronger account of the content and motivation of morality. It promises not to derive "ought" from "is," but to beg fewer normative questions at the outset than its idealistic competitors. But Hobbesian contractarians have yet to provide a well-developed and sustained account of the normative significance of hypothetical inquiry, the inquiry which distinguishes contractarianism from other approaches to political and moral philosophy. The next generation of Hobbesian contractarianism must tend to its foundations before it continues to build above ground.

Index

Entries in italic indicate subsection headings within chapters.

Index

autonomy (*continued*)
  libertarian objection to normative force of hypothetical consent, 184–5, 219, 221–3

battle-of-the-sexes example of mixed coordination game, 114–15
belief
  and epistemic justification, 75–6
  and psychological egoism, *see* psychological eogism
  role of in human behavior, 87–8
Boorman, Scott, 93 n30
Brink, David, 8 n6, 33 n21, 79 n18, 84 n23
Buchanan, Allen, 175 n10

capacities of hypothetical actors, 9
Carroll, J., 151 n5
causal effects condition, *see* punishment cadre, causal effects condition
Characterization of a set of hypothetical individuals, see hypothetical individuals, characterization of
Characterization of the hypothetical environment, see hypothetical environment, characterization of
coalition prohibition, *see* hypothetical negotiation scenario, coalition prohibition in
collective action problems, 12
  formal definition, 13–14
  lack of group coordination and, 14
  lack of information and, 14
  latent groups, 14
  as n-person PD, 14
  privileged groups, 13–14
collective goods, 12–13
  incremental goods, 125
  as single-play PD, 126
  vagueness of, 128

jointness of supply, 13, 121
nonexcludability, 13, 121
as single-play PD, 13
step goods, 125
  causal effect condition, 129–31
  essentiality condition, 130–1
  increased probability of creating good with each contribution, 128–9
  as mixed coordination game, 126
  rationality of free-riding, 126–7
collectively irrational sovereign
  and assurance problem, 178–9
  and free rider problem, 178–9
  Hobbes's solution to, 105
  Locke's response, 105–6
  rational rebellion against, 106–7, 174–82
complex objectivism, 82–3; *see also* objectivism
confederacy agreement, 155–6, 156–72
confederacy game, 163
  and contingent-move games, *see* contingent-move games, agency game
  game-theoretic structure of, 162–72, 163 n8
  incentives to comply with, 162
  as iterated PD's, 162
  and ruler-people game, *see* agency game, ruler-people game
  and sovereign-entrepreneur, 156, 156–8, 164–72
conflict in state of nature; *see also* state of nature
  and conflict in postpolitical anarchy, 64–6, 68–70
  Gauthier's account, *see* disposition as solution to single-play PD
  Hampton's account, 48–9, 56–63

Index

and weak rational reconstruction
of political authority, *16–17*,
18 n16

fairness, *see* constrained maximization theory; rational bargaining theory
Fairness and bargaining, see constrained maximization theory;
rational bargaining theory
*Fairness and constrained maximiza-
tion, see* constrained maximization theory; prisoner's dilemma, iterated PD
farsightedness, *8*
appropriately farsighted individuals, 199–200, 216 n15
Kavka's assumption of, 199,
216–18, 216 n15
longsighted individuals in
Hampton's theory, 157,
168–70, 172
Feinberg, Joel, 9 n7
*First stage of the contractarian argu-
ment, see* hypothetical environment; hypothetical individuals; hypothetical scenario
fit, *see* soundness as criterion
Flood, Merrill, 11 n9
forwardlooking individuals, *see* farsightedness, Kavka's assumption of
free rider problem, *13*
and collective goods, 13, 121–31
incremental goods, 126–7,
126 n4
step goods, 126–7
future utility discount rate, *see* discount rate; farsightedness;
shortsightedness

Gibbard, Allan, 29 n20

Hamilton, W. D., 93 n30
Hampton's solution to the sovereign-
selection problem, see sovereign-
selection problem
Hardin, Russell, 6 n4, 13, 14 n13
Hare, R. M., 29 n20
Head, J., 13 n10
healthy deliberation conception of
rationality, *see* rationality,
healthy deliberation account of
Hobbes and normative minimalism, see
normative minimalism,
Hobbesian
Hume, David
examples of pure coordination
games, 109–10, 123
Hume's hurdle, 29, 29 n20; *see
also* naturalistic fallacy; naturalistic gap
hypothetical actions
moral merit of, 185–6
normative significance of, 184–8,
200
applicability of inheritance
principle to, 243–51
and idealistic scenarios, 184,
187, 198
Kavka's justifications of, *see*
inheritance principle ac-
count; no reasonable ob-
jection account; realistic
reconstruction account
and soundness of contractarian argument, 184
*Hypothetical agreement in Kavka's
theory, see* hypothetical egotia-
tion scenario
hypothetical consent, 184–5; *see
also* autonomy, libertarian objection to hypothetical consent
hypothetical environment, characterization of, 4, 9–10; *see also*
state of nature
availability of resources, 10
scarcity in Hobbes's state of
nature, 58, 191

325

Index